Jane Austen had a life!

A Guide to Jane Austen's Juvenilia

V.S. Rutherford

*This interesting & scholarly work
is dedicated without permission
to the lovely & lively Miss Hannah Simone
by
The Author*

Published by Arcana Press, August 2020

Copyright © V. S. Rutherford 2020

The moral rights of the author are asserted. All rights reserved, no part of this book may be
reproduced or transmitted in any form, or in any means, electronic or mechanical, including
photocopying, recording or by any information storage and retrieval system, without prior permission in writing
from the publisher, the Arcana Trust.

The Australian Copyright Act 1968 allows a maximum of one chapter or 10% of this book,
whichever is the greater, to be photocopied by an educational institution for its educational purposes,

Provided that the educational institution (or body that administers it) has given a remuneration
notice to the Copyright Agency (Australia), email: info@copyright.com.au.

Every effort has been made to trace the holders of copyright material.
If you have any information concerning copyright material in this book, please

Contact the author, at info.vsrutherford@gmail.com.

ISBN: 978-0-6487631-0-9

Cataloguing-in-Publication details are available from the National Library of Australia

www.trove.nla.gov.au

Typesetting and layout by Megan Taylor

Cover: *The old and Mouldering Castle, which is situated two miles from Perth on a bold projecting Rock,
and commands an extensive view of the Town and its delightful Environs. Jane Austen Lesley Castle.*
Photograph: V.S. Rutherford, 2018.

Contents

Preface

What a delightful library!

Pride & Prejudice

You reach the Bodleian Library in Oxford via Catte Street, go through the Great Gate, cross the Old School Quadrangle, through the entrance to the Old Bodleian. One of its great treasures, more than 230 years old, the battered *Volume the First* of Jane Austen's *Juvenilia*, lives here, in its own maroon cloth-box. Her second and third volumes are in London, 55 miles away, in the British Library, on Euston Road.

Jane Austen's brother Henry wrote, *at a very early age, she was sensible to the charms of style and enthusiastic in the cultivation of her own language.*[1] Her nephew, James Edward Austen Leigh, told of *her absorbing interest in original composition*, of how Jane wrote her early stories to read to her family at dinner; she was *continually supplying her juvenile effusions for the transitory amusement of her family party.*[2]

The three volumes of her *Juvenilia* contain thirty-one pieces, short stories, plays and a poem, which Jane Austen wrote between 1788, when she was twelve, and 1793, when she was seventeen. She chose to keep these thirty-one, out of all those she had read to amuse her family on long winter evenings.

Jane Austen had a Life! is the first complete guide to Jane Austen's *Juvenilia.* That in itself is puzzling, given that the contents of her three notebooks, or volumes, have been in the public domain for almost seventy years.

Commentaries on the *Juvenilia* to date have tended to focus on a recurring handful of its thirty-one individual pieces. Several use Virginia Woolf's image of *Jane Austen Practising*[3], treating these early pieces as akin to scales and arpeggios, a means for Austen to consciously polish her technique, building up for the big concertos, her works with real meaning and value.

A few writers on Jane Austen have confronted their difficulties. Novelist and biographer, Margaret Drabble noted: *in some of the shorter fragments there are hints of another Jane Austen, a fiercer, wilder, more outspoken, more ruthless writer, with a dark vision of human motivation.*[4]

Austen's biographer, David Nokes, was known for his skill to *spot terrain missed by other biographers, and to use it to supply a psychological dimension of discomfort which his subjects concealed, while suggesting how their evasions left traces in their literary writings.*[5] He said of the Juvenilia, *there is a restless, reckless undercurrent of frustration in all her early sketches; a violent fantasizing energy, which uses the disguise of fiction to subvert the careful rules and reticences of polite rectory life.*[6]

John Halperin, another biographer, remarked: *these earliest works are startling in their hostility and cold detachment... Clearly, the Rectory at Steventon was no Garden of Eden: indeed, the monsters may have seemed, to the young writer, always on the verge of taking it over.*[7]

Poet, Richard Church, the editor of the Folio edition of Jane Austen's novels, agreed, suggesting, *it is obvious that this early savagery must have had a cause.*[8]

It is hoped this guide will provide insights into these questions and concerns.

I must relieve myself by writing *Lady Susan*

Her *Juvenilia* stories are the only record we have of Jane Austen's youth, through them we learn something of her lively teenage years and her despair at the loss of her great and enduring love. They reveal her as an imaginative creator, and, befitting the daughter of a clergyman, a truth teller, with a difficult understanding of the world.

Jane Austen, like any other writer, wrote about her own reality, she relied on her own experiences for her inspiration. The difference was her age, her awareness and her detachment. In many of her stories she uses subterfuge, writing in the third person, using satire, changing names, places and details, but still revealing a great deal of what was going on in her life. They are records of her preoccupations, her experiences, of her real desires, motivations and actions. On one solitary occasion she tells something of her story in the first person, *"I, Jane."*

The *Juvenilia* is the work of a headstrong, adolescent, finding her way to adulthood, pushing at the permissible boundaries. She wrote about escape, elopement, marriage, dissipation, drunkenness, of the great world beyond Hampshire.

It is sometimes difficult to conceive these stories were written by a young girl, between twelve and seventeen. Her stories abound with sexual attraction, love, elopements, and marriage. Many are sad and dark, ending with death, absence or exile, others contain thefts, violent scenes and murders. A number criticise parental tyranny, oppression and forced marriages, yearning for youthful independence and freedom to experience the great world.

As she read them at table, Jane Austen often hid her feelings behind parody and burlesque. As she explored and pursued her writing, she came to rely less on such comedy and humour. Her later, stronger narratives give a clear-eyed view of the world, underpinned by a more delicate irony, social satire and criticism.

This pathetic piece of family history *Persuasion*

After her death in 1817, her family burnt most of Jane Austen's letters and papers. Her elder sister, Cassandra kept some of her letters from Jane, *though she burnt the greater part.*[9] She took the scissors to the letters she saved, cutting out particular words and sections, though she did overlook two or three significant references Jane made to her youthful escapades. She kept the three notebooks of Jane's *Juvenilia*.

Cassandra Austen died in 1845. She left *Volume the First* to her youngest brother Charles, *Volume the Second* to her brother Frank, and *Volume the Third* to James Edward Austen Leigh, son of her eldest brother James.

As the popularity of Jane Austen's novels continued to grow, readers sought information about their anonymous author, but her family chose not to respond to their enquiries. Eventually, fifty-one years after her death, her nephew James Edward Austen-Leigh published his *Memoir of Jane Austen*. He was seventy-one, the senior spokesman for the Austens, he had been a clergyman for forty-eight years,

If, with all our caution, some rumour of the truth should get abroad
Persuasion

Austen-Leigh acknowledged that few of her readers *knew even her name and none knew more of her than her name, adding, I doubt whether it would be possible to mention any other author of note, whose personal obscurity was so complete.* He said very little about Jane Austen's youth or the influence of her formative years on her writing. He described her life as *singularly barren: few changes and no great crisis ever broke the smooth current of its course,* and *there was no definite tale of love to relate.*[10]

Austen-Leigh may have thought he had the last word, but several of his female relatives decided he had gone too far. His sister Caroline Austen, his half sister, Anna Lefroy, and her third daughter Fanny Caroline in particular, did not expect anyone to believe Jane had never known romantic love. They set about uncovering a selection of secret romantic encounters, in which Jane's suitors were mainly nameless clergymen, met during holidays on the coast, who disappeared without a trace.

Her niece Caroline analysed a brief, obscure note in her mother, Mary Austen's pocketbook, and announced that Jane was once engaged, though only overnight, to Mr Bigg Withers, who proposed, was accepted, then rejected by Jane, the morning after.

Fanny Caroline, concerned her great aunt would be seen as *shallow and cold-hearted*, declared she had indeed known *the pangs of disappointed love.* She reported Jane's acquaintance with two brothers, over *a week, or a fortnight at most, time not only for love to arise, but to have it struck its roots deeply into the heart.* Jane's favourite, according to Fanny, was a clergyman, who died unexpectedly.[11]

Austen Leigh's *Memoir* was published thirty years before Sigmund Freud's first analysis of the subconscious. The odd thing is that after more than a century of study of the human mind and creativity, the authority and accuracy of his *Memoir* remains largely unquestioned.

What an exquisite possession a good picture of her would be! *Emma*

A contemporary of Jane Austen, Mary Russell Mitford (1787-1855), left two very different snapshots of her. Twelve years younger than Jane, she lived in Hampshire, and like her, had attended Abbey House School.

She quoted her mother, who had grown up at Ashe, a tiny parish near Steventon, where her father was rector, from 1729 to 1783: *Mamma says that she was then the prettiest, silliest, most affected, husband-hunting butterfly she ever remembers.*

Mary Russell Mitford also proffered some gossip she had from an unnamed friend, a description of Jane Austen in her early forties: *a friend of mine, who visits her now, says that she has stiffened into the most perpendicular, precise, taciturn piece of "single blessedness" that ever existed, and that, till 'Pride and Prejudice' showed what a precious gem was hidden in that unbending case, she was no more regarded in society than a poker or a fire-screen, or any other thin upright piece of wood or iron that fills its corner in peace and quietness. The case is very different now; she is still a poker – but a poker of whom every one is afraid.*[12]

Solicitous for the credit of the family

Critics have observed the control exercised by the Austen family over her history. Bruce Stovel noted: *the major biographies of her for more than one hundred years after her death in 1817 were written by family members, and biographies since then have relied largely on unpublished or obscurely published family manuscripts. Furthermore, the Austen family has been determined from the start to present its most famous member to the world as a figure of exemplary gentility and piety... The public's curiosity was satisfied, and yet the author's dignity was preserved.*[13]

Paul Poplawski described Austen-Leigh's Jane Austen, as: *no more (and no less) than a construction, and very much an idealized Victorian construction of what a good Christian maiden aunt ought to be like. This was inevitable, given Austen-Leigh's place in time and position in society as an elderly clergyman, and, by creating a figure congenial to Victorian sensibilities, the Memoir certainly facilitated the growth of critical debate and publication around Austen's work. However, it may also have had a stalling effect on the development of a truly sophisticated and searching style of Austen criticism, in that the demure "dear Aunt Jane" figure of the Memoir tended to encourage a congruently decorous type of criticism that largely eschewed detailed analysis and serious moral or ideological debate in favor of a generalized appreciation of Austen's "genius" and "perfection". This genteel and self–consciously amateurish form of criticism somewhat dominated the field in this period, and it eventually became known as the Janeite tendency in Austen studies.*[14]

John Halperin, a biographer of Jane Austen, commented on *the unsubtle, ritual closing of ranks among the family.* He thought it *helped explain why so many have laboured so long to discover what was hidden. Surely something was being hidden...Could this life, could any life, be so devoid of "events," of "crisis," of "attachment"?*

And what about all that burning and pruning of her letters carried out so assiduously by Cassandra?..The effect of the destruction was to suppress anything of a peculiar intimacy. As one critic surmised "the gaps in the letters can be expected to correspond with crises in their author's life." But she was not supposed to have had any crises.[15]

On the subject of books
Sense & Sensibility

In his *Memoir*, Austen-Leigh justified the Austen family's suppression of Jane's *Juvenilia*: *"The family have rightly, I think, declined to let these early works be published.. Her earliest stories are of a slight and flimsy texture, and are generally intended to be nonsensical...Instead of presenting faithful copies of nature, these tales were generally burlesques, ridiculing the improbable events and exaggerated sentiments which she had met with in sundry silly romances... It would be as unfair to expose this preliminary process to the world."*[16]

It was not until 1922, more than a hundred years after her death, that *Volume the Second* of the *Juvenilia*, was released. Perhaps by then, her family believed it unlikely anyone would ever connect her to the people and events in her stories.

For Virginia Woolf, they were a revelation. She wrote in 1923: *I prefer to present her not in the modest pose which her family determined for her, but rather, as she most frequently presented herself, as rebellious, satirical and wild.*[17] She described: *A sense of meaning withheld, a smile at something unseen, an atmosphere of perfect control and courtesy mixed with something satirical, which, were it not directed against things in general rather than against individuals, would be almost malicious.*[18]

Zona Gale wrote in the New York Times Book Review, *here she is, human, laughing, alive, taken unaware, as she must so often have longed to be taken. Never before has she quite escaped from the rectory.*[19]

By 1927, novelist E.M.Forster was enquiring testily about the other volumes: *I am a Janeite...There exist at least two manuscript-books of Jane Austen...what else lies hidden? It is over a hundred years since the authoress died, and all the materials for a final estimate ought to be accessible by now.*[20]

In 1933, eleven years after *Volume the Second*, *Volume the First* was published. In his Preface, G.K.Chesterton seemed impressed by its natural exuberance, he declared Austen was: *the very reverse of a starched or a starved spinster; she could have been a buffoon like the Wife of Bath if she chose.* He downplayed *the contents, as her first and feeblest, her crudest early experiments.*

In 1951, a further eighteen years later, a hundred and thirty-four years after Jane Austen's death, *Volume the Third* was finally released. Today, her *Juvenilia* remains little known or appreciated, the contents considered little more than childish cartoons or exercises she undertook to develop her writing skills.

She wished to declare only the simple truth *Sense & Sensibility*

Jane Austen's readers have long observed her *preoccupation with truth, her selection of material only from among observed facts tested by personal experience.*[21] Her first independent editor noted her writing was *exceptionally and even surprisingly dependent on family and biographical truth as the basis of imaginary construction.*[22]

Brian Southam, Austen scholar, reflecting on the challenge readers have faced in understanding the meaning of her early stories, said he found them, *a mixture of fantasy and family history...for the most part the references are sunk too deeply for us to identify biographical details.*[23]

No doubt of her being in love *Emma*

Scholars have searched at length for the great love of Jane Austen's life. John Halperin trawled through her surviving letters, examining every man mentioned. In the first of these, dated 9 January 1796, she mentions Tom Lefroy's birthday and jokes about flirting with him at a Ball, *dancing and sitting down together.* Halperin declared Tom Lefroy to be *Jane Austen's first romantic interest.*[24]

Jon Spence, after reviewing all the information he could find, conceded defeat, he had failed to find the real lover of Jane Austen. He could only find Tom Lefroy: *Jane Austen and Tom Lefroy engaged in a high-spirited flirtation for a couple of weeks in January 1796, and then Tom left Hampshire to study law in London. They never met again.* Spence concluded, even if they met when Jane was in London in 1796, it was still *not proof of a serious relationship.* He was never convinced that Tom Lefroy was Jane's lover.[25]

The flaw in these endeavours was to begin at 1796, rather than in Jane's *Juvenilia*, written, in the main, more than five years before her earliest surviving letter, or any mention of Tom Lefroy.

All in one unison: words, conduct, discretion & indiscretion, told the same story   *Emma*

Jane Austen wrote about real people, real episodes, events and conflicts, disguising them as fiction. Over two centuries, sensitive readers and critics have guessed they were dealing with true stories, but they lacked the key to unlock them. Her family kept her secrets closely guarded for generations, somehow deflecting critics and historians from probing key names and events in her novels. The story of the great love of Jane Austen's life, D'Arcy Wentworth, remained hidden in plain sight for almost two hundred and thirty years.

The whole of his history   *Pride & Prejudice*

We know a great deal more today about Jane Austen's situation during the years she wrote her *Juvenilia*. It is easier to understand the emotions that burn through a number of her stories, undercutting her wit and satire with anger and despair.

In 2017, two hundred years after her death, the story of their romance was finally made public, by a Wentworth family member, Wal Walker. His *Jane & D'Arcy,* in two volumes, *Folly is not always Folly*, and *Such Talent & Such Success*, revealed Jane Austen's brief period of great happiness and freedom, cut short over Christmas 1789, soon after she turned fourteen.[26] In the limited time they spent together it seemed that all her planets were in alignment.

D'Arcy Wentworth, a young Irish surgeon from County Armagh lived in England between mid 1785 and January 1790. Jane Austen met him at the Bear Inn in Reading in August 1786. She saw him again in mid 1788, when they found themselves at the same ball in Basingstoke. They spent Christmas together in 1789, three weeks before D'Arcy sailed from Portsmouth for New South Wales. Jane Austen wrote many of her *Juvenilia* pieces during and shortly after this period.

I can see it in no other light than as an offering of love   *Emma*

Her love affair with D'Arcy Wentworth was the great inspiration for Jane Austen's writing. The brief period of their early relationship became the crucible of her creative inspiration, it supplied characters, conversations, incidents and remembrances for her novels and the backdrop to many of her *Juvenilia* stories.

From 1788, she wrote a number of absurdist, picaresque stories, containing bright shards of the story of Jane and D'Arcy, giving her perspective on the events of that tumultuous autumn and winter.

Jane did not write them to obtain closure, she wanted to rescue her story from damnation and oblivion. Her writing was the outlet for her grief and frustration, feelings that lay raw and exposed in the *Juvenilia*. She recorded them with comic, improbable plots and absurdist humour, sparkling with knowingness, full of action, romance and misfortune.

But why all this secrecy? Why any fear of detection?   *Pride & Prejudice*

In her novels, Jane Austen gave many leads to her relationship with D'Arcy Wentworth. She named him, she revealed his connection to Earls Strafford and Fitzwilliam, and she included characters from his adventures on the King's Highway.

In *Pride & Prejudice*, in a scene with Mr Darcy and his cousin, a *Colonel Fitzwilliam, the younger son of his uncle Lord* — she revealed he was a cousin of Earl Fitzwilliam. In *Persuasion*, disregarding Sir Walter's disdainful assertion, *Mr Wentworth was a nobody, I remember; quite unconnected to the Strafford family. One wonders how the names of many of our nobility become so common* she reaffirmed D'Arcy was a connexion of the Earl of Strafford.

When *Pride & Prejudice* was published, Jane worried about her brothers' reaction. Henry Austen, in London, arranged for a copy to be sent to each of his brothers. Jane warned Cassandra, who was staying in Steventon with James, *it might be unpleasant to you to be in the Neighbourhood at the first burst of the business.*[27] Her brother Frank's response to his copy was reassuring, though it seems he had cautioned her of the pitfalls of telling her secret history. Jane thanked him, and assured him, *I was previously aware of what I should be laying myself open to.*[28]

He seemed by this connexion between the families, quite to belong to her

Emma

Jane Austen's use of names connected to the Wentworth family began in the *Juvenilia*. She used the names of many noble families, but none are more prominent than those of the inter-connected Wentworth, Watson and Fitzwilliam families.

In her *Juvenilia*, her novellas and major novels, Jane Austen recorded names from every branch, bough and twig of the Wentworth family tree, but particularly that of Thomas Wentworth, 1st Earl of Strafford, one of the few heroes of her *History of England, that noble and amiable man, who never forgot the duty of the Subject, or swerved from his attachment to his Majesty.*

The heroic Earl of Strafford was a connection of her enduring love, D'Arcy Wentworth, and a distant connection of Jane herself, through her distaff line, her mother's family. Jane Austen wanted to record the happiness of her relationship with D'Arcy Wentworth, she identified herself as a Wentworth, and was proud of their connection through the Earl of Strafford.

The *meaning withheld, the smile at something unseen,* that Virginia Woolf observed in the *Juvenilia*, was undoubtedly the pride Jane Austen took in her relationship with D'Arcy Wentworth.

The publication of *Jane & D'Arcy* in 2017, has provided her readers with an understanding of the context in which Jane Austen wrote her *Juvenilia*. It has illuminated the meaning behind stories that have been opaque and puzzling to readers since their first release. For readers of Jane Austen, long interested and intrigued by the *Juvenilia*, it has proven to be a most exciting and illuminating history.

This guide to the three volumes of Jane Austen's *Juvenilia* is not a catalogue of received opinions. I hope you will bask in the light it shines on her *Juvenilia*, and her life.

V. S. Rutherford
January 2020

Juvenilia,
Volume the First

Jane Austen's *Volume the First*, housed in the Bodleian Library, is the earliest record we have of her writing. Her nephew, James Edward Austen Leigh, revealed the existence of her old copy books, *containing tales, some of which must have been composed when she was a young girl.* He wrote: *it is impossible to say at how early an age she began to write,* noting, *her earliest stories are of a slight and flimsy texture, they were, generally intended to be nonsensical, and amounted to a considerable number by the time she was sixteen.*

From 1773 to 1796, the Austen household included a small number of students studying with her father, preparing to become clergymen. Their training included rhetoric and the art of speaking in public. Life in the rectory included entertainments, writing and performing rhyming charades, performing plays during the festive season, and reading aloud, after dinner at table, from books and from their own writing. Austen Leigh wrote that Jane was *continually supplying amusing pieces to the family party.* [29]

The *considerable number* of stories Jane Austen read to amuse her *family party* were likely written on loose paper. In 1790, she obtained a quarto size notebook, most likely one from stock for her father's students. She had decided to make a more lasting record of her favourite and most meaningful pieces. On the cover, she wrote *Volume the First*, and underscored it with a flourish, and inside, she prepared a Contents page.

Over the next three years Jane transcribed sixteen short pieces, adding each title and the number of its starting page to the Contents.

All but one of the stories in *Volume the First* is introduced with a formal dedication and a description of the genre. They include five *Novels* (one *unfinished*), five *Tales* (one *unfinished*), one *unfinished performance,* one *beautiful description* and a *fragment*. As well, it contains two short plays, both comedies, one *unfinished*, and a poem, an *Ode to Pity*.

Jane continued to record pieces in *Volume the First* after she began working on *Volume the Second,* in the second quarter of 1790, and *Volume the Third* in 1792. *Volume the First* includes the earliest and the last pieces of Jane Austen's *Juvenilia*.

The first nine pieces in *Volume the First*, written during 1788 and 1789, are not in chronological order. The two plays, *The Visit*, from 1790 and *The Mystery*, 1791, were written after the Austen family theatricals ceased in the winter of 1788-89. *The Three Sisters* was likely recorded before the original was sent to her brother Edward and his bride, to celebrate their wedding in Kent at the end of December 1791.

Eighteen months later, on 2 June 1793, Jane transcribed *Detached Peices*, dedicated to her newborn niece Anna Austen, into *Volume the First*. The following day, 3 June, she added a poem, *Ode to Pity*, her last entry in *Volume the First*. It marked the completion of her entire *Juvenilia* project.

The Bodleian Library's description of *Volume the First*, notes it *exhibits signs of heavy and early use*, that *the marbled paper to both boards is abraded with loss of surface and the spine is damaged with extensive losses of covering leather.*[30] Jane Austen had undoubtedly shared it with her friends, for their fun and amusement, as she did later with her manuscript of *First Impressions*.[31]

1

Frederic and Elfrida
a novel – in five chapters

To whom this work is dedicated

Jane Austen dedicated *Frederic and Elfrida* to *Miss Lloyd, My dear Martha, as a small testimony of the gratitude I feel for your late generosity to me in finishing my muslin Cloak.*

Martha Lloyd (1765-1843), ten years older than Jane Austen, was the eldest of the three daughters of Reverend Nowes Lloyd, rector of Enborne in West Berkshire, and a first cousin of Cassandra's beloved, Tom Fowle.

Martha's mother, also Martha, was the daughter of Charles Craven, Royal Governor of South Carolina from 1712 to 1715. Her cousin, Baron William Craven, owned the livings of Enborne and Kintbury, her husband was the rector of Enborne, and her elder sister Jane was the wife of Reverend Thomas Fowle, rector of Kintbury.

In 1775, Nowes Lloyd had nursed his family through an outbreak of smallpox in the parish. Pock-marked by the *speckled monster,* they recovered, all except his only son Charles, aged seven. His father buried him in Enborne's St Michael's & All Angels, with an inscription above his tomb, saluting his *pleasing form, with gentlest manners join'd; an infant temper, with a manly mind.*[32]

Brothers-in-law Nowes Lloyd and Thomas Fowle were friends and colleagues of George Austen. Between 1778 and 1789, Thomas Fowle's four sons attended Reverend Austen's private school at Steventon, to prepare them for entry to Oxford.

Nowes Lloyd died mid-February 1789. His widow and two unmarried daughters, Martha and Mary, after seventeen years residence, left Enborne. George Austen, Jane's father, was rector of two Hampshire parishes, Steventon and Deane. The three Lloyd women moved into the vacant Deane rectory as his tenants.

In 1797, Martha's sister Mary (1771-1843) became the second wife of Jane's eldest brother James, two years after the sudden death of his first wife, Anne Mathews.

In April 1805, after her mother's death, Martha, now 40, moved to Bath to live with Jane, Cassandra, Reverend Austen and his wife. Jane wrote in 1808, *with what true sympathy our feelings are shared by Martha... she is the friend & sister under every Circumstance.*[33] Martha remained part of the Austen household after George Austen's death, in 1806 she moved to Southampton with the Austen women, and to Chawton Cottage with them in July 1809.

In July 1828, Martha Lloyd, sixty-three, became Lady Austen, when she married Jane's brother Frank, fifty-four, now Vice-Admiral Sir Frances Austen. Frank's first wife, Mary Gibson, had died five years earlier, leaving five daughters and six sons, including her newborn, Cholmeley, who lived just six months.

Six weeks before he married Martha, Frank's eldest daughter Mary Jane, twenty-one, had married Lieutenant George Purvis, RN. His four younger daughters, aged from seven to fourteen, and their eight year old brother were still at home.

Martha and Frank were old friends, Jane was close to both of them, she reveals herself in her letters to them, quite different in tone from her breezy, gossipy letters to Cassandra. Martha Lloyd was not only good at needlework, her detailed collection of recipes,[34] ninety-nine in all, declare she was a capable household manager and cook, she would have made Frank a fine wife.

Gathering her work together

Pride & Prejudice

Frederic and Elfrida is a funny, rollicking story of the differing approaches to courtship and matrimony of four young women: Elfrida Falknor, her intimate friend Charlotte Drummond, and Jezalinda and Rebecca Fitzroy, two sisters who had recently arrived in the neighbourhood.

The intimacy between the Families of Fitzroy, Drummond, and Falknor daily encreased till at length it grew to such a pitch, that they did not scruple to kick one another out of the window on the slightest provocation.

Elfrida and Frederic were first *cousins...born in one day & both brought up at one school.* They loved each other *with mutual sincerity but were both determined not to transgress the rules of Propriety by* owning their attachment.

Frederic did not propose to Elfrida, his parents proposed to Elfrida's parents. *Being accepted with pleasure, the wedding cloathes were bought and nothing remained to be settled but the naming of the day.*

Charlotte Drummond, daughter of the local Rector of Crankhum-dunberry, had *an earnest desire to oblige every one.*

The elder Miss Fitzroy, Jezalinda, with an *engaging Exterior & beautiful outside,* ran off early in the story *with the Coachman,* and that is the last we hear of her. Her younger sister Rebecca is amiable, her *Wit & Charms* shine *resplendent,* despite her *forbidding Squint, greasy tresses & swelling Back.*

The amiable Rebecca was asked in marriage by Captain Roger of Buckinghamshire. Her mother Mrs. Fitzroy did not approve of the match on account of the tender age of the young couple, Rebecca being but 36 &

Captain Roger little more than 63. To remedy this objection, it was agreed that they should wait a little while till they were a good deal older.

The *lovely Charlotte,* with her *willingness to oblige every one,* accepted an invitation from her Aunt in London, leaving her friends *with a heavy heart and streaming Eyes.* She had scarcely sat down with her Aunt, when *an aged gentleman with a sallow face and old pink Coat* entered and fell at her feet, *declaring his attachment to her & beseeching her pity in the most moving manner. Not being able to resolve to make any one miserable, she consented to become his wife.*

A short time later a young & Handsome Gentleman with a new blue coat, entered & intreated ... permission to pay to her, his addresses. With *the natural turn of her mind to make every one happy,* Charlotte *promised to become his Wife the next morning.*

It was not till the next morning that Charlotte recollected the double engagement she had entered into...the reflection of her past folly operated so strongly on her mind, she threw herself into a deep stream which ran thro' her Aunt's pleasure Grounds in Portland Place. Her body floated to Crankhumdunberry, where she was buried, her epitaph composed by Frederic, Elfrida and Rebecca.

The three returned with Captain Roger to see Mrs Fitzroy. Throwing themselves at her feet they announced that as seven days had now expired, she could no longer object to the union of Rebecca and Captain Roger on account of their tender years.

They offer Mrs Fitzroy a *smelling Bottle as a reward if she agrees,* and *a dagger steeped in her heart's blood* if she refuses. She replies, *the arguments you have used are too just & too eloquent to be withstood,* and agrees to them marrying in *3 days time.* After the ceremony, Rebecca and Captain Roger set out for his *seat in Buckinghamshire.*

Elfrida's parents, knowing her delicate frame of her mind, do not press her to name the day for her marriage to Frederic. *Weeks & Fortnights flew away...the Cloathes grew out of fashion.* When Captain Roger, Rebecca and their eighteen year old daughter Eleanor come to visit her, almost twenty years later, we find that Elfrida and Frederic are still unmarried.

Elfrida decides Captain Roger and Rebecca are *growing too old & too ugly to be any longer agreeable.* She is eager to befriend *so pretty a girl as Eleanor,* but finds herself being *treated by her as little less than an old woman.*

Elfrida notices a *growing passion in the Bosom of Frederic* for Eleanor. She *flies to Frederic & in a manner truly heroic* and splutters out she intends to be *married the next Day.* Frederic boldly replied, *Damme Elfrida – you may be married tomorrow but I won't.*

His answer *distressed* Elfrida *too much for her delicate Constitution.* She collapsed into a *succession of fainting fits, scarcely recovering from one before she fell into another.* Frederic, *his heart as soft as cotton, flew to her, and finding her better than he had been taught to expect, he was united to her Forever–.*

Conjecturing as to the date *Pride & Prejudice*

Frederic and Elfrida was the first of three stories Jane Austen wrote in London in 1789. It was begun mid-year , while she and Cassandra were staying with Anne Lefroy and her children in Mayfair.

An early visit to London *Lady Susan*

Amidst the marvels of London, freed from her daily chores and the confines of the rectory, Jane wrote a story centred on a group of young women, each reflecting an aspect of her own experience and feelings.

There was something in the name *Emma*

Jane Austen drew the names for her story from various sources. Elfrida was the second wife of King Edgar, the great grandson of Alfred the Great, first king of all England, who ruled from 959 to 975.[35] Eliza

Nugent Bromley used the name *Elfrida* in her 1784 novel, *Laura & Augustus*, in which Laura and Augustus Montague attend a play in London called, *Edgar and Elfrida*.[36] Jane used each of these names in her *Juvenilia*.

Jane probably included the name Charlotte in the story to acknowledge Charlotte Brydges, who lived at the Deane Rectory with her brother Egerton between 1786 and 1788, and for a period was involved with James Austen.

Falknor was the name of one of the proprietors of *Collyer's Flyers* who ran a coach service from several centres in Hampshire to London.

The Drummonds were a noble Scottish family that produced two queens of Scotland. In Jane Austen's day, Robert Drummond (1728-1804), third son of the 4th Viscount Strathallan, was a director of Drummond's Bank in Charing Cross. He owned a grand estate in Hampshire, *Cadland*, near Fawley, two and half thousand acres on the shoreline of the Solent, looking over to the Isle of Wight. There he employed 'Capability' Brown to design him a garden of twenty-seven acres.

In her vignette of Miss Fitzroy, who ran off with the coachman, Jane was referring to a Wentworth family scandal. In 1764, Lady Harriet Wentworth had eloped with William Sturgeon, one of Lord Rockingham's coachmen. The couple left England shortly after to live in France.

Drawn from her own family *Pride & Prejudice*

Elfrida's request to Charlotte for a new and fashionable bonnet, was a reference to Jane Austen's aunt, Philadelphia, who had trained as a milliner.

Philadelphia Hancock, her daughter Eliza, Countess de Feuillide, and her grandson Hastings lived in Orchard Street, Marylebone, not far from Portland Place. Jane may have seen the Tyburn on a fleeting visit she made with her parents to dine with them, in August 1788.

The Tyburn, one of London's lost rivers, flowed down from Hampstead

Heath to the Thames, through Regents Park, following a course along the curves of Marylebone Lane between Euston Road and Oxford Street. From there it flowed underground in conduits to the Thames. The Great Conduit, built in 1236 from elm trunks, carried water to Cheapside, in the City. The area beside the Tyburn, once open fields, by 1788 flowed through a grid of streets, west of Harley and Wimpole Streets. *The pleasure Grounds* of Charlotte's aunt would have extended westward from Portland Place to the Tyburn.

Falling in love with her when she is thirteen *Emma*

Jane turned thirteen in December 1788, certain that in D'Arcy Wentworth, she had found her true love. Under the *Marriage Act of 1753, an Act for the Better Preventing of Clandestine Marriage,* she needed her parents' permission to marry.

In *Frederic and Elfrida,* maintaining a comic voice, she blames her mother for standing in her way, by insisting *they should wait a little while till they were a good deal older.*

In her day, it was the normal practice, particularly where families owned property, for parents to arrange their children's marriages. Elfrida does not argue or object to her parents agreeing to a marriage proposal from Frederic's parents, she simply refuses to name a day for the wedding.

Elfrida's passive resistance continued nearly two decades, until she realised she was growing old and that Frederic had developed a *growing passion* for a *pretty girl.* Elfrida promptly claims him as hers, declaring she will marry him tomorrow. When he refuses she has *scarcely patience enough* to stage the series of fainting fits that persuade him to change his mind.

An advertisement in the medical line, extensive business, undeniable character, respectable references *Sanditon*

From November 1787, to maintain his privacy and avoid the press, D'Arcy Wentworth used several aliases when in London, including the name *Fitzroy*. On 4 November 1788, he placed an advertisement in *The Times* under the name *Charles Fitzroy*, seeking a partnership as a surgeon or apothecary. Later he used the name to hire horses and to rent lodgings in London.[37]

Reading it aloud
Northanger Abbey

In 1790, if Jane read *Frederic & Elfrida* aloud to them at table, did her parents recognise she had put them on notice that she was not too young to know her own heart, that she wanted them to respect her independence?

2

Jack and Alice
a novel – in nine chapters

To whom this work is dedicated   *The History of England*

Jane Austen dedicated *Jack and Alice* to her brother, *Francis William Austen Esqr Midshipman on board his Majestys Ship the Perseverance.* Francis Austen (1774-1865) was nearly two years older than Jane, they were close in age and were always good friends.

In 1786, Frank had entered the Royal Naval Academy in Portsmouth, and in December 1788, he joined *HMS Perseverance* to begin his practical training. In December 1789, after active service in the East Indies, during the French Revolutionary Wars, he was promoted to midshipman. He returned home four years later, in December 1793.

Conjecturing as to the date   *Pride & Prejudice*

Jane Austen wrote *Jack and Alice* in November 1789 while staying in London. She would have sent the original to Frank, in the East Indies, the following year, to celebrate his promotion to midshipman on *HMS Perseverance.*

Gathering her work together

Jack and Alice is a funny, fast-moving black comedy of unrequited love. Its two naïve young heroines, Alice and Lucy, are infatuated with the dazzling, heartless, narcissistic Charles Adams.

A warning, this story contains scenes of drunkenness, violence, intrigue and manipulation!

It begins with a Masquerade party to honour the fifty-fifth birthday of Mr Johnson, father of Jack and Alice, *a family of Love, though a little addicted to the Bottle & the Dice.* When the party ends, everyone is *carried home, Dead Drunk.*

Being a Masquerade, each guest wears a mask. Charles Adams, *an amiable, accomplished & bewitching young Man, of so dazzling a Beauty that none but Eagles could look him in the Face,* wears the one most *universally admired,* an image of the sun.

Jane Austen ridicules him with her wild exaggerations: *The Beams that darted from his Eyes were like those of that glorious Luminary tho' infinitely Superior. So strong were they that no one dared venture within half a mile of them; he had therefore the best part of the Room to himself, its size not amounting to more than 3 quarters of a mile in length and half a one in breadth.*

The beams and the *brightness of his Wit subdued the hearts of so many,* but it was Alice Johnson who could not *withstand the power of his Charms.*

Alice *could think of nothing but Charles Adams, she could talk of nothing but him. Somewhat heated by wine she sought relief from her disordered head & Love-sick Heart in the Conversation of the intelligent Lady Williams.* Alice *spoke so openly that Lady Williams soon discovered the unreturned affection she bore him.*

Lady Williams suggests that she and Alice walk from her *pigstye to Charles Adam's Horsepond.* On the way they come upon *a lovely young*

Woman lying apparently in great pain beneath a Citron tree, and ask her about her *Life & adventures.*

Lucy tells them that she first saw Charles Adams six months ago, in her village in Wales. She *could not resist his attractions, she wrote him several letters, offering him with great tenderness her hand & heart.* Her first letter *received an angry & peremptory refusal,* after that she heard nothing.

When Charles Adams returned home, Lucy wrote that she would shortly do herself *the honour of waiting on him.* When he did not reply, she chose to take his *Silence for Consent.* Without telling her aunt, Lucy travelled alone from Wales. She had arrived that morning and was on her way to call on Charles Adams, when, just in sight of his house, her leg was *seized, caught in one of the steel traps so common in gentleman's grounds.* A servant heard her screams and released her from the trap, but her leg was *entirely broken.*[38] Alice exclaims, *Oh! cruel Charles to wound the hearts and legs of all the fair.*

Lady Williams goes to Lucy's assistance, *examining the fracture* and setting her leg *with great skill.* Lucy rose up *from the ground & finding she could walk with the greatest ease, accompanied them to Lady Williams's House.* Next morning, she accepted an invitation from the eldest Miss Simpson to stay with her and her two sisters, in Bath.

Alice, meanwhile, was finding herself more violently attached to Charles Adams each day. Her father, Mr Johnson, agreed *to propose a union between them to Charles, and being a man of few words his part was soon performed.*

Charles Adams replied that he considered the proposal an affront. He provided a lengthy list of his perfections: *Beauty, Manners & Address,* accomplishments in *every Language, every Science, every Art and every thing,* more than anyone in Europe.

After calling Mr Johnson a *drunken old Dog,* he told him his daughter was *neither sufficiently beautifull, sufficiently witty, nor sufficiently rich.* He declared, *I expect nothing more in my wife than my wife will find in me – Perfection. After hearing this sad account from her father, the unfortunate Alice, flew to her Bottle, & it was soon forgot.*

After a fortnight in Bath, Lucy has also with *tolerable Ease,* forgotten Charles. She wrote to Lady Williams, telling her she had an offer of marriage from the Duke of –, an elderly Man of *Rank & Fortune* with a *home.* Lucy asked her advice, her aunt in Wales is too incensed by her *imprudent departure* to have her back, and she wished *most earnestly* to leave the Miss Simpsons, as the 2ⁿᵈ Sister, the *envious & malevolent Sukey, is too disagreable to live with.*

Lady Williams sends a very confused reply: *never shall my Lucy be united to such a one! He has a princely fortune, how nobly you will spend it...Why will you not at once decide this affair by returning to me & never leaving me again?*

Lucy never received the letter, it reached Bath *a few Hours after she breathed her last,* a victim of Sukey Simpson's *Envy & Malice. Jealous of her superior charms,* Sukey poisoned Lucy, taking her *from an admiring World at the age of seventeen.*

A report circulated through Pammydiddle *of the intended marriage of Charles Adams. To the astonishment of every one, he was publicly united to Lady Williams.*

Her own share in the story   *Emma*

Jack and Alice lampoons youthful infatuation. It has none of the intricacies of courtship or the burden of parental influence found in *Frederic and Elfrida.*

Neither Lucy nor Alice, the two young heroines, have a mother. Lucy was given by her father into the care of an aunt. Alice's father is present, though he seems to have little influence over his daughter.

Lucy is a young woman of independent mind, she acted according to her feelings when she wrote to Charles Adams offering him her hand and heart. Jane Austen endorsed young women taking the initiative in affairs of the heart. Leading by example in her comic letter to *The*

Loiterer,[39] from *Margaret Mitten*, she informed the editor of she was *destined to be your future Helpmate*.

Telling him, *merit, like yours, deserves to meet every encouragement,* Ms Mitten explained that, *under some particular circumstances the Poet tells us: A maid unask'd, may own a well-plac'd Flame*.

Jane omitted the next line: *Not loving first, but loving wrong is shame,*[40] though it was a sentiment she would certainly have endorsed.

Margaret Mitten described herself: *a person of the very tallest size, not incumbered with the coarse redundance of plumpness, or flushed with the vulgar glow of health;...I have preserved my figure in the unbending Majesty of prim perpendicularity, uncorrupted by the present fashionable lounge of our modern Girls, who always appear to me as it they were going to tumble on their noses. – Such is my person, nor is my mind unworthy of it, for except for an unfortunate propensity to tittle tattle, and an hereditary love of the bottle, I have few failings, and am wanting in no virtue except Candour, Generosity, and Truth*.

In *Jack and Alice*, Lucy travelled alone from Wales to Pammydiddle. She then set off to walk alone and uninvited to Charles Adams' house. Alice and Lady Williams accept her story without comment or criticism. Neither Lucy or Alice question Lady Williams' motives, as she pumps them with questions about their feelings for Charles Adams. Neither realise she has an ulterior motive, that she is their rival for Charles Adams' affections.

In *Pride & Prejudice*, Jane Austen describes how society judged such independent behaviour. When Elizabeth Bennett walks alone, across the muddy fields to Netherfield, the Bingley sisters are scandalised: *To walk three miles, or four miles, or five miles, or whatever it is, above her ankles in dirt, and alone, quite alone! What could she mean by it? It seems to me to shew an abominable sort of conceited independence, a most country town indifference to decorum*.

Jane Austen exercised great independence of spirit in her teenage years. She wrote later of a father, who *was not in the least addicted to locking up his daughters.*[41] In *Jack and Alice,* Jane may have been referring to some of her own escapades.[42]

To form that ground-work

Jane portrayed characters and situations in *Jack and Alice*, that she would develop more fully in her mature novels.

Lucy's need for a safe roof over her head and for congenial friends, anticipates the peripatetic Lady Susan, and sisters Anne and Lucy Steele in *Sense & Sensibility*, who also seem to have no place of their own. They display *constant and judicious attention* to their hosts, and pay *their court through such foibles* to make themselves *agreeable.* Mary Crawford in *Mansfield Park*, is similarly rootless, she stays with her brother from time to time, and has a series of other visits planned, none of which she expects to enjoy.

Lady Williams is a forerunner to Lady Greville, who bullies Miss Maria endlessly in *A Collection of Letters.* Lady Catherine de Bourgh, another of these noble ladies, meets her match in Elizabeth Bennet, in *Pride and Prejudice.*

Lady Williams, a *widow with a handsome Jointure & the remains of a very handsome face*, is the story's most complex character. We are told she is too sensible to fall in love with one so much her junior, but to everyone's surprise she wins the hand, though perhaps not the heart of Charles Adams.

After making great efforts to eliminate any competition from Lucy and Alice, Lady Williams has won herself a trophy of her success, a glowing young man. Charles Adams with his wealth, his sense of entitlement and his *cold and indifferent heart*, chooses Lady Williams to nurture his childish selfishness and ego; theirs is not a relationship to develop through love and understanding.

See how she takes it – whether she colours   *Emma*

While Lady Williams uses kindness towards Lucy, she attacks Alice relentlessly. She declares to Alice that *a Lady of Fashion* has *too much colour.* Alice reddens with anger and Lady Williams realising she has struck a sensitive chord continues to provoke and demean her. She taunts Alice half dozen times with references to: *a great deal of red in their Complexion, too red a look, too great a proportion of red in her Cheeks,* etc, until Alice, *heated with wine & raised by Passion, could have little command of her Temper.*

On their stroll to the *Horsepond*, Lady Williams starts once more, she repeats her story of the woman with too much colour, and continues provoking Alice up to the very moment they come upon Lucy *beneath a Citron tree.*

Reading it aloud   *Northanger Abbey*

Undoubtedly, if Jane Austen read *Jack and Alice* aloud after dinner, its zany settings and characters would have roused lots of laughter and enjoyment. Her family would have noted the dismal fates of the two lovesick heroines, particularly Lucy, poisoned by the envious Sukey.

Her audience would have enjoyed the crescendo effect of Lady Williams comments to Alice about her *colour.* Jane Austen had rosy cheeks, her brother Henry wrote that her *eloquent blood spoke through her modest cheek,*[43] and *others noticed her high or brilliant colour.*[44] Contemporaries described hers *complexion of rich colour;*[45] *her great colour;*[46] and observed she had a *good deal of colour in her face – like a doll.*[47]

We can guess Jane Austen knew the embarrassment of blushing, that she had been teased about it, and that being teased had made her cross. In *Jack and Alice* she responded, satirising and exaggerating Lady Williams' repeated teasing of Alice, into an idiotic malicious repetition.

At one point, *the Dispute at length grew so hot on the part of Alice that "From Words she almost came to Blows."* Luckily her father entered and forced *her away from Lady Williams, Mrs Watkins and her red cheeks.*

A few days later, Lady Williams, walking with Alice, accuses her of being *nearly dead drunk*, and provokes her again *with the renewal of the old story of too much colour.* Alice reacts, *"Again! Lady Williams: this is too much --"* The narrator interrupts, *"I know not what might have been the consequence of it, had not their attention been engaged by another object. A lovely young Woman lying apparently in great pain beneath a Citron tree."*

Jane's tormentors had been warned, next time you tease her about her red cheeks, don't expect her to be polite or easily distracted!

3

Edgar and Emma
a tale – in three chapters

Edgar and Emma has no dedication. It is a story that describes, and gently ridicules, the overflowing grief of a young girl, at the absence of her would-be suitor.

Gathering her work together
Pride & Prejudice

Edgar and Emma involves two families, the Marlows and the Willmots. Sir Godfrey and Lady Marlow own *three good Houses in some of the finest parts of England,* but for the past two years they have been living *crowded in deplorable Lodgings, three pair of stairs High, in a paltry Market town* with their two daughters.

Unable to agree who was *most to blame* for their decision to move there, the Marlows *prudently laid aside the debate,* and next morning leave for their seat in Sussex. News of their return home spreads quickly, and local families call to congratulate them.

When Mr and Mrs Willmot arrive with nine of their twenty or more children, Emma, the younger Marlow daughter, watches from her *Dressing-room window.* She harbours a secret passion for the Willmots' eldest son, she is *in anxious Hopes of seeing young Edgar descend from the carriage.* As the Willmots with *their three eldest Daughters first appear,* Emma began to *tremble.* She turned *pale* as four Willmot sons followed, and Edgar was not among them. When the last of the children were *lifted from the Coach,* she sank *breathless on a Sopha, her heart too full to contain its afflictions.*

Emma confided her *melancholy Disappointment* to Thomas, the footman, but when she asked his advice, he declined to get involved. Ordering him to keep her complaints secret, she descended *with a heavy heart into the Parlour* to join the party.

Emma summoned up enough courage to ask after the rest of the Willmot family, but her voice was so low and faltering, no-one heard her. When Mrs Willmot asked one of her daughters to ring the bell for their Carriage, Emma seized the bell-pull, and declared resolutely, *"Mrs Willmot, you do not stir from this House till you let me know how all the rest of your family do, particularly your eldest son."*

Mrs Willmot replies that all her other children were well, she reported the whereabouts of the eleven not at home, including Edgar, who was at college. Emma managed to remain tolerably composed and to refrain from tears until the Willmots had gone, *when having no check to the overflowing of her greif, she gave free vent to them, & retiring to her own room, continued in tears the remainder of her Life.*

Conjecturing as to the date   *Pride & Prejudice*

Jane Austen most likely wrote *Edgar and Emma* at the end of 1788. She was falling in love with D'Arcy Wentworth, a young Irish surgeon, working as a locum for an Alton apothecary. Like Emma, she tried unsuccessfully to keep her feelings for him a secret.

In late September, D'Arcy had left suddenly for London, to apply for a position in the East India Company. He returned to Hampshire in early November,[48] and in the months that followed their romance blossomed. This story may have been her gift to him on his return. Her father had ruled that D'Arcy, and her relationship with him were never to be mentioned, which could explain why she did not include a dedication when she recorded the story in *Volume the First*.

The names of people that fill up my time *Mansfield Park*

The name Marlow was likely Jane's acknowledgement of Reverend Dr Michael Marlow, a friend of her eldest brother James Austen[49] at Oxford. They were fellow scholarship students at St. John's College.

From 1795 to 1828, Dr Marlow served as President of St. John's; in 1789 he was appointed vicar of St Giles, Oxford; and from 1798 to 1802, he was Vice-Chancellor of Oxford University.

The story of the Willmot family, with *their children too numerous to be particularly described,* nine visiting the Marlows with their parents, eleven away from home and *all the rest,* was a satirical reference to *Farmer George,* King George III, and his wife, Queen Charlotte of Mecklenburg.

Their great Royal brood of fifteen children: George Augustus Frederick, Prince of Wales, b.1762; Frederick Augustus, Duke of York and Albany, b.1763; William Henry, Duke of Clarence and St Andrews, b.1765; Charlotte, Princess Royal, b.1766; Edward Augustus, Duke of Kent and Strathearn, b.1767; Augusta Sophia, b.1768; Elizabeth, b.1770; Ernest Augustus, Duke of Cumberland and Teviotdale, b.1771; Augustus Frederick, Duke of Sussex, b.1773; Adolphus, Duke of Cambridge, b.1774; Mary, Duchess of Gloucester and Edinburgh, b.1776; Sophia Matilda, b.1777; Octavius, b.1779; Alfred, b.1780; and Amelia, b.1783; nine sons and six daughters, was a standing joke of the time.

Jane took the name *Willmot* from Eliza Nugent Bromley's novel *Laura and Augustus,* by, published in 1784. In the story, Augustus kills the villain Boswell in a duel, then flees with Laura from the West Indies to London, where they assume the name *Willmot*.

Jane Austen's use of an assumed name for Emma's beloved was an allusion to D'Arcy Wentworth. After he was acquitted of highway robbery in 1787, D'Arcy became a celebrity, pursued by the press. When in London, to avoid their intrusions, he often used an assumed name.

Her own share in the story   *Emma*

Reading *Jack and Alice* and *Edgar and Emma,* we realise that twelve year old Jane Austen had experienced the pleasure, the dreams and desperation of a teenage crush.

In 1788, reading *Edgar and Emma* aloud after dinner, closing with the *overflowing of* Emma's *greif* that would continue *the remainder of her Life,* Jane was telling her parents of her desire to see D'Arcy Wentworth again. At this point, she had her family's full support.

Her mother in particular, was full of encouragement, delighted with Jane's interest in a handsome young man from such a noble family:

> *Good gracious! Lord bless me! only think! dear me! Mr. Darcy! Who would have thought it! And is it really true? Oh! my sweetest! how rich and how great you will be! What pin-money, what jewels, what carriages you will have!* [50]

4

Henry and Eliza
a novel

To whom this work is dedicated   *The History of England*

Jane Austen dedicated *Henry and Eliza* to her cousin Jane Cooper, four and a half years her senior. Jane Cooper's late mother, also named Jane, was her mother, Mrs Austen's elder sister. Despite the difference in their ages, Jane Cooper was a true friend and confidante to Jane Austen.

Gathering her work together   *Pride & Prejudice*

Henry and Eliza is a dark absurdist story about parents, rewards and punishment, and the fate of young women out in the world.

It opens with a vigorous introduction to Sir George and Lady Harcourt, who are *inspecting the Labours of their Haymakers*. They reward the industrious ones with smiles of approbation and punish the idle by bludgeoning them with a cudgel. Beneath a haystack, the couple find a baby girl, *not more than 3 months old. Having no Children of their own*, they resolve to take her home *to educate her with care and cost*.

Eliza grows up *beloved by Lady Harcourt, adored by Sir George and admired by all the World,* but at eighteen her happiness is interrupted. She is caught stealing a £50 banknote and *turned out of doors.*

Eliza seeks help from Mrs Wilson, an Innkeeper at *the red Lion. A most amiable creature,* she recommends Eliza to the *Dutchess of F.* as a companion for her daughter, Lady Hariet, who is *on the point of marriage with a young man of considerable fortune,* Henry Cecil.

Eliza and Henry Cecil fall in *Love,* he *declared his first and prevailed on Eliza to consent to a private union,* a quick marriage option, that did not require parental permission or the reading of marriage banns over three weeks, from the pulpit.

One evening, when the Dutchess and Hariet were absent, Henry and Eliza prevailed on the Dutchess's chaplain, who would *do anything to oblige* Eliza, to marry them. They departed immediately afterwards, leaving a note for the Dutchess:

Madam,
We are married and gone.
Henry and Eliza Cecil.

After reading the note, the Dutchess *flew into the most violent passion.* She sent *300 armed Men* after them with orders to bring them back to her, dead or alive. If they were alive, she would have them *put to Death in some torturelike manner, after a few years Confinement.*

Henry and Eliza fled to France, away *from the dreadful effects of the Dutchess's vengeance.* They lived there, *to the utmost extent of their Income.* Three years later, Henry died, and Eliza and their two sons were left in poverty. Eliza returned to England, and was apprehended as soon as she stepped *on Shore at Dover.* She was imprisoned in the Dutchess' *snug little Newgate, erected for the reception of her own private Prisoners.*

With some difficulty, Eliza and her children escaped. She sold her clothes, *the last reliques of her former glory, and bought playthings for her Boys and a gold Watch for herself.*

Too late, after her children chewed off two of her fingers, Eliza realized they were hungry, and she had no money for food. She decided to return to *her old freinds, Sir George and Lady Harcourt, whose generosity she had so often experienced and hoped to experience as often again.*

As their hospitable Mansion was 40 miles away, Eliza walked *30 without stopping.* She reached an *inn she remembered with so much delight,* and took up *a post at the Innyard,* hoping *to receive some Charitable Gratuity* from patrons going *in and out.*

Eliza recognised Lady Harcourt in a carriage leaving the yard, and called to her. Sir George, who was with his wife, demanded Eliza explain her *Situation.* Lady Harcourt, *in transports of Joy,* told him Eliza was their *real Child,* born while Sir George was in America. She had dreaded his *just resentment* at the child not being a boy, and left the baby beside a Haycock. *Satisfied within myself of the welfare of my Child, I soon forgot I had one.*

When they found Eliza there, she tells Sir George, *I had no more idea of her being my own, than you had, and nothing I will venture to say could have recalled the circumstance to my remembrance, but my thus accidentally hearing her voice which now strikes me as being the very counterpart of my own Child's.*

Sir George accepted his wife's *rational and convincing Account of the whole affair,* and freely forgave Eliza for *the robbery she was guilty of.* The three were reconciled, Eliza entered their carriage with her children, and returned home, after an absence of *nearly four years.*

No sooner was she reinstated in her accustomed power at Harcourt Hall, than she raised an army, with which she entirely demolished the Dutchess's Newgate, snug as it was, and by that act, gained the Blessings of thousands, & the Applause of her own Heart.

Conjecturing as to the date

Pride & Prejudice

Henry and Eliza was the last of the three *novels* Jane Austen wrote in London in 1789, it was written in November of that year.

There was something in the name   *Emma*

The title was a remembrancer of Christmas 1786, when Eliza de Feuillide, her son Hastings and her mother Philadelphia Hancock came to stay with the Austens at Steventon rectory, along with Jane Cooper and her brother Edward.

Eliza was twenty-four, lively and flirtatious, and Henry Austen, fifteen, was smitten. Jane noticed, she was nursing a partiality for a handsome young apothecary in Alton.

Though she used their names for the title, her story *Henry and Eliza* had nothing to do with Henry Austen, and very little with Eliza de Feuillide. The back-story, like most of the *Juvenilia*, is about Jane herself.

Perhaps she titled the story *Henry and Eliza* as a knowing, sisterly gesture to commiserate with her beloved brother Henry, even encourage him. Her intuition, naming them as a couple, proved correct, eleven years later, in 1797, Henry Austen and Eliza de Feuillide were married.

Such a fund of vivacity & good humour   *Kitty, or the Bower*

At the end of 1786, Jane had returned home from Abbey House School in Reading in disgrace, never to return. Her sister Cassandra would go back to school the following year without her. Jane was to remain at home in the rectory, under the firm control of her mother.

Despite these omens, Christmas 1786, was the happiest occasion. Eliza, Philadelphia and Eliza had last visited the Austens ten years earlier, when Jane was Hastings' age.

Eliza was a bright star in the night sky of Steventon. She captivated Jane with tales of faraway places, she was a flirt, her knowledge of India, the French Court and London society, and her élan vital were an inspiration. She brought French manners, insouciance and an attitude of laissez-faire to the parsonage. Above all, she recognised the importance of love.

Eliza believed that during cold weather, *dancing was the only effectual method of rendering one's existence less uncomfortable,*[51] Her birthday was three days before Christmas, six days after Jane. George Austen borrowed a fortepiano for her to play, and she filled the rectory with carols, songs and lively dance tunes for them all.

She was *delicately fair*, slight and full of life, her countenance *absolutely sweet and her voice and manner winningly mild.*[52] She captivated Jane with tales of faraway places, and with her pleasantries, that could rouse the heart of any young man.

Born in Calcutta in 1761, Eliza was proud of being *early accustomed to the vagabond life.*[53] She was three when her parents returned to England with her and their Indian servants. They stayed with the Austens at the Deane rectory in the summer of 1766, at the time Jane's second brother George was born. Eliza's father, Tyso Hancock, was proud to be made his godfather.

At fifteen, Eliza and her mother left England for Europe, travelling through Flanders and Germany for two years before settling in Paris at the end of 1779, the city she described as *magnificence beyond conception.*[54] At twenty, Eliza had married a titled, handsome, French Captain, ten years her senior, Jean-Francois Capot, Comte de Feuillide, with estates in the south west of France.

Jane included a reference to Eliza's escape from the French Revolution with her baby son and her mother Philadelphia. They left France in the first week of July 1789 without incident, a week before the storming of the Bastille. Eerily, Jane's story predicted the death of Eliza's husband, Comte Jean Capot de Feuillide, guillotined in Paris in February 1794.

Eliza's arrival in Steventon in December 1786, lifted Jane's spirits, it began a friendship between the two that lasted until Eliza's death in 1813. She was *the most remarkable visitor during Jane Austen's childhood.*[55] Perhaps it was her vivacity and good humour, and the world of other possibilities she presented, that Jane found so liberating.

What its ancient date might occasion *Northanger Abbey*

Two years elapsed from the time Jane Austen wrote *Henry and Eliza* until she recorded it in *Volume the First*. In that time both her own and Eliza de Feuillide's lives altered irrevocably.

What its ancient date might occasion *Northanger Abbey*

Jane continued to revise *Henry and Eliza*, after recording it in *Volume the First*, making more than twenty changes to the text.

Wilson brought me word of it *Lady Susan*

She changed the name of the woman *who kept the red Lion,* from *Jones,* to Wilson,[56] *the most amiable creature on earth, was an innkeeper in a small market town.*

Jane knew a Mrs Willson, wife of William Willson, proprietor of the *Crown Inn*, in Basingstoke, a market town eight miles from Steventon, an important staging and refreshment point for coaches.

The *Crown*, and the *Red Lion* were among five large inns in Basingstoke that competed for contracts to provide the refreshment services. The *Crown*, with its frontage of 54 feet and a depth of 120 feet, was also used for public meetings, for hearings of the Assizes — the circuit court that heard criminal cases; and on the Thursday nearest full moon, for meetings of the select Hants Club.

From 1770 to 1790, the *Crown Inn* ran the annual Basingstoke Races. In February 1798, it took over the management of Basingstoke's regular monthly ball, held in the *Angel Assembly Rooms*. The Willsons advertised it in the *Reading Mercury,* sold tickets, provided refreshments, hired the musicians and managed the door.

For decades, the Austens regularly attended the Basingstoke Assemblies. Jane gossiped about them in her letters: if she planned to attend; and when she did, who was there, and with whom; what she wore and her partners. Jane Austen and Mrs Willson would certainly have known each other.

Jane, not yet thirteen, accompanied her sister and brothers to the Basingstoke Ball in the late spring of 1788.

D'Arcy Wentworth had obtained a position as a locum with an apothecary in Alton. He was staying at *Kempshott Park*, three miles from Dummer, rented by his friend, William Wickham.

Wickham came from *Cottingley Hall*, near Bingley, in the West Riding of Yorkshire. He was a friend of the Prince of Wales, introduced to him by a former tutor of the Prince, Cyril Jackson, Wickham's Dean at Christ Church, Oxford. When Wickham left for Europe in July 1788, the Prince took over his lease of *Kempshott Park*.

Wickham's father, Henry, was Honorary Deputy Lord Lieutenant of the West Riding to Lord Rockingham, until Rockingham's death in 1782. He was presently Honorary Deputy to Charles Howard, Duke of Norfolk, After the Duke was removed in March 1798, he would serve Earl Fitzwilliam in the same role.

D'Arcy and Wickham met in York in 1785, through Fitzwilliam, and had remained friends. Wickham's two sisters Anne and Harriet were also staying at *Kempshott*. The four of them decided to pass the evening at the Basingstoke Assembly. The Austen party was already settled when they arrived.

Jane looked down the long room at the Angel and saw a *great tall fellow*[57] with Wickham. She recognized him immediately, she had met D'Arcy two years earlier, at the *Bear Inn* in Reading, when she, Cassandra and Jane Cooper dined there with Edward Austen and Edward Cooper. D'Arcy and the two Edwards were in Reading for the Bulmershe races.[58]

At the end of October 1789, when Jane and D'Arcy Wentworth returned to London from Scotland, they took lodgings at 23 Clipstone Street, Marylebone, under the name of Wilson.[59]

Her own share in the story *Emma*

Jane Austen was sent away from home for five of her first eleven years. Fostered out as a baby, she did not return to her family until she could walk and talk. Her story of a baby girl found under a haystack may well reflect her own insecurity.

Perhaps she justified her mother's coldness and anger towards her by imagining she was not really her daughter, but had been found as a baby, exposed out of doors. At the same time, Jane Austen was raising serious questions about the extent of female infanticide in England, the deliberate killing of newborn baby girls.

Infanticide was considered to be the crime of an unmarried woman, an "unhappy wench," poor, in insecure employment at best, who could not support a child. Jane Austen presented a quite different picture, of a titled, wealthy, married woman who left her baby for dead because she was female, not the male child her husband wanted. Jane did not have Lady Harcourt actively murder her daughter, rather she leaves her exposed, laying her down in a field *beneath a Haycock*.

The law against child killing in England, dealt solely with the murder of illegitimate children. The objective of the law, the *Infanticide Statute of 1624, was, to prevent the destroying and murthering of bastard children.* It stated, *many lewd Women that have been delivered of Bastard Children, to avoid their Shame, and to escape Punishment, do secretly bury or conceal the Death of their Children.*[60]

It ruled that if the death of the baby was concealed, the mother would be presumed guilty of infanticide and would be subject to the death penalty, unless she could prove, with at least one witness, that her baby was born dead.

There is exquisite pleasure in subduing an insolent spirit *Lady Susan*

There was no love lost between Jane and her mother, she was the *least dear to her of all her children.*[61] Very young, just learning to form her letters, Jane scrawled in the margin of a book: *Mothers angry fathers gone out.*[62]

Jane wrote later: *Mothers certainly have not yet got quite the right way of managing their daughters. I do not know where the error lies. I do not pretend to set people right, but I do see that they are often wrong.*[63]

Jane Austen's depiction of the *Dutchess of F.* details the deterioration of her relationship with her mother after her return home from school in Reading. She saw herself as confined in the Dutchess's *snug little Newgate, erected for the reception of her own private Prisoners.*

The Dutchess was a reference to her mother, mocking her much vaunted connection to the 1st Duke of Chandos, her great uncle. Jane described her as a woman of *most violent passion,* of *Enmities unconquerable.* In 1786, when Eliza's visit to Steventon provided inspiration for the story, Mrs Austen was forty-seven, in *Henry and Eliza,* Jane gave her age as, *about 45 and a half.*

In the story, Eliza raised *an Army with which she entirely demolished the Dutchess's Newgate.* This was not an impossible prospect, just a few years earlier, in June 1780, Newgate Prison was destroyed during the Gordon Riots. Perhaps though, Jane was simply putting on record that Eliza had succeeded in overthrowing the Dutchess's tyranny in a far more subtle and abiding way.

Determined to manage it with eoconomy & not to spend it either with folly or Extravagance
Love and Freindship

In *Henry and Eliza,* Jane described the difficulties that confronted young people in managing their money wisely: *Henry and Eliza were able to save but a trifle, having lived to the extent of their Income.* To raise money, Eliza sold her clothes, but she failed to keep enough money for food for herself and the children, and was reduced to begging outside an inn.

My father's opinion of me does me the greatest honour
Pride & Prejudice

Jane's reference to the dutchess's chaplain, who would do anything to oblige Eliza, was an ironic allusion to her father, Reverend George Austen.

In late 1789, Jane and D'Arcy Wentworth eloped to Scotland. They returned to Steventon at Christmas to visit Jane's family. Her father agreed to marry them, to legalize their Scottish marriage, but after James Austen returned from Oxford, he changed his mind.

I want to be married at home and my brother will not consent to it
Sir Charles Grandison

James reported to his father the stories he had read in the London newspapers about D'Arcy Wentworth. Convinced about the impact of Jane and D'Arcy's relationship on the Austen family's reputation, and on the future careers of his sons, Reverend Austen withdrew his consent.[64]

In the course of the Christmas week
Mansfield Park

Over Christmas 1789, Jane was persuaded by her father to abandon her relationship with D'Arcy Wentworth. He believed she had escaped the *most irremediable of evils, a connection for life with an unprincipled man.*[65]

D'Arcy Wentworth sailed from England three weeks later for the other side of the world, without her. Jane's family closed ranks around her, her father ruled the affair and D'Arcy's name were never to be mentioned. Jane remained within the family confines until her death in 1817.

During the first years after she returned home, Jane felt imprisoned, she wrote later, she was *allowed no liberty*, no *society, no amusement, till my father's point was gained.*[66]

5

The Adventures of Mr Harley
a short, but interesting Tale

To whom this work is dedicated　　　　　　　　　　　*The History of England*

Jane Austen dedicated *The Adventures of Mr Harley*, with all imaginable respect, to her brother *Mr Francis William Austen Midshipman on board his Majestys Ship the Perseverance.* Twenty months older than Jane, closest in age to her of all her siblings, they were always good friends.

Conjecturing as to the date　　　　　　　　　　　*Pride & Prejudice*

In December 1789, after a year in training aboard *HMS Perseverance*, Frank Austen was made a midshipman, he served in that post until November 1791. The two stories Jane dedicated to him, *Jack and Alice* and *The Adventures of Mr Harley*, were written during this period. She would most likely have included them in her letters to Frank, as he did not return home from the East Indies until the end of 1793.

Gathering her work together　　　　　　　　　　　*Pride & Prejudice*

A few weeks after his marriage to Emma, Mr Harley went to sea as a naval chaplain, on board a Man of War. Six months later he returned to England and took *the Stage Coach for Hogsworth Green*, where Emma lived.

In the Stagecoach, were *A man without a Hat, Another with two, An old maid and a young Wife.* Mr Harley noticed the *young Wife.* She was *about 17 with fine dark Eyes and an elegant Shape. Mr Harley soon found out, that she was his Emma and recollected he had married her a few weeks before he left England.*

Names, facts, every thing mentioned
Pride & Prejudice

Mr Harley was named for Harley Street in London. Its terraces and mansions were laid out and built in the early years of the eighteenth century, transforming the green fields around the village of Marylebone into London's West End. It became the prime location in London for medical specialists to have their consulting rooms.

Edward Harley, 2nd Earl of Oxford (1689-1741) and his wife Lady Henrietta Cavendish Holles (1694-1755) led and financed the development of Harley Street, Cavendish Square and other surrounding streets including Wimpole and Wigmore, that bear their family names. Lady Henrietta was a connexion of Lady Arabella Holles, the second wife of Thomas Wentworth, 1st Earl of Strafford, executed during the reign of Charles I.

Her own share in the story
Emma

Harley Street had other connotations for Jane Austen. In July 1788, Lord Saye & Sele, a connection of her mother, succeeded there in his second attempt to take his own life. It was said he committed suicide after his doctor told him that his unbearable headaches were caused by an incurable disease.

In March 1789, in Cavendish Square, at the southern end of Harley Street, a fire broke out in the house of Henry and Deborah-Jemima Maxwell. Deborah-Jemima, the sister of Jane's friend and neighbour, Anne Lefroy, was badly burned.

Slumbering on one side of the fire   *Emma*

Deborah-Jemima had been sitting by the fire in the drawing room, *after dinner, engaged in writing cards of invitation,* wearing *a round calico gown, with an apron of fine muslin, very full and wide.*[67]

A poker fell from the fireplace onto the hem of her gown, and quickly set fire to her clothes. She tried to put out the flames by rolling herself in the carpet, but it was nailed to the floor, she could not lift it.

She ran up the stairs to her bed-chamber, her dress on fire. Servants following her tried to put out the flames with their coats and the bed curtains, but failed. In a few moments the bed, the wainscot and window shutters had all caught fire. The whole household was screaming.

After it was extinguished, Deborah-Jemima lay in bed until early morning, badly burnt, *conscious and uncomplaining.* She died just before dawn, leaving her daughter, eight months old, and her husband, distraught.[68]

A week after her funeral, Anne Lefroy decided she must go to London, to do what she could. Henry Maxwell was depressed, unapproachable, withdrawn. The house in Cavendish Square needed urgent repairs and attention. Her mother wrote that the baby was in the house, with her nurse, but failing to thrive. Her mother was very concerned, but seemed unable to help or intervene.

In April, George Austen took Jane and Cassandra to London to stay with Anne Lefroy in Cork Street, at the house of Benjamin Langlois, an uncle of Reverend Lefroy. Mrs Lefroy brought her six children and nursemaids with her. She had invited the Austen sisters as company for her children, particularly her daughter Jemima-Lucy, aged ten.

All the terrors of expectation   *Northanger Abbey*

Jane wrote *The Adventures of Mr Harley* in 1790, filled with allusions to her own circumstances. D'Arcy Wentworth was an apothecary and a surgeon, a member of the medical fraternity moving into Harley Street.

Like Emma and Mr Harley, Jane and D'Arcy Wentworth had married several weeks before D'Arcy sailed from England. Mr Harley's wife is seventeen when he returns, Jane would be seventeen in December 1792.

As she read the story aloud to her family, her father would have heard Jane's hopes that D'Arcy would soon return, and her fear that he could have forgotten her.

6

Sir William Mountague
an unfinished performance

To whom this work is dedicated   *The History of England*

Jane Austen dedicated *Sir William Mountague* to her brother *Charles John Austen Esqre*, the youngest member of her family, four years her junior.

Conjecturing as to the date   *Pride & Prejudice*

It is generally agreed *Sir William Mountague* was written in 1788, when Charles Austen was nine. He was twelve when Jane dedicated the story to him and transcribed it into *Volume the First* of her *Juvenilia*.

In July 1791, following his brother Frank into the Navy, Charles commenced his studies at the Royal Naval Academy in Portsmouth. It is likely Jane celebrated the event by dedicating two of her stories to him. Certainly *Sir William Mountague* would have had greater appeal to a boy of twelve entering the world than to a nine year old schoolboy.

Gathering her work together *Pride & Prejudice*

Sir William Mountague is a fun and funny story satirizing the inconstancy of a young man's passions, his indecision in romance, his fickle fancies and his love of shooting.

It opens by announcing his noble connections, with a brief genealogy of seven of his titled antecedents. At *about 17,* on the death of his father, Sir Henry Mountague, Sir William inherited a handsome fortune and a fine estate, *well stocked with Deer.*

Over two pages, he falls in love with seven young women, and looks ahead to an eighth. A fortnight after marrying the sixth, he falls most violently in love with a seventh, rejoicing that through her he could gain *free access to Miss Wentworth.*

Jane Austen ended the story at that point, the narrator's voice trails off with a long ellipsis of five dots. As she finished reading her *unfinished performance* to her family, they knew as we readers do, exactly where Sir William was heading.

Sir William falls in love with every girl he sees, but his love of shooting drives him even harder. He feels *Sorrow and Affliction* at having to cancel his first wedding arrangements when they clash with the opening of the shooting season. He knows he should be *much more grieved* by this turn of events but cannot restrain his feelings of *Joy* and *Happiness* at not *losing such a Day.*

There are no oppressive parents or broken hearts in *Sir William Mountague.* Rather, there is a seemingly inexhaustible supply of young women ready to humour Sir William, who appears to cut a swathe through them.

Jane Austen did allow for a measure of resistance from three of his seven conquests. Lady Perceval refuses to change her wedding date, and *enraged*, returns to London. Miss Arundel refuses Sir William at first, despite her uncle Mr Brudenell being his friend and a *sensible Man.* Emma Stanhope asks for fourteen shillings compensation after Sir

William shoots her brother, but when he offers her a slightly better deal, *himself and his Fortune,* she accepts and marries him.

The names of people that fill up my time

The name, Mountague, echoes the hero of Shakespeare's *Romeo and Juliet,* a Montague. It also acknowledged Augustus Montague, the hero of Eliza Bromley's novel *Laura and Augustus.* Jane Austen varied the spelling to the more ribald *Mountague,* suggesting perhaps the sexual preoccupation, even prowess, of her hero.

Arundel was a Wentworth family name. Elizabeth Wentworth, daughter of Sir William Wentworth, 2nd Earl of Strafford of the 2nd Creation (1722-1791) married John Arundell, 4th Baron Arundell of Trerice (1701-1768). His estate passed to her nephew, Frederick Thomas Wentworth, 3rd Earl of Strafford (1732-1799).

The name also referenced Charles Howard, 11th Duke of Norfolk (1746-1815), Earl of Arundel, a friend and colleague of D'Arcy Wentworth's cousin, Earl Fitzwilliam, whose seat was Arundel Castle in Sussex. Jane Austen refers to him again in *Evelyn,* in *Volume the Third.*

Jane used a second Wentworth family name, Stanhope, in the story. Anne Stanhope, Lady Clare, was the mother of Arabella Holles, the wife of Thomas Wentworth, the first Earl of Strafford (1593-1641). Admiral Sir Henry-Edwin Stanhope (1754-1814) a contemporary, was a distant connexion of both Jane Austen's mother and D'Arcy.

A number of characters have the names of important families of the time. Perceval was a reference to the Earls of Egmont, Anglo-Irish peers. Jane's contemporary, Spencer Percival, (1762-1812), seventh son of John Perceval, 2nd Earl of Egmont (1711-1770) was later Prime Minister, from October 1809 to May 1812. He remains the only Prime Minister of England ever to be assassinated.

Of all people and all names in the world   *Persuasion*

Why the story ends with the possibility for Sir William of free access to Miss Wentworth, is still a mystery. In 1788, when she wrote *Sir William Mountague,* Jane Austen's romance with D'Arcy Wentworth had hardly begun. Was she flirting with him, using a nickname, 'Miss Wentworth' to emphasise their family connexion?

7

Memoirs of Mr Clifford
an unfinished tale

To whom this work is dedicated

The History of England

Jane Austen dedicated *Memoirs of Mr Clifford* to her brother Charles. He was so pleased with *Sir William Mountague,* she was encouraged to dedicate a second unfinished tale to him, *as unfinished as the first.*

Conjecturing as to the date

Pride & Prejudice

It is believed Jane wrote both *Memoirs of Mr Clifford* and *Sir William Mountague* in 1788, and recorded them in *Volume the First* in the second half of 1791.

Memoirs of Mr Clifford satirises an enthusiast, devoted to his diverse wheeled vehicles. In today's world, we would probably recognise him as a fanatical collector of antique cars, seen occasionally, motoring along, perched high in the slow lane, with the wind in his hair.

Gathering her work together

Pride & Prejudice

Mr Clifford owned *a great many Carriages* and an amazing fine stud of Horses. The narrator can remember less than half the names of his different carriages: *a Coach, a Chariot, a Chaise, a Landeau, a Landeaulet, a Phaeton, a Gig, a Whisky, an italian Chair, a Buggy, a Curricle and a wheelbarrow,* and the colours of his nineteen horses, *six Greys, 4 Bays, eight Blacks and a poney.*

Mr Clifford sets out from Bath in his *Coach and 4 Bays* at 5 o'clock on a Monday Morning the 1st of May, for London, t*o feast his eyes with a sight of that great Metropolis.*

On his first day on the road he covers *no less than nineteen miles,* and it was *pretty tight work.* He arrives in Devizes by 11pm and after eighteen hours on the road he needs the comfort of a good hot Supper. We note a certain stinginess when he orders *a whole Egg to be boiled for him and his Servants.*

Mr Clifford sets off again next morning and after *3 days hard labour,* presumably tinkering and adjusting the mechanisms of his coach all the way, he *reached Overton.*

His progress is tediously slow, he has travelled forty-two miles in three days, just fourteen miles a day. Nevertheless, he finds himself *seized with a dangerous fever the Consequence of too much violent Exercise.* He remains five months in Overton under the care of a *celebrated Physician who at length compleatly cured him of his troublesome Desease.*

Mr Clifford gets back on the road, still very weak, he travels only three miles on the first day. Stopping at Dean Gate, he stays a few days before resuming his journey. Clearly he is avoiding violent Exercise, he does not want a recurrence of *his troublesome Desease.*

Setting off again, in easy stages, he arrives at Clarkengreen: half a mile from Deane Gateon the first day, on the next he reaches Worting: two and a half miles from Clarkengreen, the third takes him to bottom of Basingstoke Hill, and the fourth to Mr Robin's Crown Inn and Post House in Basingstoke, where obviously he stops for refreshment. In the four days since he left Deane Gate, he has covered almost six miles.

Jane ends her story here, probably with mock resignation or disbelief, her voice trailing away over an ellipsis of four dots. She is leaving Mr Clifford at Basingstoke to soldier on alone over the next fifty to sixty miles to London. If he can maintain his present speed, travelling every day without a break, it could take him five to six weeks, depending where in London he is heading. Who knows if he will make it?

The names of people that fill up my time *Mansfield Park*

Jane Austen gave a Wentworth family name to the hero of the story. Lady Margaret Clifford, daughter of the 4th Earl of Cumberland and Grisold Hughes, was the first wife of Sir Thomas Wentworth, 1st Earl of Strafford (1593-1641), D'Arcy's most distinguished relation.

Oh, these odious gigs! How I detest them *Northanger Abbey*

Jane seems to have enjoyed those characters who appreciate speed and know how to put a vehicle through its paces, we meet another, John Thorpe in *Northanger Abbey*.

Do but look at my horse; did you ever see an animal so made for speed in your life?" "Such true blood! Three hours and a half indeed coming only three-and-twenty miles! Look at that creature, and suppose it possible if you can."

"He does look very hot, to be sure."

"Hot! he had not turned a hair till we came to Walcot Church; but look at his forehand; look at his loins; only see how he moves; that horse cannot go less than ten miles an hour: tie his legs and he will get on.

What do you think of my gig, Miss Morland? A neat one, is not it? Well hung; town-built; I have not had it a month. "Curricle-hung, you see; seat, trunk, sword-case, splashing-board, lamps, silver moulding, all you see complete; the iron-work as good as new, or better. He asked fifty guineas; I closed with him directly, threw down the money, and the carriage was mine."

Her own share in the story *Emma*

Jane wrote *Memoirs of Mr Clifford* in her sunny year of 1788. It was a delightful gift for her youngest brother, nine year-old Charles Austen, a fun and funny story that would have had him and all at the table in peals of laughter as Jane read it to them. The long road Mr Clifford travelled was familiar to them all, they might have interjected at points in the story, urging him along where they knew the lane narrowed or the slope was slippery, even calling a warning of a big pothole ahead.

8

The beautifull Cassandra
a novel in twelve Chapters

To whom this work is dedicated   *The History of England*

Jane Austen dedicated *The beautifull Cassandra, by permission to Miss Austen,* her sister, with a paean of praise: *You are a Phoenix. Your taste is refined, Your Sentiments are noble, and your Virtues innumerable. Your Person is lovely, your Figure, elegant, and your Form, majestic. Your Manners, are polished, your Conversation is rational and your appearance singular.* Jane hopes her story will give Cassandra *one moment's amusement.*

Cassandra Austen (1773-1845) was two years older than Jane, her only sister in a family dominated by six brothers. The two were close and seem to have remained so.

Gathering her work together   *Pride & Prejudice*

The beautifull Cassandra was a spoof report from Jane to her family on her sister's encounters and adventures, as she explored the expanse and the delights of London.

In *Chapter the First,* Jane tells her listeners this story is about a different

Cassandra, the daughter of a milliner. In Chapter the 2^d they learn that she, like Cassandra Austen, had *attained her 16th year.* Jane has prepared them for a story that is a mix of fact and fiction.

This done, she compresses a whole series of events into nearly 7 hours on a single day. She can exaggerate Cassandra's exploits or expose her mischievous behaviour for the amusement of the family, without offence, doubtless encouraging Cassandra to correct any errors of fact, to take up the story and to tell her family what she really did in London.

Cassandra, the fictional heroine, begins her day at her mother's hat shop in *Bond Street.* She puts on a Bonnet *her Mother had just compleated for the Countess of –*, and she leaves the *shop to make her Fortune.*

Despite her good intentions, over the next eight chapters, Cassandra does very little to make her fortune, but she does have encounters her namesake would never have had at home in Steventon.

In Chapter the 3rd she meets a young Viscount, celebrated for his *Accomplishments, Virtues, Elegance and Beauty,* she curtseys and walks on.

In the next chapter, we learn where she is heading, to a *Pastry-cooks* for an ice-cream. One is not nearly enough, Cassandra devours six ices, and on a sugar-high, *refuses to pay,* knocks down the Cook and walks off.

She moves faster, goes further afield, hiring a Hackney Coach to go to Hampstead then ordering it to turn around. Arriving back at *the same spot,* the Coachman demands to be paid. Cassandra searches her pockets *again and again* but finds no money. He grows *peremptory,* she takes off her valuable bonnet, places it on his head and runs away.

After proceeding *thro' many a street,* without meeting *the least Adventure,* on *turning a Corner of Bloomsbury Square,* Cassandra meets Maria. They tremble, blush, turn pale and pass in *mutual Silence.* A Widow hails her from a window, Cassandra curtseys and keeps going.

A quarter of a mile on she reaches her home in Bond Street. She has been *absent nearly 7 hours.* Her mother presses her to her bosom. Cassandra smiles to herself, *"This is a day well spent."*

Conjecturing as to the date   *Pride & Prejudice*

The beautifull Cassandra was most likely written in mid-1789, when Jane and Cassandra were staying in London with Madam Lefroy, in Cork Street. It was polished and recorded in *Volume the First* in 1791.

Her own share in the story   *Emma*

Jane Austen included a reference to her aunt, Philadelphia Hancock, in the story, as the *celebrated Millener in Bond Street*. In her youth Philadelphia had completed a seven year apprenticeship to a milliner. Jane praised her as *celebrated*, a master milliner in London's most elegant and fashionable street.

Jane presents the milliner as a kind and affectionate mother, a *worthy woman*. Cassandra arrives home to a big hug, not a scolding, her mother makes no mention of the Countess's missing bonnet.

In making Cassandra the milliner's *only Daughter,* Jane found a spot in her story to refer to her cousin Eliza, Philadelphia's only child.

Jane introduces *the beautifull Cassandra*, as she did *Sir William Mountague*, by way of her parentage and noble associations. Here she uses them for more obvious comic effect, the Duchess, Countess and Viscount of the first three chapters suggest Cassandra's encounters with nobility of steadily declining rank.

Jane Austen satirised her parents relationship in *The beautifull Cassandra*. "*The Dutchess*" may well have been a nickname the Austen children used amongst themselves to refer to their mother, a granddaughter of Mary Brydges, sister of the 1st Duke of Chandos.

In her reference to Cassandra's father's claim to *noble Birth as a near relation of the Dutchess of – 's butler,* Jane poked fun at her father, George Austen. She suggests he is of lowlier stock, someone who recognises his wife's loftier social status and waits on her. It was done with a light touch, but doubtless there was some truth in it.

Adventure will not befall a young lady in her own village *Northanger Abbey*

In London, Cassandra entered a different world from Steventon and its surrounding villages. She experiences the pleasure of wearing a fashionable bonnet and eating delicious ice creams. She walks and rides along miles of paved streets that open suddenly into gracious squares. There she might meet a Viscount, or hail a Hackney Coach and order the Coachman to take her wherever she pleases.

Jane focuses on alterations in Cassandra's confidence and feelings as she explores unfamiliar places with unfamiliar rules. The downside of ordering ices and carriage rides is that she needs money to pay for them. Cassandra has no money to pay for her ices, she knocks *down the Pastry Cook* and walks away; when the Coachman demands payment, she places her stolen bonnet on his head and runs off.

Meeting Maria in Bloomsbury Square restores Cassandra to herself, the two girls look at each other, embarrassed, each seems to recognise herself in the other. They tremble, blush, turn pale, and pass each other in *mutual silence*. Cassandra is a girl of sixteen again, out of her depth in the big city. No longer *out to make her Fortune* or to seek *Adventure*, she begins to make her way home.

The beautifull Cassandra is a warm, funny, fast moving story. By elegantly presenting it in twelve tiny chapters, Jane creates the illusion of her sister's progress around London.

London, *the great world,*[69] fills Jane Austen's *Juvenilia*, she knew the city, its layout and the nuances of class at play within its central districts, Bloomsbury Square, Bond Street, Brook Street, Grosvenor Street, Portland Place, Portman Square, Queen's Square, Ranelagh Gardens and Sackville Street; and further afield: Hampstead, Holborn, the King's Bench and Newgate Prisons.

The beautifull Cassandra was a story designed to be read to amuse her family, its success and the shared memories it evoked were good reasons for Jane to record it in her *Juvenilia*.

9

Amelia Webster
an interesting and well written tale

To whom this work is dedicated   *The History of England*

Jane Austen dedicated *Amelia Webster* to her mother, Mrs Austen, with *permission*.

Gathering her work together   *Pride & Prejudice*

Amelia Webster, made up of seven short letters, tells how the three Hervey siblings, Matilda, George and Sally, meet their future partners. The last letter confirms the success of their different approaches, with a public report of their marriages.

Matilda and George act as matchmakers for each other. Matilda tells her friend Amelia Webster that her brother is home from abroad. He is a good looking young man of interest, *never did I see a finer form*.

Amelia replies, using Matilda's nickname, Maud, she is happy to hear of his arrival, she has a thousand things to say, but her paper has run out.

Amelia writes again, perhaps the following week, she does not mention George's return. Her letter, she says, is just to *inform you that I did not stop at your house in my way to Bath last Monday.* She signs off as before, many things to tell Maud, but running out of paper.

George Hervey's letter to his friend Henry Beverley, on the other hand, is quite direct. He has returned home to a hearty reception, his sisters are *both fine girls – particularly Maud, who I think would suit you as a Wife well enough.* He asks for his response – *What say you to this?* He deals with the question of Maud's financial position – *She will have two thousand Pounds.* He concludes with a little push – *If you don't marry her you will mortally offend.*

We hear nothing from Maud, neither what she thinks of Henry Beverley, nor of the prospect of marrying him, not even what happens next.

The middle letter in the series, Letter the 4th, is a surprise. Much longer, from Benjamin Bar, addressed to Miss S. Hervey, Maud's younger sister. He calls her Sally, we soon learn they have a private correspondence. Benjamin seems to set the rules – where to leave their letters, how far Sally should walk, he seems concerned about her health. There is no hint of overt romance, no affection. We realise they are a couple, and their relationship is a secret.

In another surprise, the cool, detached Amelia Webster receives a letter from *an humble Admirer,* addressing her as lovely *Fair one.* He saw her through his telescope, on her way to Bath, and was *so struck by her Charms,* that since then he has not *tasted human food.* It is signed, George Hervey.

Where is all this heading? The last letter answers our every question. It is from Tom, who read *the list of Marriages* in the morning paper, he is writing to Jack, to report on three of them: *George Hervey Esqre to Miss Amelia Webster; Henry Beverley Esqre to Miss Hervey; and Benjamin Bar Esqre to Miss Sarah Hervey.*

Her own share in the story *Emma*

In *Amelia Webster,* Jane made a salient point to her mother: young people do not need their parents to arrange their marriages, they can do it quite well for themselves. She highlighted the importance of brothers and sisters in widening the circle of potential partners for each other, and illustrated the different social codes applying to the young women and the young men involved.

Amelia Webster is a remarkably accomplished story, clever, elegant and spare. Four of the seven undated letters are just one sentence long, the first has two sentences, the longest five. Each is a miniature snapshot of the writer and recipient, adding new possibilities to the story.

What is not said is as significant as what is. The atmosphere becomes more highly charged, the suspense builds, as George Hervey and Benjamin Bar declare their interest, while Amelia maintains a disinterested stance and the others remain silent. The 7th and last letter, between bystanders Tom and Jack, resolves the anticipation and uncertainty in a final tableau, a snapshot of three young couples, facing towards the future.

The names of people that fill up my time *Mansfield Park*

Jane Austen's use of the name Hervey acknowledged a contemporary of her father, Frederick Augustus Hervey, 4th Earl of Bristol and Lord Bishop of Derry. George Austen and Frederick Hervey were both ordained in 1754, after taking their Master of Arts degrees, Jane's father at St John's Oxford, Hervey at Corpus Christi College, Cambridge. Reverend Hervey was appointed a Royal Chaplain in 1763 and was elected the Bishop of Cloyne in Ireland in 1767.

As Bishop, Hervey encouraged his clergy to pursue a healthy lifestyle, requiring overweight priests who applied for promotion to compete against each other in midnight runs through bogs and marshlands. He received news of his appointment as Lord Bishop of Derry while engaged in a round of leapfrogging with his chaplains on his front lawn.[70]

Benjamin Bar suggests that he and Sally use *a very convenient old hollow log for their private Correspondence.* This strategy was a reference to Paul Wentworth, D'Arcy's distant cousin and *particular friend*, born on

Barbados, educated in New Hampshire, and in 1766 appointed Colonial Agent for New Hampshire in London.

In 1766, after Benjamin Franklin was sent to the Court of Louis XVI, in France, as ambassador for the American Colonies, Paul Wentworth arranged for contacts in Franklin's household to prepare weekly reports, written in invisible ink. On Tuesday afternoons, they were left for him in a boxwood tree on the southern edge of the Tuileries Garden.[71]

De Beaumarchais, the French Foreign Minister said of Paul Wentworth, *He is related to the Marquis of Rockingham; is a particular friend of Lord Suffolk; is employed by the minister in difficult matters ... This Mr Wentworth speaks French like you and better than I do; he is one of the cleverest men in England.*[72]

Conjecturing as to the date   *Pride & Prejudice*

Amelia Webster was written in late 1788, close to the time Jane turned thirteen. It could have been a Christmas gift for her mother. The clue to its date lies in the first letter, where Maud reports *the return of my amiable brother from abroad.*

Edward Austen returned from his two year, Grand Tour in late Autumn 1788. Opening her story with a reference to his return gave an added significance to Jane's gift to her mother, creating a connection between the characters in the story and the Austen family.

The choicest gift   *Persuasion*

Amelia Webster was a pointed gift from Jane to the woman most eager to see her married. Just months earlier, Mrs Austen had applauded her romance with a cousin of Earl Fitzwilliam: *I am so pleased – so happy. Such a charming man! – so handsome! so tall! – A house in town! Every thing that is charming!.. Ten thousand a year! Oh, Lord! What will become of me. I shall go distracted.*[73]

His library, & all the Parish to Manage *Emma*

In late Autumn 1790, confined in the rectory, forbidden to mention D'Arcy, Jane decided to record her marriage in her father's parish register, the official record of all marriages conducted and banns read at St Nicholas, Steventon between 1755 to 1812.[74] At the front of the volume, there were specimen sheets provided, setting out the data required, to ensure it was accurate and complete. On one of these Jane Austen wrote, in her tiniest hand, her own marriage banns.

It was a defiant gesture, she was interfering with the official record, it is surprising her entry survived. Clearly, in the eleven years George Austen was its custodian, and James Austen's eleven years that followed, neither of them noticed it. If either had read Jane's make believe banns, the page would have disappeared. Instead, in 1812, James formally submitted it as part of the Steventon parish record.

Jane wrote in the parish register that the banns were issued, that Jane Austen was married at St. Nicholas, Steventon. She did not record the date, or give the real name of her husband, rather, she gave three different names.

Publishing the Banns of Marriage between John Smith & Mary Brown *Sense & Sensibility*

The Banns of Marriage between Henry Frederick Howard Fitzwilliam of London and Jane Austen of Steventon.

Edmund Arthur William Mortimer of Liverpool and Jane Austen of Steventon were married in this Church.

This marriage was solemnised between us Jack Smith & Jane Smith late Austen, in the Presence of Jack Smith, Jane Smith.[75]

Jane Austen's Banns announced she was to marry a connection of Fitzwilliam, with Christian names of his friends and of heroes from English history, names she later used for lovers and heroes in her novels.

Frederick Howard, 5th Earl of Carlisle, was a school-friend from Fitzwilliam's first days at Eton and a fellow Whig. Charles Howard, 11th Duke of Norfolk, a Tory, was Lord Lieutenant of the West Riding of Yorkshire from 1782 to 1798.[76] Jane could have been introduced to them at *Wentworth Woodhouse* in September 1789.

An earlier Howard, Charles, 1st Earl of Nottingham, 2nd Baron Howard of Effingham, was a nephew of the 3rd Duke of Norfolk, a first cousin of Queen Elizabeth and of Ann Boleyn. In 1588, as Lord High Admiral, he commanded the English fleet in the longest naval battle in history, the defeat of the Spanish Armada.

More important, from Jane's perspective, Howard stood up to Elizabeth I. After his victory over the Armada, to reduce expenditure, she demanded he demobilise the crews and send them home. Howard refused to discharge them unpaid. It was *too pitiful to have men starve after such service*, he wrote, he was sure Her Majesty would not want it so. Howard paid out many of the men from his own pocket, he distributed *wine, cider, sugar, oil and fish* amongst the ships at Plymouth. He wrote to the Queen: *God knows I am not rich, but I would rather have never a penny in the world than that they should lack.*

Jane wrote a second name for her intended, Edmund Arthur William Mortimer, *a name of heroism and renown; of kings, princes, and knights; and seems to breathe the spirit of chivalry and warm affections.*[77]

Shakespeare depicted Edmund Mortimer, 5th Earl of March, 7th Earl of Ulster, in *Henry IV, Part I*, as a claimant to the throne, a survivor and a lover, who declared, *I understand thy kisses & thou mine.*[78]

Jane's third entry in the register was most revealing. Here she named herself and D'Arcy as Jane and Jack Smith, whose marriage was solemnised in their own presence, not by her father, nor any clergyman. John Smith was a name D'Arcy sometimes used in London.[79]

10

The Visit
a comedy in 2 acts

To whom this work is dedicated The History of England

Jane Austen dedicated *The Visit* to her eldest brother, Reverend James Austen. In Spring 1790, James had returned home to Steventon, after eleven years at Oxford, to become curate in the nearby parish of Overton. He had left Steventon in 1779, at age fourteen, when Jane was a mere three and a half, to take up a Founder's Kin scholarship at St John's College Oxford.

At St John's, James became a Scholar, then a Fellow of the College. He graduated as Bachelor of Arts in 1783, was ordained a Deacon in December 1787 and obtained a Master of Arts in 1788. From July 1788, he commuted from Oxford to a curacy in Stoke Charity, outside Winchester, and in June 1789 was ordained a priest at Oxford.

In July 1788, Henry Austen, seventeen, joined James at St John's, like him, on a Founder's Kin scholarship. In January 1789, the two brothers started a weekly student magazine, *The Loiterer,* that ran for sixty issues. It ceased in March 1790, when James left Oxford to take up the curacy at Overton.

55

James was in excellent spirits

Northanger Abbey

James was ten years older than Jane, the favoured Austen son and heir. At times her sibling rivalry was roused, she would poke fun or challenge him. We know of two letters-to-the-editor she sent him at *The Loiterer,* the first, signed Sophia Sentiment, was published in March 1789.

The Loiterer's motto was *Speak of us as we are,* and Jane, as Sophia Sentiment, complied. She told James she found his magazine, *the stupidest work of the kind I ever saw... your subjects are so badly chosen, that they never interest anyone... Only conceive, in eight papers, not one sentimental story about love and honour, and all that. Not one Eastern Tale full of Bashas and Hermits, Pyramids and Mosques.*

She suggested he create *a little bustle*, make his stories more interesting, that he *get a new set of correspondents, from among the young of both sexes, but particularly ours...If you see fit to comply with this my injunction, you may expect to hear from me again, and perhaps I may give you a little assistance.*[80] Sophia signed off, *Your's as you behave,* suggesting Jane's writing had received James' critical analysis.

The universities did not admit women, but James gave her letter pride of place, below a quotation from Ovid: *non venit ante suum nostra querela diem – you will find my complaint comes not before its time,* which may imply he did not disagree with her.

Her own share in the story

Emma

During the 1780s and early 1790s James was the mainstay of the Austen family theatricals, produced at Steventon over Christmas and New Year. In her dedication, Jane noted *The Visit was inferior to those celebrated Comedies called "The school for Jealousy" and "The travelled Man."* She hoped it would *afford some amusement to so respectable a Curate as yourself.*

There is no record of the two *celebrated comedies* Jane mentions. She appears to be teasing James, alluding to events from his past she could

56

have dramatised, that would made for racier comedy and embarrassed *so respectable a curate*. *The travelled Man* suggests incidents from James' Grand Tour in 1786 -87, *The School for Jealousy* his rivalry with his brother Henry for Eliza de Feuillide's attentions.

In *The Visit,* Jane included a short quote from *High Life Below Stairs*,[81] produced over Christmas 1788-1789, the last year of the family theatricals. The quote, *"the more free, the more Welcome,"* may have alluded to these romantic intrigues.

Gathering her work together   *Pride & Prejudice*

The Visit is set in the family home of young Lord Fitzgerald. He and his sister, Miss Fitzgerald, have their cousin Stanly to stay. The Hampton family, Sir Arthur and Lady Hampton, their daughter Sophia, nephew Willoughby and niece Cloe, have been invited for dinner.

The comedy arises mainly from the inadequacies of the Fitzgeralds' hospitality. Lord Fitzgerald makes an elaborate excuse to Stanly for the beds being too short for him, explaining that their Grandmother was *a very short woman*, who had beds made to suit *her own length*.

When the Hampton party arrives, Miss Fitzgerald notices they have insufficient chairs for their guests, *Bless me! There ought to be 8 Chairs and these are but 6…I am really shocked at crouding you in such a manner.* She too explains that Grandmother was the problem, as she never had *a very large Party and did not think it necessary to buy more chairs*.

None of the guests appear concerned, and Miss Fitzgerald finds a solution. She suggests Lady Hampton takes Sir Arthur on her lap. Her daughter Sophy sits Lord Fitzgerald on hers, and declares him, *very light*. During introductions, seating and assembling for dinner, the young people are busy assessing each other, with asides about who is attractive or who attracted to whom.

A servant interrupts, announcing *Dinner is on the table.* The spread is pure Yorkshire cuisine, with the choice of red herrings, Tripe, Suet pudding, Liver and Crow and fried Cowheel and Onion. The drinks include Elder wine, Mead, warm ale with toast and nutmeg and Grandmother's home-made Gooseberry Wine.

Lady Hampton refuses every dish her husband is offered, she declares the Tripe is too savoury for him, the Suet pudding and Gooseberry Wine, too high. Cloe tries a little fried Cowheel and Onion, Willoughby enjoys the red herrings, but overall, the meal is a failure. Miss Fitzgerald asks, *Will no one allow me the honour of helping them?* Receiving no answer, she tells the servants to remove the food and bring the wine.

The guests are not offered dessert, and Lord Fitzgerald apologises once more, explaining that his Grandmother had *destroyed the Hothouse in order to build a receptacle for the Turkies.*[82] Lady Hampton begs him to make no apologies. Willoughby calls, *Come girls let us circulate the Bottle.* Stanly is already drinking *draughts of Love from Cloe's eyes.*

Lord Fitzgerald asks the *amiable Sophia to condescend to marry* him, and taking her hand he leads her to the front. Cloe accepts Stanly's offer to make him *blessed,* they too *advance* to the front. Miss Fitzgerald tells Willoughby, since he is *the only one left, she cannot refuse his earnest solicitations,* and she gives him her hand. Clever Miss Fitzgerald! She has had her eye on Willoughby all evening. The play ends in a tableau of the three happy couples at front of stage, with Lady Hampton's salutation, *And may you all be Happy!*

One very superior party   *Emma*

Jane wrote *The Visit,* in 1790, to entertain her family with satirical glimpses of her visit to *Wentworth Woodhouse,* the Yorkshire estate of D'Arcy's cousin, the 4th Earl Fitzwilliam, and burial place of Thomas Strafford, 1st Earl of Strafford, in August-September 1789.

Fitzwilliam had invited Jane and D'Arcy to a grand garden party at *Wentworth Woodhouse,* held to honour the visit to the North of the Prince of Wales and his brother, the Duke of York.[83]

To receive so flattering an invitation! To have her company so warmly

58

solicited! Everything honourable and soothing, every present enjoyment, and every future hope was contained in it; and her acceptance with the only saving clause of Papa and Mamma's approbation, was eagerly given. – "I will write home directly," said she, "and if they do not object, as I dare say they will not." [84]

The previous year, King George III, had become mentally unbalanced. In November 1788, he was too ill to deliver the King's Speech, to open Parliament. It was feared his judgement and his capacity to exercise his royal authority would not recover for a considerable time, if at all.

The Whigs considered the King's eldest son, the Prince of Wales, was entitled to act as Regent, in the King's place. This was opposed by the Tories and by Pitt, the Prime Minister, who was afraid he would lose office if the Prince was made Regent. He had a *Regency Bill* drawn up to limit the power of the Prince of Wales, and had the Great Seal of the Realm attached to the Bill without royal endorsement. The *Regency Bill* was passed by the House of Commons, but before it passed the Lords, the King recovered.

During the crisis, the Prince and his lifestyle were the subject of widespread concern and criticism. His tour of the North was a move to rally loyalty and improve his image. The Whigs supported his entitlement, and allied themselves with him in anticipation of his future support.

The Whitehall Evening Post reported, Fitzwilliam had *his gates thrown open to the loyalty and love of the surrounding country. The vast concourse of people regaled in the park* were estimated to number twenty thousand. Inside *the house were about 200. The dinner was in the highest stile of magnificence, and the Fete concluded with a Ball.* [85] Jane's observation that there were insufficient chairs was likely quite correct.

Fitzwilliam received the royal party at *Wentworth Woodhouse*, his grand Palladian villa, twice as wide as Buckingham Palace, it covers a hectare. The East Front, 607 feet long, is the longest country house façade in Europe. It has 365 rooms, five miles of passageways and over a thousand windows. In *Pride and Prejudice*, Jane Austen named it *Pemberley*.

Jane and D'Arcy travelled to *Wentworth Woodhouse* with jurist Thomas Erskine and his wife Frances, along with numerous coaches on the Great North Road, carrying guests to the party. Jane recalled her *admiration of the style in which they travelled, of the fashionable chaise-and-four, postilions handsomely liveried, rising so regularly in their stirrups, and numerous out-riders properly mounted.*[86]

In great spirits, the party travelled to Leicester and Nottingham, through *all the celebrated beauties of Matlock,*[87] *Bakewell,*[88] *Chatsworth, the Peak; from Dove Dale*[89] into South Yorkshire, to Sheffield, and thence to Rotherham and *Wentworth Woodhouse.*

Jane was shown up several staircases to her room, above the grandest guests. Quite possibly she was given a child's bed. In this story, Jane Austen makes fun of dinner in an aristocratic household, an old house with old furniture, and a kitchen serving only the local delicacies.

The names of people that fill up my time *Mansfield Park*

Jane changed Fitzwilliam's name to Fitzgerald, obeying her father's dictum that her romance with D'Arcy Wentworth would never again be mentioned.

The name Stanly was also connected to the Wentworth family. Henrietta Mary Stanley, daughter of James Stanley, 7th Earl of Derby was the wife of William Wentworth, the 2nd Earl of Strafford (1626-1695).

Willoughby was a name from Jane Austen's mother's family. Both her mother and sister were named Cassandra, in honour of their forebear, Cassandra Willoughby, second wife of her wealthy cousin James Brydges. In 1719, she became a Duchess when he was created the 1st Duke of Chandos. They had no children. Jane Austen used the name Willoughby again, most importantly for Marianne's faithless lover in *Sense and Sensibility.*

11

The Mystery
An unfinished comedy

To whom this work is dedicated   *The History of England*

Jane Austen dedicated *The Mystery* to her father, Reverend George Austen. It is a tiny piece of absurdist theatre, a one-act play mocking the dead hand of collusion in family secrets.

Gathering her work together   *Pride & Prejudice*

In *The Mystery*, Jane Austen predated absurdist playwrights of the twentieth century, such as Genet, Beckett, Artaud, Arrabal, Pinter, Pirandello, Stoppard, Albee, et al. Nothing specific is said, the dialogue is full of half stated, unspoken and whispered hints, the characters all understand they are not to speak them aloud.

The Mystery contains three short scenes. In the first, set in a garden, Old Humbug confirms that his son is convinced of the *propriety* of his advice and will follow it. His son, Young Humbug assures his father *he will certainly act in the manner you have pointed out to me.*

The second scene is the Parlour of Humbug's house, where Mrs Humbug and Fanny sit sewing. Mrs Humbug asks if Fanny understands her. Fanny says, *Perfectly*. Fanny asks Mrs Humbug to continue her story, but she has *nothing more to say on the subject*. Daphne enters and announces, *t'is all over*. The three converse in broken phrases. When Daphne is asked a question, she whispers her answer, unheard by the audience. One character asks, *and is he to?* It seems a man has gone. An answer is whispered, the whisperers understand each other but nothing is made clear.

The audience and the reader catch only broken phrases. We are not to know who he is, where or why he has gone. Is he in some unmentionable predicament? It is a family secret discussed in whispers, never out loud.

The scene ends after Daphne whispers *all she knows of the matter* to Mrs Humbug and Fanny. Fanny replies, *Well! Now I know everything*.

In the third scene Sir Edward Spangle is asleep, Colonel Elliott enters, *My daughter is not here I see...there lies Sir Edward.. Shall I tell him the secret?...No, he'll certainly blab it... But he is asleep and wont hear me...So I'll e'en venture*. The play ends with the Colonel whispering something into the ear of Sir Edward, still fast asleep. Nothing is resolved.

Conjecturing as to the date
Pride & Prejudice

Jane Austen wrote *The Mystery* in 1791, after finishing *Lesley Castle*. It is clear she was conscious those around her were whispering about her past, gossiping about her romance with D'Arcy Wentworth.

She called *The Mystery*, ironically, *an unfinished comedy*. Her nephew James Edward Austen-Leigh later described it as *the kind of transitory amusement which Jane was continually supplying to the family party*.[90]

Perhaps Jane wrote *The Visit* and *The Mystery* with the Austen Christmas theatricals in mind. But as it turned out, the performances over Christmas-New Year 1788-89 had marked the end of the family theatricals. The tumultuous events of the following Christmas would have ruled out such family celebrations, and by Christmas 1790-91, James, now a curate in Overton, had responsibilities of the season to its parishioners.

Jane's story in *Mansfield Park* of the Bertram family theatricals, the flirtatious rehearsals of *Lover's Vows*, and Sir Thomas Bertram's anger at his family's behaviour, might suggest additional reasons for the demise.

The names of people that fill up my time   *Mansfield Park*

The Humbug family: Old Humbug, Mrs Humbug and Young Humbug, share a comical name suggesting sham and hypocrisy. Spangle could be that of a circus performer, or perhaps a reference to Lord Sparkle, a dishonest character in *Which is the Man*, the play Eliza suggested for the Austen theatricals in 1787-88.

Together their names suggest deceit, dissembling and trickery. Jane Austen used these names for those near to her who were gossiping about her behind her back.

A profound secret, not to be breathed beyond their own circle   *Persuasion*

Beneath the surface of what appears to be a comedy, was the great tragedy of Jane Austen's life. The mystery, the secret being whispered, was the end of her relationship with D'Arcy Wentworth. It was the family secret her father insisted be maintained to protect the Austen's good name, but Jane knew it was constantly whispered about.

She wrote *The Mystery* in the form of a play, without her having to add commentary or an explanation. Here, she catches them in the act, producing evidence that might be obtained today from a dashcam or CCTV. We can only guess who the three men and three women exchanging views about an unspoken secret were intended to represent.

D'Arcy Wentworth sailed to New South Wales without her, three weeks after her father persuaded her to break with him. The day before he left, Henry Austen published a piece in *The Loiterer*, applauding the world for getting rid of *its superfluous inhabitants, both Poets & Pick-pockets Prudes & Prostitutes, in short all those who have too much cunning or too little money...shipped off with the very first cargo of Convicts to Botany Bay.*[91]

Her family regarded Jane and D'Arcy's relationship as scandalous. Having chosen to hide the truth they continued to deny it, never discussing it with Jane, or mentioning D'Arcy Wentworth in her presence. Jane knew that regardless, they were gossiping to each other, and to who knew who else, about them both.

She had become hardened to such affronts   *Persuasion*

Jane dedicated the play to her father, making it plain that while he had forbidden D'Arcy's name to be mentioned, their story was constantly whispered about. Making it a secret had only served to subject her to racier and endless gossip.

12

The three Sisters
a novel

To whom this work is dedicated

Jane Austen dedicated her *unfinished Novel, The three Sisters,* to her third brother Edward, seven years her senior. It was probably written in 1791, the year Jane turned fifteen, sometime between the beginning of March, when Edward's engagement to Elizabeth Bridges was announced, and their wedding day, at the end of December.

Elizabeth was the third of six Bridges sisters. The three elder sisters were all married in 1791, Fanny, the eldest, to Lewis Cage, and Sophia, the second, to William Deedes, in a joint ceremony with Elizabeth and Edward Austen.

Conjecturing as to the date   *Pride & Prejudice*

It is believed *The three Sisters* was a wedding present from Jane Austen to Edward and his wife,[92] a comic story, perhaps *to contrast the matrimonial plans of the Bridges girls with those of three quarrelling sisters who had certainly never learnt any good manners or social graces.*[93]

Gathering her work together   *Pride & Prejudice*

The story of the three Stanhope sisters is told in four letters, the first two from Mary Stanhope to her married friend Fanny, the last two from Mary's sister Georgiana to her friend Anne.

In her first letter, Mary asks Fanny for her advice, whether she should accept an unexpected marriage proposal from Mr Watts. She is elated, *it is the first I have ever had.* Her feelings towards Mr Watts are quite negative, but she considers their marriage would be a triumph over her sisters and her friends, the Duttons.

Mary declares, *Mr Watts is quite an old man...so plain I cannot bear to look at him.* He is extremely disagreeable, she hates him more than any body else in the World. He has a large fortune and will make great Settlements on me, but then he is very healthy...If I accept him I know I shall be miserable all the rest of my Life...I would refuse him at once if I were certain that neither of my Sisters would accept him, and that if they did not, he would not offer to the Duttons. I cannot run such a risk...

Mr Watts, like Reverend Collins in *Pride & Prejudice*, is quite definite that he wants a wife, but not too fastidious about whom he marries. The first girl who accepts him will do.

In her second letter, Mary tells Fanny her mother had asked her intentions. Her mother, anxious not to lose a potential husband for one of her daughters, plays on the rivalry between them, telling Mary that if she does not accept Mr Watts tomorrow, *he intends to pay his Addresses to Sophy,* her sister. If Sophy does not accept him, she tells Mary, *then Georgiana must, for I am determined not to let such an opportunity escape of settling one of my daughters so advantageously.*

The third letter, from Georgiana Stanhope to her unmarried friend Anne, tells her how, after their mother told them she will not let Mr Watts go farther than our family for a Wife, she and Sophy had *been practising a little deceit on our eldest sister.*

Mr Watts does not appeal to either of the younger sisters, they find him *hideous in person and without one good quality.* They are pleased not to be in Mary's predicament, but deviously, they tell Mary if she does not accept Mr Watts, they will. Faced with this dilemma, Mary decides to accept him, but on her terms.

She has a list of demands: *a new Carriage... blue spotted with silver, a new Saddle horse, a suit of fine lace, an infinite number of the most valuable jewels, a cream coloured Phaeton with 4 of the finest Bays in the Kingdom, the house newly furnished, two new Footmen, two waiting women, an elegant Greenhouse stocked with plants, every Winter in Bath, every Spring in Town, every Summer taking some Tour, every Autumn at a Watering Place, and at home the rest of the year, you must do nothing but give Balls and Masquerades, build a room for that purpose and a Theatre to act Plays in. The first Play we shall have will be* Which is the Man, *and I will do lady Bell Bloomer.*[94]

When Mr Watts asks what he can expect in return, Mary replies, *you may expect to have me pleased.* Mr Watts promptly decides Mary's expectations are too high, and turns his attention to her sister Sophy. She assures him her expectations are *to the full as high as my Sister's; for I expect my Husband to be good tempered and Chearful; to consult my happiness in all his Actions, and to love me with Constancy and Sincerity.*

Mr Watts stared. "These are very odd Ideas truly Young lady. You had better discard them before you marry, or you will be obliged to do it afterwards.

Meanwhile, Mrs Stanhope has taken Mary aside. Mr Watts is about to turn his attention to Georgiana, when *in a voice half humble, half sulky,* Mary tells him she was not in earnest with her list of demands, though she must have a new Chaise.

After a little more negotiation it was *settled that they should be married,* and *a common License was at last agreed on.*

The final letter, from Georgiana to Anne, describes how, next day, Mary made a fool of herself. She called on her neighbours, the Dutton sisters, to brag about her new status, and found them in the company of a very pleasing, handsome, well-mannered young man, Mr Brudenell. Mary was jealous of his attention to them.

When Mr Watts next comes to court her, Mary can't resist telling him *she had met a Man much handsomer than he*. He flies *into a great passion*, calls her a *Vixen* and complains to her mother about her behaviour, but in the end, he goes *to Town to hasten the preparations for the Wedding*.

Absolutely on the catch   *Lady Susan*

Although *The three Sisters* is presented as a comic tale, the rivalry between the sisters, and the intrigue and duplicity of Georgiana and Sophy, who gang up against Mary, make it brutally realistic.

Mary's musings on the benefits of accepting Mr Watts' proposal and her attempts at negotiating the terms of her acceptance, echo Mary Wollstonecraft's description of marriage as prostitution, published in 1790. [95]

Richard Church noted Jane Austen's *characteristic subtlety in the portrait of the frivolous, heartless little worldling, Mary Stanhope. The interplay of her greed, social apprehension, and pitiable ignorance is so skilfully drawn out by the young author that it becomes a swift-running triple fugue. She is limbering up for the later devastations and refinements of cruelty.*[96]

Here you are in your own family   *Pride & Prejudice*

In the story, Mary Stanhope writes to her married friend, Fanny, and one of Mary's sisters is named Sophy. Elizabeth Bridges' two elder sisters' names were Fanny and Sophia. Was this pure coincidence? Or was Jane Austen hinting, perhaps, that her brother Edward, like Mr Watts, had it in mind to marry one, any one, of the Bridges sisters?

It is not hard to imagine Edward Austen and Elizabeth Bridges, in the midst of their marriage plans, finding *The three Sisters* too clever, quite un-funny, even affronting.

Detached Peices

To whom this work is dedicated   The History of England

In 1793, Jane Austen, now seventeen, experienced the joy of becoming an aunt, welcoming two nieces born within three months of each other, a first child, a daughter for each of her brothers, James and Edward.

By the time of her death, in July 1817, Jane Austen had fourteen nieces and eleven nephews. James Austen had three children, two daughters and a son; Edward had five daughters and six sons; Frank had three daughters and four sons; and Charles, four daughters. Henry had no children.

Frank's family continued to increase until 1823, adding two more sons and two daughters, Charles had another daughter and three more sons. By 1826, four of Jane's six brothers and their wives had produced thirty three children, seventeen girls and sixteen boys.

Edward and his wife Elizabeth had their first child, Fanny Catherine Austen, on 23 January 1793, at *Rowling* in Kent. On 15 April 1793, at Deane, closer to home, her eldest brother James and his wife Anne, had their first and only child, Jane Anna Elizabeth Austen, known to her family as Anna.

Jane Austen dedicated these three little stories to *My Dear Neice*, Anna. She called them *Miscellanious Morsels,* but listed them in the index to *Volume the First,* as *Detached Peices.*

Jane proffered a little advice to Anna with these morsels: *if you seriously attend to them, You will derive from them very important Instructions, with regard to your Conduct in Life. Adding: if such my hopes should hereafter be realised, never shall I regret the Days and Nights that I have spent in composing these Treatises for your Benefit.*

Conjecturing as to the date

On 2 June 1793, seven weeks after Anna's birth, Jane recorded the *Miscellanious Morsels* in the first volume of her *Juvenilia*. It was two and a half years since she had added anything to this volume. On the following day she made the last and final entry, her poem, *Ode to Pity*, and with that, she completed not only *Volume the First,* but all three volumes of her *Juvenilia*.

13

A fragment – written to inculcate the practise of Virtue

A fragment, the first *Miscellanious Morsel*, is just four sentences long. Its intent is *to inculcate the practise of Virtue*. It was a gift from the daughter of one clergyman to the daughter of another. As someone in a similar position, Jane Austen had some insights to offer her *neice*.

By the time she wrote *A fragment,* Jane would have attended nearly a thousand church services: at St Nicholas, Steventon under her father's eye, at chapels and churches in Oxford and Southampton in the care of Mrs Cawley, and at St Lawrence's Church in Reading during 1785 and 1786, when she was a pupil at the Abbey House School.

By June 1793, she would probably have heard nearly a thousand sermons, and as many prayers of intercession, interceding or pleading on behalf of another, deemed a great and necessary part of Christian devotion. In *A fragment,* Jane Austen contemplated the failure of such devotions to instill the practice of virtue in the faithful.

Gathering her work together
Pride & Prejudice

A fragment reads like an introduction to a sermon, or to the intercession of the day. The pastor reminds his congregation of the many who are *unfortunate in their progress through the world,* and asserts it is their duty to seek out these unfortunates, to study their wants, and *to leave them unsupplied.* The pastor declares that, *to leave them unsupplied is the duty, and ought to be the Business of Man.*

There is some disagreement amongst readers of *A fragment,* as *to whether to leave them unsupplied* means: to leave them without wants, ie to satisfy their needs, or, *to leave their wants unsupplied,* ie not to satisfy their needs.[97] Proposing the second option might be a step too far for the daughter of a clergyman, perhaps it was meant as a double entendre.

In the two final sentences, Jane directs our gaze away from the pastor, towards his congregation. With this shift, the speaker's rhetoric loses its vigour; his notions of *duty* and the *Business of Man* become mere *employments.* The wants of unfortunates within their midst are disregarded, *few have the time, fewer still have the inclination, and no one has either the one or the other for such employments.*

Jane gives a comic snapshot of the *employments* consuming the time and energy of the *company.* They are busy perspiring *away their Evenings in crouded assemblies,* so busy they have no time *to bestow a thought* on the less fortunate. Those unfortunates, in their progress through the world, do not *perspire,* they *sweat under the fatigue of their daily Labour.*

A fragment gives a glimpse of an earnest clergyman's wasted efforts to *inculcate the practise of Virtue* in his flock. If it contained an *important Instruction* for Jane's small *neice* Anna, *with regard to her Conduct in Life,* it was probably, to maintain a realistic view of the gulf between the efforts of clergymen like her father and grandfather, *to inculcate the practice of Virtue* in their flock, and the likelihood of them ever succeeding.

Jane Austen later rejected this *Treatise,* striking it out with horizontal, diagonal and vertical lines. Perhaps Anna's father, James Austen, had objected to it.

14

A beautiful description of the different effects of Sensibility on different Minds

In this *Miscellanious Morsel,* Jane Austen turned her satirical eye on the preoccupation of popular novels of the time with *Sensibility.*[98] *A beautiful description* employs many of the affectations and postures of novels of sensibility, which she sends up for comic effect.

In *A beautiful description*, we observe the different effects of *Sensibility* on the nine characters in the story. Melissa[99] lies in bed, with an unnamed illness, her seven concerned friends are placed around in a tableau, each with a particular emotional posture, when Dr Dowkins makes a house-call to check on her progress.

We learn nothing about Melissa's illness, though we do gather a great deal about what she is wearing: *a book muslin bedgown, a chambray gauze shift, and a French net night-cap.* The narrator, one of her visitors, tells us she has attended *many Bedside, and never saw so affecting an object* as Melissa.

Her six other visitors all exemplify the popular cult of Sensibility; facile and affected, they are unable to do much more than sigh, exclaim or lament. Filled with florid and exaggerated sentiment, they seem unable to think rationally or to offer any practical help, in the house or sickroom.

Sir William is constantly at Melissa's bedside, he has had only five minutes repose in a fortnight, and that an *imperfect Slumber,* for he starts up *every Moment exclaiming Oh! Melissa, Ah! Melissa.* The narrator does note though, that *he raises his left arm and scratches his head.*

Poor Mrs Burnaby is *beyond measure afflicted,* though the narrator observes that *she sighs every now & then, that is about once a week.* The *melancholy Charles* is so anxious about her, he *says every Moment "Melissa how are you?"*

Melissa's *lovely Sisters,* Julia, Maria and Anna, *are much to be pitied.* Julia *ever lamenting the situation of her friend,* does try to help, she lies behind Melissa's pillow & supports her head. Maria is *more mild in her greif,* she *talks of going to Town next week,* while Anna is *always recurring to the pleasures we once enjoyed when Melissa was well.*

The narrator alone remains unaffected by this malaise of sensibility. Practical and efficient, she is *usually at the fire cooking some little delicacy for the unhappy invalid.* She prepares Melissa's *favourite dishes, hashing up the remains of an old Duck, toasting some cheese or making a Curry.* Her choice of such rich, spicy, even indigestible food suggests Melissa has quite a robust appetite, which raises questions about how ill she really is, and how sound the judgement of her friends?

Dr Dowkins arrives, he asks *How is she?* The *fainting Melissa* replies, *very weak indeed.* Dr Dowkins, quite unconcerned, asks about her progress, responding to her replies and those of her friends with a pun or a play on their words. When he asks, *Does she think of dieing?* When he receives the response — *She has not the strength to think at all,* he suggests her malaise might be all in her mind, *Nay, then she cannot think to have strength.*

Jane Austen made it clear in *A beautiful description* that she intended to be a decidedly unsentimental novelist.

15

The Generous Curate –
a moral Tale, setting forth
the Advantages of being
Generous and a Curate

Gathering her work together *Pride & Prejudice*

The Generous Curate, lightest of the three *Morsels*, is made up of little anecdotes that allude to the members of Anna's family. Her father James had been the curate of Deane parish for a little over a year, her grandfather George was *a very worthy Clergyman*, rector of Deane and of Steventon; her uncle Frank was in the Royal Navy, and her uncle Edward, who was adopted by a neighbour.

In her letter to the editor of *The Loiterer*, signed Margaret Mitten, Jane introduced herself as *the daughter of a country Clergyman. As one, who between prayers and scandal, sermons and cards, leads a tolerably happy life.*

With mock seriousness, Jane changed the names and locations of her family members, even making sure the mischievous schoolboy at the story's end attended a *twopenny Dame's School in the village*, certainly not her father's private boarding school.

Their father is a clergyman & their brother is a clergyman, & they are all clergymen together *Mansfield Park*

Mr Williams, *a very worthy Clergyman,* earns an income of £200 per annum from his living, comparable to the combined earnings of £210, from George Austen's two parishes. Like Mr Williams, George Austen has been the rector of Deane for just *above twenty years.*

Mr Williams was the *father of six very fine children,* while Reverend Austen had seven. His second child, George, is disabled, and may not have been included among the *very fine.* George was sent away from home when he was thirteen, into the care of another family. Jane was four years old, she would have missed her big brother.

A large Newfoundland puppy *Northanger Abbey*

Mr Williams' eldest son was *placed in the Royal Academy for Seamen when about thirteen years old* and from *thence discharged on board one of the Vessels of a small fleet destined for Newfoundland.* He sends a large *Newfoundland dog every month to his family.*

Frank, George Austen's fifth son, commenced his studies at the Royal Naval Academy at Portsmouth in 1786 when he was twelve. By 1793, he was a lieutenant on board *HMS Despatch,* on active duty in the East Indies, during the French Revolutionary Wars.

Some famous day's sport with the fox hounds *Northanger Abbey*

Anna's father, James Austen, enjoyed riding to hounds, and it is quite likely he kept a dog or two at the Deane rectory.

Newfoundland dogs, working dogs bred to haul small carts and sledges, to drag wood and pull in fishing nets, can grow up to two feet tall and weigh 100 to 150 pounds. Jane's tall tale of one arriving every month at the rectory would have raised her family's laughter. It was a visual joke Anna would enjoy, in time.

Some active, respectable young man, as a resident curate   *Persuasion*

In February 1789, James had placed a mock advertisement in *The Loiterer*, the student magazine he edited at Oxford with his brother Henry:

Wanted — A Curacy in a good sporting country, near a pack of fox-hounds, and in a sociable neighbourhood; it must have a good house and stables, and a few acres of meadow ground would be very agreeable--To prevent trouble, the stipend must not be less than £80. — The Advertiser has no objection to undertaking three, four, or five Churches of a Sunday, but will not engage where there is any weekly duty.[100]

He is moreover heir to a very large Estate   *A Collection of Letters*

In 1783, Edward, the Austen's third son, aged sixteen, was adopted by Thomas Knight, a cousin of George Austen, a former MP and Steventon's biggest landowner. He and his wife, the former Catherine Knatchbull, were wealthy and childless. In 1786, they had sent Edward on the Grand Tour, he had spent time in Italy, Switzerland and Dresden.

In *The Generous Curate* –, Mr Williams' second son is *adopted by a neighbouring Clergyman,* who had a *Curacy of fifty pound a year.* Unlike Mr Knight he could not support his *very large family.* Young Williams knew *nothing more at the age of 18 than what a twopenny Dame's school in the village could teach him...He was addicted to no vice, or ever guilty of any fault beyond what his age and situation rendered perfectly excusable.*

Though young Williams had *sometimes been detected flinging Stones at a Duck or putting brickbats into his Benefactor's bed,* his adopted father, the *Generous Curate* of the story saw *these innocent efforts of wit* as simply *the effects of a lively imagination.* His punishment was *in general no greater than that the Culprit should pick up the Stones and take the brickbats away—*

Her own share in the story *Emma*

The Austen family would have had many stories about the misdemeanours and practical jokes of their father's students at the Steventon rectory. It seems he suffered such pranks with good humour and tolerance, perhaps even brickbats in his bed.

The story reflects Jane's love and affection for her father, as she shared family stories about his life at the rectory with his new grandaughter the new generation of Austen children.

16

Ode to Pity

Conjecturing as to the date *Pride & Prejudice*

On Sunday, 2nd of June 1793, Jane Austen recorded *Detached Peices* in *Volume the First*, dedicated to Anna, James Austen's first child.

On the same day, after entering *Scraps*, five short pieces dedicated to Edward Austen's first child, Fanny, she ended *Volume the Second* of her *Juvenilia*, adding *Finis, End of the Second Volume.* Ten months earlier she had completed *Volume the Third, Kitty, or the Bower.*

Next day, Monday 3rd of June 1793, Jane Austen wrote the final entry in her *Juvenilia*, the short poem, *Ode to Pity*. She placed it at the end of *Volume the First*, and below it she wrote: *End of the first volume.*

To whom this work is dedicated *The History of England*

Jane Austen dedicated *Ode to Pity* to her sister Cassandra, *from a thorough knowledge of her pitiful nature.* She used the word *pitiful* to mean full of pity, a sense that is now obsolete. Today, for the same meaning, we would use the word, *compassionate.*

Gathering her work together

The ode is a form used in ancient Greece for poems of praise, usually in honour of a person or an object, describing their qualities and the feelings they arouse in the poet.

Jane Austen was familiar with her father's students, mastering Greek and Latin for university entry, studying the odes of the Greek lyric poet Pindar, celebrating victors at the Olympics and other Hellenic competitions;[101] and the more reflective odes of the Latin poet Horace. Henry Austen recalled, *producing a translation of a well-known Ode of Horace to my father's criticism.*[102]

George Austen's library would most likely have held examples of more recent English odes, such as those by Abraham Cowley (1618-1667), John Dryden (1631-1700), Thomas Gray (1716-1771) and William Collins (1721-1759). Jane had doubtless read Collins' *Ode to Pity*, though her poem of the same name, written half a century later, differs in tone, structure and content.

In her *Ode to Pity*, Jane used the word *pity* to mean, a *regrettable fact or circumstance, a cause for regret or disappointment.*[103] Today, that usage is obsolete.

In William Collins' *Ode to Pity*, he made Pity a *maid, a virgin,* he calls to her, *Come, Pity, come, enter my thoughts.* In Austen's ode, the speaker directs her own thoughts, delighting in ever musing on the events that led to her present disappointments and regrets.

Ever musing I delight to tread
The Paths of honour and the Myrtle Grove

Musing, she treads the *Paths of honour:* reflecting on those events brings her happiness, she honours them, they should be honoured, there is nothing there to be ashamed of. Her *tread* takes her to *the Myrtle Grove*, in classical mythology a place sacred to the goddess of love.

Whilst the pale Moon her beams doth shed
On disappointed Love.

The moon, a feminine symbol, reflects female creativity, intuition and wisdom, its cycle is female, representing the rhythm of life and of time. Under the *pale* light of the *moon*, the speaker's great regret is revealed as *disappointed love.*

While Philomel on airy hawthorn Bush
Sings sweet and Melancholy, And the Thrush
Converses with the Dove.

In Greek mythology, *Philomel* was transformed into a nightingale after her tongue was cut out by her attacker.[104] In the poem, she sits on a *hawthorn Bush,* the Celtic symbol of love and protection, singing *sweet and Melancholy.*

Like Philomel, Jane has been silenced. Her eldest brother and her father, those who hold the power in her family, have forbidden her to speak of D'Arcy Wentworth, of the most important events in her life, the times she spent with him.

Jane used two birds to signify her enduring love for D'Arcy. The appearance of a thrush to two lovers was a signal their relationship would endure, never break down. The dove was a symbol of devotion, care and peace.

After having revealed, in the first stanza, that the subject of the ode, the *cause for regret or disappointment* is *disappointed love,* in the second stanza, the speaker *is ever musing,* looking with the eye of the moon at *lovely scenes* never to be forgotten. There is a new energy in the opening lines:

Gently brawling down the turnpike road
Sweetly noisy falls the Silent Stream –

A turnpike road was a main road, perhaps a couple travelling the road in a carriage, gently squabbling or arguing, have paused beside the stream and enjoy the sweetness of its sounds. In these lines Jane Austen revisited a scene in *Love and Freindship,* where Laura and Sophia, exhausted, sit *by the side of a clear limpid stream... Before us ran the murmuring brook and behind us ran the turn-pike road.* Perhaps they are travelling south to London from Scotland, as Jane and D'Arcy did in late 1789.

Delighted to connect anything with history already known, or warm her imagination with scenes of the past *Mansfield Park*

The turnpike road was significant in the story of Jane Austen's disappointed love. D'Arcy Wentworth had been arrested when he stopped at the Notting-Hill Turnpike to pay the toll, he was charged with highway robbery, removed to Newgate and remanded for trial in the Old Bailey.[105]

The Moon emerges from behind a Cloud
And darts upon the Myrtle Grove her beam.
Ah! Then what Lovely Scenes appear,
The hut, the Cot, the Grot, and Chapel queer

The moon lights up the speaker's musings once more in this stanza. It reveals *Lovely Scenes,* places where the Jane and D'Arcy had paused during their ramble across Scotland together, a hut, a cottage, a grotto, a chapel.

And eke, the Abbey too a mouldering heap,
Conceal'd by aged pines her head doth rear
And quite invisible doth take a peep.

The moonlight peeps at an earlier scene, the *mouldering* ruins of Reading Abbey, *conceal'd by aged pines,* in the grounds of the Abbey House School where Jane had once sat talking to D'Arcy Wentworth.[106]

On Monday, 3 June 1793, after six and a half years of work, Jane Austen, now seventeen, closed her *Juvenilia* with this poem. She made it the endpiece of the first volume of her *juvenilia*, in which she had recorded so much heartbreak.

In the poem she affirms her enduring love for D'Arcy Wentworth, she honours her memories of their exciting and happy times together, and declares her separation from him remains the greatest cause of regret and disappointment in her life.[107]

Juvenilia,
Volume the Second

In 1790, a few months after Jane Austen began transcribing her stories into *Volume the First*, George Austen gave her a second quarto notebook, much thicker, 276 pages long, almost a hundred pages more than *Volume the First*. Jane wrote a Latin phrase, *Ex dono mei Patris*, above the Contents page, *a gift from my father*.

While Jane continued to add short pieces to *Volume the First*, her new notebook was reserved for longer, more personal stories. *Volume the Second* is the longest of the three volumes, it contains thirteen pieces, twelve in prose, ten of these written in the form of letters, and the first act of a play.

The first two stories, *Love and Freindship*, a *Novel in Letters*, and *Lesley Castle*, an *unfinished Novel in Letters*, are set mainly in Scotland, where Jane and D'Arcy rambled in the Autumn of 1789.

The next, an illustrated history of England from Henry IV to Charles I, was a project she undertook with her sister Cassandra, written to amuse her father's students at the end of term, before Christmas 1791. The following December, she added a collection of five letters, dedicated to her beloved cousin Jane Cooper.

The last five pieces Jane Austen recorded in *Volume the Second* were a collection of four stories, three letters and a tale, and a short play, *The first Act of a Comedy*, sent to Edward Austen and his wife, Elizabeth, to celebrate the birth of their daughter Fanny, Jane's first niece.

It seems Jane wrote most of the pieces in *Volume the Second* directly into her notebook, rather than copying them from an earlier draft. One consequence of this is the greater number of corrections she made to the text, and the twelve leaves of paper she cut from the volume. When Jane finalised the table of contents, *Volume the Second* had lost twenty-four pages.

It is unlikely that the stories in this volume were read aloud at table. Other than one or two of the shorter *Scraps*, these were probably too long, and at times too dark, to be read aloud at the rectory table. George Austen would certainly have read them, and there are parts of them Jane may well have written to inform him about her travels with D'Arcy, her travails and her experience of the world.

Cassandra Austen left *Volume the Second* to her younger brother Frank. When she died in 1843 he was a Vice Admiral, and by the time of his death in 1865, he had served as Admiral of the Fleet. Frank left *Volume the Second* to his youngest daughter, Frances Sophia. It was the first volume of the *Juvenilia* to be made public. Frank's granddaughter, Janet Sanders, approved its publication in 1922, under the title, *Love and Friendship*.

The manuscript remained in Frank Austen's family until July 1977, when his great granddaughter, Rosemary Mowll, put it up for auction in London at Sotheby's, it was listed it in the catalogue as *The Property of a descendant of Jane Austen* and purchased by the British Library for £40,000. Today, *Volume the Second* is housed in the British Library in London.

17

Love and Freindship
a novel in a series of letters

To whom this work is dedicated

Jane Austen dedicated *Love and Freindship* to her cousin Eliza, Madame la Comtesse de Feuillide. Eliza was living in London in August 1789, when Jane Austen and D'Arcy Wentworth left for Rotherham, in Yorkshire, to attend Earl Fitzwilliam's garden party at *Wentworth Woodhouse,* She was there in London when they returned from Scotland, she was privy to the entire history of their *Misfortunes and Adventures.*

Eliza would have recognised the references in *Love and Freindship* to love at first sight, to thefts of money, travelling north by coach, a carriage turning over on the road, visiting generous relatives, to the romance of Jane and D'Arcy, and the short duration of their marriage.

Gathering her work together

Love and Freindship is an exaggerated, fantastical and mischievous burlesque, complicated and fast moving. Using many zany subterfuges, Jane created a spoof of her adventures with D'Arcy, never revealing the secret of their romance, but recording the truth of her feelings, and something of their escapades.

She told the story in fifteen undated letters, the first from Isabel to Laura, sent on Laura's 55th birthday, Laura answers Isabel in the second, and she writes the following thirteen letters to Isabel's daughter, Marianne.

Letter the First. Isabel's opening letter contains no birthday greetings or good wishes, it is just another of her *repeated intreaties* to Laura to give her daughter *a regular detail of the Misfortunes and Adventures of your Life.*

Until now, Laura has refused, saying she would prefer to wait until she is out of danger of repeating her dreadful Misfortunes. Isabel contends that by age 55, Laura must surely be safe *from the determined Perseverance of disagreeable Lovers and the cruel Persecutions of obstinate Fathers.*

In *Letter 2ᴰ*, Laura does not agree, but not wanting to be seen as obstinate or ill-natured, she agrees to satisfy Marianne's curiosity, hoping the *fortitude with which I have suffered the many Afflictions of my past Life may prove to be a useful Lesson in her own.*

Letter 3ʳᵈ. Laura opens her first letter to Marianne with something of her history: *My Father was a native of Ireland and an inhabitant of Wales; my Mother was the natural Daughter of a Scotch Peer by an Italian Opera-girl – I was born in Spain and received my Education at a Convent in France.*

At eighteen, recalled home to Wales, her mind was filled with *every Virtue, good Quality and noble sentiment. She was beautiful, the Mistress of every accomplishment of her sex, her only fault, if a fault it could be called was a sensibility too tremblingly alive.*

Letter 4ᵗʰ. Yearning to experience life, Laura asked Isabel, her only friend in Wales—*What probability is there of my ever tasting the Dissipations of London, the Luxuries of Bath, or the stinking fish of Southampton? I who am doomed to waste my Days of Youth and Beauty in an humble Cottage in the Vale of Uske.* Laura little thought she would quit that Cottage so soon for *the Deceitful Pleasures of the world.*

In Laura's following thirteen letters to Marianne, Jane Austen parodied and sent up the postures of sensibility in popular novels of her day. Laura's letters are filled with palpitating fervour, youthful skits, shifts and swift turns of fortune. But the older Laura cannot disguise her sense of loss as she revisits the scenes of her youth.

Letter 5th. One winter evening there was a *violent knocking on the outward door of the rustic Cot,* where Laura lived with her parents. The servant announced *a young Gentleman and his servant,* lost and very cold, who *begged leave to warm themselves by our fire.*

Laura declares the young Gentleman was *the most beauteous and amiable Youth, I had ever beheld... My natural Sensibility had already been greatly affected...no sooner did I first behold him, than I felt that on him the happiness or Misery of my future Life must depend.*

Letter 6th. The noble Youth, Edward Lindsay, tells Laura and her family that he is *the son of an English Baronet,* who, *seduced by the false glare of Fortune and the Deluding Pomp of Title,* had *insisted on him giving his hand to Lady Dorothea.*

Laura and her family admire the *noble Manliness* of his reply: *"No never exclaimed I. Lady Dorothea is lovely and Engaging; I prefer no woman to her; but Know Sir, that I scorn to marry her in compliance with your wishes. No! Never shall it be said that I obliged my Father.*

Edward had mounted his Horse and set off for his Aunt's house in Middlesex, but somehow he became lost, *'tho I flatter myself with being a tolerable proficient in Geography, I know not how it happened,* he now finds himself in South Wales.

At the end of his story, he takes Laura's hand, and asks her:
"Oh! when will you reward me with yourself?"
"This instant, Dear and Amiable Edward." (replied I). We were immediately united by my Father, who tho' he had never taken orders had been bred to the Church."

Letter 7h. After an *affecting Farewell* to her family, Laura accompanies

Edward to his Aunt Philippa's house in Middlesex. His aunt receives them *both with every expression of affectionate love,* though their marriage was *a most agreeable surprise to her.*

There Laura meets members of Edward's family, who arrive one after another. In Edward's sister, Augusta, she notes a *Disagreable Coldness and Forbidding Reserve... None of that interesting Sensibility or amiable Simpathy in her Manners and Address... her expressions of regard were neither animated nor cordial: her arms were not opened to receive me to her Heart, tho' my own were extended to press her to mine.*

Laura overhears Augusta telling Edward that he will need to ask for his father's help, to support his new wife. Edward replies

"Never, never Augusta will I so demean myself. Support! What support?"... "Only those very insignificant ones of Victuals and Drink." (answered she.) "Victuals and Drink!" (replied my Husband in a most nobly contemptuous Manner) Can you not conceive the Luxury of living in every Distress that Poverty can inflict, with the object of your tenderest affection?"

Lady Dorothea, *a very Handsome young woman,* is ushered into the Room. Laura feels that, *altho' Lady Dorothea's visit was nominally to Philippa and Augusta, yet I have some reason to imagine that (acquainted with the Marriage and arrival of Edward) to see me was a principal motive in it.*

Laura judges that *tho' Lovely and Elegant in her Person and tho' Easy and Polite in her Address, Lady Dorothea is of that inferior order of Beings with regard to delicate Feeling, tender Sentiments, and refined Sensibility... She staid but half an hour and neither in the course of her Visit, confided to me any of her Secret thoughts, nor requested me to confide in her, any of Mine...I could not feel any ardent Affection or very sincere Attachment for Lady Dorothea.*

Letter 8th. Next, Edward's father, Sir Edward Lindsay arrives, *doubtless to reproach him for having dared to unite himself to me without his Knowledge. Edward, foreseeing his design, approached him with heroic fortitude as soon as he entered the Room, and addressed him in the following Manner.*

Sir Edward, I know the motive of your Journey here – you come with the base Design of reproaching me for having entered an indissoluble engagement with my Laura without your Consent – But Sir I glory in the Act – . It is my greatest boast that I have incurred the Displeasure of my Father!

Edward takes Laura to his father's carriage and orders *the Postilions to Drive to M—to the seat* of his *most particular friend, a few miles distant.*[108]

There, his friend's wife Sophia, welcomes them: *she was all Sensibility and Feeling. We flew into each others arms and after having exchanged vows of mutual Freindship for the rest of our Lives, instantly unfolded to each other the most inward Secrets of our Hearts.*

Edward's friend Augustus arrives. *"My life! My Soul!" (exclaimed the former). "My Adorable Angel!" (replied the latter) as they flew into each other's arms. – It was too pathetic for the feelings of Sophia and myself – We fainted Alternately on a Sofa.*

Letter the 9th. After the affectionate entreaties of Augustus and Sophia to consider their House as our Home, Edward and Laura *determine never more to leave them. In the society of my Edward and this Amiable Pair, I passed the happiest moments of my Life; Our time was most delightfully spent, in mutual Protestations of Freindship, and in vows of unalterable Love, in which we were secure from being interrupted, by intruding and disagreeable Visitors.*

By *Letter the Ninth,* Laura has offered Marianne few if any *useful Lessons* for her future life. Laura's assessment of the worth of others relies on her measure of their *true feeling,* her *noble Sentiments* reject reason and precept, her letters are filled with romantic adventures. True feelings, for Laura, are expressed with deliberately worked up sentimentality and cloying sweetness, in a facile and affected manner.

By now, Laura's story has achieved the mood of palpitating fervour, so essential to the novel of sensibility. But things go rapidly wrong, misfortune follows misfortune, as she and her friends fall hapless victims to their resolve to live according to impulse and inclination.

Sophie and Augustus have been living on a *Considerable Sum of Money, which Augustus had gracefully purloined from his Unworthy father's Escritoire, a few days before his union with Sophia.*

Their Expenses were considerably encreased with the arrival of Laura and Edward, tho' their means for supplying them were then nearly exhausted. They, Exalted Creatures! Scorned to reflect a moment on their pecuniary Distresses and would have blushed at the idea of paying their Debts.

Alas! What was their Reward for such disinterested Behaviour! The beautiful Augustus was arrested and we were all undone...Ah! what could we do but what we did! We sighed and fainted on the sofa.

In *Letter 10th*, Edward goes to visit Augustus in Newgate prison, *to lament over his misfortunes,* leaving Laura and Sophia to *consider the most prudent step to be taken.*

The two young women decide *to leave the House, as the Officers of Justice* are expected at any moment to seize the contents on behalf of the unpaid creditors. *With the greatest impatience they wait for Edward to return, but no Edward appeared...no Edward returned.*

At length collecting all the Resolution she was Mistress of, Laura packs some necessary apparel for Sophia and herself. I dragged her to a Carriage I had ordered and we instantly set out for London.

'Where am I to Drive?' said the Postilion. 'To Newgate Gentle youth (replied I) to see Augustus.' 'Oh! no, no, (exclaimed Sophia) I cannot go to Newgate; I shall not be able to support the sight of my Augustus in so cruel a confinement – my feelings are sufficiently shocked by the recital of his Distress, but to behold it will overpower my Sensibility.

Laura directs the Postilion *to return into the Country.* By now, she is *destitute of any Support, and unprovided with any habitation.* Her parents had died a few weeks after she left with Edward, so she cannot return home, She was the lawfull *Inheritress of their House and Fortune. But alas! The House had never been their own and their Fortune had only been an Annuity on their own Lives. Such is the Depravity of the World!*

She tells Marianne, *to your Mother I should have returned with Pleasure... introduced to her my Charming Sophia and passed the remainder of my Life in their dear Society,* but Isabel, by then, had married and removed to a *Distant part of Ireland.*

Letter 11th. Sophia remembers that she has a *Relation in Scotland...who I am certain would not hesitate in receiving me.* They travel north, and pause at an inn near his house, to write a *very elegant and well-penned Note to him containing an Account of our Destitute and melancholy Situation, and of our intention to spend some months with him in Scotland.*

In an increasingly chaotic narrative, a *Gentleman considerably advanced in years,* arrives at the inn, in a *coroneted Coach & 4.* Laura throws *herself on her knees before him and besought him to acknowledge her as his Grand-Child.* By now, readers had perhaps forgotten Laura's *Mother was the natural Daughter of a Scotch Peer by an Italian Opera-girl.* The Scottish Lord St. Clair recognises Laura, then Sophia, and two other young men at the inn as his grandchildren, and he gives them each a £50 note.

Letter the 12th. Laura and Sophia faint *in each others arms,* and when they recover, find the young men, Philander and Gustavus, have disappeared with all four banknotes. Sophia's cousin, Macdonald, arrives at the inn, and invites Sophia, and Laura, as her *freind,* to Macdonald Hall. There they meet Janetta, his fifteen year old daughter, *Mistress of the Mansion, naturally well disposed, endowed with a susceptible Heart, and a simpathetic Disposition.*

Laura and Sophia are horrified to learn Janetta is engaged to Graham, a *Sensible, well-informed and Agreable* young man recommended by her father. They are *certain that Janetta could feel no affection for him.* They succeed in convincing her it is impossible she could love Graham, that it is her *Duty to Disobey her Father.*

The pair find it a little more difficult to interest Janetta in the only other young man she can think of, Captain M'Kenzie. They apply their efforts to convincing her she is *violently in love* with him and that *the attachment must be reciprocal.* Sophie writes M'Kenzie an anonymous letter of encouragement, he flies *on the wings of Love* to Macdonald-Hall, and he and Janetta *depart for Gretna-Green.*

In *Letter the 13th*, a *couple of Hours* later, Macdonald enters the Library to find Sophia *majestically removing a 5th Bank-note from his Drawer to her own purse.* He reproaches her, *the gentle sweetness of her Nature* is provoked, and Sophie takes revenge *by informing him of Janetta's Elopement.* Macdonald tells Sophia and Laura they have thrown his daughter *into the arms of an unprincipled Fortune-Hunter,* and orders them to leave.

After packing *their wardrobe and valuables* they depart Macdonald Hall. They walk for *about a mile and a half* and sit beside a *clear limpid stream to refresh their exhausted limbs.* Meditating on the beauty of nature around them, Laura asks, *Alas why are not Edward and Augustus here to enjoy its Beauties with us?*

Sophia cries, *Ah my beloved Laura, for pity's sake forbear recalling to my remembrance the unhappy situation of my imprisoned Husband. Alas, what would I not give to learn the fate of my Augustus! – to know if he is still in Newgate, or if he is yet hung.*

Laura tries to change the subject, but anything she says reminds Sophia of Augustus. *The feelings of Sophia were at that time so exquisite, and the tenderness she felt for Augustus so poignant that I had not the power to start any other topic.* Suddenly, on the road behind them, a Gentleman's fashionably high Phaeton overturns. They hasten towards the spectacle of *two gentlemen most elegantly attired weltering in their blood...it is Edward and Augustus.*

Sophia shrieked and fainted on the Ground, while Laura *screamed and instantly ran mad.* Like proper heroines of novels of sensibility, the two young women face their unfolding misfortunes with touchingly sentimental incompetence. They are paralysed into inactivity in this crisis, by the poignancy of life.

An hour and a quarter later, *Edward (who alone retained any share of Life)* lets out a groan. Laura and Sophia postpone their *Lamentations,* run to him and *implore him not to die.* Laura makes a futile effort to keep him conscious, she asks him to tell her what has befallen him since the *unhappy Day* they were separated. *"I will" (said he) and instantly fetching a Deep sigh, Expired.*

Sophia *sunk into a swoon.* Laura's *Voice faltered,* her *Eyes assumed a vacant Stare, her face became as pale as Death,* and *her Senses were considerably Impaired,* she raves incoherently *for two Hours.* Finally, Sophia recovers from her swoon, she warns Laura that *Night was now approaching and that the Damps began to fall.*

The two young women seek shelter in a nearby cottage for the night, where a widow gives them a *Night's Lodging.* Laura's description of the widow's daughter displays her snobbery, despite her desperate situation: *She was very plain and her name was Bridget…. Nothing therefore could be expected from her – she could not be supposed to possess either exalted ideas, Delicate Feelings or refined Sensibilities–. She was nothing more than a mere good-tempered, civil and obliging Young Woman; as such we could scarcely dislike her – she was only an Object of Contempt.*

Letter the 14th. In the morning, Sophia wakes with a *violent pain in her delicate limbs and a disagreeable Head-ake, caused by continual fainting in the open Air as the Dew was falling the Evening before…She grew gradually worse…Her disorder turned to galloping Consumption and in a few days carried her off.*

Laura consoles herself, reflecting that she had *paid every Attention to her that could be offered, in her illness. I had wept over her every day – had bathed her sweet face with my tears and pressed her fair Hands continually in mine. My beloved Laura (said she to me a few Hours before she died) take warning from my unhappy End… Beware of fainting fits…Beware of swoons Dear Laura…a frenzy fit is not one quarter so pernicious; it is an exercise to the body, and if not too violent, is I daresay conducive to Health in its consequences. Run mad as often as you chuse: but do not faint!*

After attending Sophia *to her Early Grave,* Laura *left the detested Village in which she died. I had not walked many yards before I was overtaken by a Stage-coach in which I instantly took a place, determined to proceed in it to Edinburgh.*

It is so dark inside the coach, Laura cannot see the passengers, *I could only perceive that they were many.* She gives herself *up to her own sad Reflections. A general Silence prevailed, interrupted only by the loud and repeated Snores of one of the Party.*

As light comes up, Laura realises she is *surrounded by her nearest Relations and Connections.* The snorer is Sir Edward, who shares the seat with his daughter Augusta. Laura sits opposite, sharing her seat are Isabel and Lady Dorothea. In front, on the Coach-box, are Philippa and her husband, in the luggage-basket at the rear, are the two grandsons from the inn, Philander and Gustavus. The coach is overcrowded, designed for a maximum of six passengers, it carries eight plus the driver.

At Augusta and Sir Edward's request, Laura relates *to them every Misfortune which had befallen her since they parted.* Isabel finds *fault* with Laura's *behaviour in many of the situations in which she had been placed,* but Laura pays *little attention to* Isabel's opinion, she is *sensible that she had always behaved in a manner which reflected Honour on her Feelings and Refinement,.*

Letter the 15th. Laura learns what each of her fellow passengers has been doing since she last saw them. When they arrive in Edinburgh, she accepts Sir Edward's offer of £400 a year, as *the Widow of his Son.* Laura moved to the Scottish Highlands, where she still lives in *melancholy Solitude.*

Love and Freindship ends in a neat tableau as Laura brings Marianne up to date with all the characters in her story. Augusta married Graham, abandoned by Janetta; Sir Edward married Lady Dorothea, rejected by Edward, and has a new Heir; Philander and Gustavus, actors, have found fame in Covent Garden; Edward's aunt, Philippa, is long dead, but her husband still drives a Stage-Coach from Edinburgh to Sterling.

Somehow, telling her story seems to give Laura new energy and optimism. Before bidding Marianne, *Adieu,* she tells her: *my Adventures are now drawing to a close my dearest Marianne: at least for the present.*

Though Laura is fifty-five, her marriage and her youthful adventures in Scotland remain the high point of any meaning in her life. At fifteen,

Jane Austen wrote as if she could not imagine or aspire to anything more meaningful in her own future.

Conjecturing as to the date

Pride & Prejudice

Jane Austen wrote *Love and Freindship* in June 1790. Just six months earlier, she had been persuaded to renounce her involvement with D'Arcy Wentworth. In her fifteenth year, with *so feeling a heart, so sweet a temper, to be so easily persuaded by those she loved,*[109] *she had agreed to bury the tumult of her feelings under the restraint of society.*[110]

Three months before, *The Loiterer*, the student magazine produced by James and Henry Austen at Oxford, published its last issue. During its run of sixty issues, from January 1789 to March 1790, a prime target of its weekly commentaries, designed to entertain the all-male student body, was the literature of sensibility and its sentimental heroines.

Henry Austen had blamed the sentimental novel for the spread of *degenerate and sickly refinement,* and warned, *all who adopt their opinions will share their fate; they will be tortured by the poignant delicacy of their own feelings, and fall the Martyrs to their own Susceptibility.*[111]

There was something in the name

Emma

In August 1789, Henry published his advice on love and friendship in the *The Loiterer: let every Girl who seeks for happiness conquer both her feelings and her passions. Let her avoid love and friendship as she wishes to be admired and distinguished. For by these means she will always keep her own secrets and prefer her own interest.*[112] It was far too late for Jane to heed him, she was already head over heels in love with D'Arcy Wentworth.

Deceived in friendship and betrayed in love, the subtitle of *Love and Freindship*, was the last line of a song, that ended:
> Far from the world's illusion let me rove
> Deceiv'd in Friendship, & betray'd in Love.

Reading it aloud *Northanger Abbey*

Love and Freindship is an exciting story, told with confidence and verve. We listen to it with Marianne in mind, and can imagine her to be inspired by Laura's adventures and her exciting life, regardless of the misfortunes that followed.

In many ways, *Love and Freindship* was a report to her family of her adventures with D'Arcy Wentworth. Jane Austen wanted to record the most important and catastrophic events of her young life. Forbidden to mention them, she disguised them in a lively and amusing account for her family's entertainment.

Laura's *Misfortunes and Adventures* refer to events and escapades of the period Jane and D'Arcy spent together, with flashbacks to their journey to Yorkshire, their elopement to Scotland, their rambles there, and on their return to London, D'Arcy's imprisonment in Newgate.

Love and Freindship is a memoir of suffering as well as sentiment. Behind its parody of the excesses of sensibility, Jane Austen set down how she had been carried away by love and friendship, how it came crashing down around her, leaving her alone, with no future, unable to feel anything. Beneath the burlesque and humour, Jane laid out her own feelings of loss and despair.

My father's opinion of me does me the greatest honour *Pride & Prejudice*

George Austen had ruled, if her association with a notorious highwayman became known, it would damage the reputation of the Austen family, his private school at the Steventon Rectory, and the career prospects of her brothers. D'Arcy Wentworth's name was never to be mentioned, it was *a profound secret, not to be breathed beyond their own circle.*[113]

If she read *Love and Freindship* to her family, Jane was assuring them she had always faced her difficulties with fortitude, her sole fault had been *a sensibility too tremblingly alive ... yet now I never feel for those of another.*

She told of her passion for D'Arcy, her involvement in his world, her disdain for her father's rejection of him. She told her father that her story had value, even as a cautionary tale. George Austen would have felt her censure.

Mine is a misery which nothing can do away *Sense & Sensibility*

In the first months of 1790, after D'Arcy Wentworth disappeared from her life, Jane Austen came dangerously close to mental breakdown.

In *Love and Freindship*, she told *My Greif was more audible. My voice faltered, My eyes assumed a vacant Stare, My face became as pale as Death, and my Senses were considerably impaired... I die a Martyr to my greif.*

Her first novel, *Sense & Sensibility*, first drafted in 1795, set out with clinical precision the dreadful impact of losing him.

At first, she *shed no tears; but after a short time they would burst out, tears of agony,* in *violent affliction, violent sorrow.* She cried uncontrollably, *a continual flow of tears, agitation and sobs,* and *frequent bursts of grief, tears which streamed from her eyes with passionate violence. Covering her face with her handkerchief, she almost screamed with agony.. such grief, shocking as it was, such violent oppression of spirits.. her voice entirely lost in sobs.. she was without any desire of command over herself.*

Dreadfully white...in silent agony, too much oppressed even for tears, her *violence of affliction sunk into a calmer melancholy,* she would experience *a sort of desperate calmness, immediately followed by a return of the same excessive affliction.*

Her own share in the story *Emma*

In *Love and Freindship*, Jane Austen revealed she had travelled to Scotland. In her day, to say that a young girl had gone to Scotland, meant only one thing. That she had travelled north to take advantage of Scottish law, which, unlike the English *Marriage Act of 1753, an Act for the Better Preventing of Clandestine Marriage,* permitted youths to marry without parental consent, without the posting of banns over three weeks, and without a formal ceremony conducted in a parish church or chapel of the Church of England.[114]

In *Letter the 10th*, Jane included a brief reference to Janetta's (or little Jane's) elopement to Gretna Green. In *Letter the 6th*, she made sure that Laura was married before she left home with Edward. Married by her father who was *bred to the Church*, though as he had *never taken orders,* the marriage is not strictly lawful. In *Letter the 10th*, she returns to her own story, her elopement to Scotland with D'Arcy Wentworth. Forbidden to discuss or to reveal the event of greatest importance to her, she rescued it from damnation, recording it in her notebook as the story of Janetta, little Jane, and her Scottish marriage.

Having so nobly disentangled themselves from the shackles of Parental Authority, by a Clandestine Marriage   *Love and Freindship*

In September 1788, a year earlier, Jane Austen's cousin Thomas Twisleton and Charlotte Wattell, both under twenty-one, had eloped to Gretna Green. Their families approved them remarrying under English law, and a few weeks later, on 4 November 1788, their elopement was regularised, at St Marylebone.

On 29 January 1790, twelve days after D'Arcy sailed on the *Neptune*, Thomas' younger sister, the Hon. Cassandra Twisleton, not yet sixteen, eloped to Gretna Green with Edward Jervis Ricketts, the eldest son of Viscount St Vincent. Her mother, Lady Saye & Sele, said her family *winked approvingly* at their continued attachment, if not the elopement.[115]

The restraint which her father imposed   *Mansfield Park*

In Letter 6th, Laura told Marianne that after she accepted Edward's proposal, *we were immediately united by my Father, who tho' he had never taken orders had been bred to the Church.* In Letter the 9th, she praises the marriage of Augustus and Sophia, *contrary to the inclinations of their Cruel and Mercenary Parents.*

George Austen would have felt his daughter's judgement. When they returned to Steventon at Christmas 1789, he had agreed to legalise Jane and D'Arcy Wentworth's Scottish marriage under English law. But after James Austen's arrival from Oxford, he changed his mind and refused to do so. His betrayal had destroyed her chance of happiness. It may explain the words *Betrayed in Love* she wrote beneath the title.

Wickedness is always wickedness, but folly is not always folly   *Emma*

In *Love and Freindship*, Jane Austen made it clear how difficult it was for young people to *disentangle themselves from the shackles of parental authority*. To do so required sufficient resources and skills to live independently.

At first, Augustus and Sophia seem to have succeeded, but their money, which Augustus had *gracefully purloined from his Unworthy father,* soon ran out. Edward and Laura do not appear to understand or to assist. Augustus' debts mount up and he is arrested and imprisoned.

In *Love and Freindship,* parents are castigated for their wickedness in attempting to persuade their children into arranged marriages. Their interference is deemed worse than stealing money, which is presented as mere folly, particularly if stolen for a life of freedom or romance.

The story makes light of thefts of money by young people. Sophia unlocks *a private Drawer in Macdonald's Library,* and finds bank notes of a considerable amount. She and Laura agree, next time either of them *happen to go that way,* they will remove one or more of them. They show no remorse when Sophia is caught *majestically removing the 5th Bank-note.*

Philander and Gustavus steal the two £50 notes given to Laura and Sophia by Lord St Clair, their mutual long lost grandfather. Laura does not criticise them, nor dispute their claim they had obtained the £200 for themselves. Nor does she comment when they tell her they stole the last of their mothers' savings, and that their mothers, Bertha and Agatha had starved to death.

Laura describes for Marianne, their method of managing their money *with eoconomy,* they divide it *into nine parcels, one of which we devoted to Victuals, the 2d to Drink, the 3rd to House-keeping, the 4th to Carriages, the 5th to Horses, the 6th to Servants, the 7th to Amusements, the 8th to Cloathes and the 9th to Silver Buckles.*

You will not refuse to visit me in prison?　　　　*Mansfield Park*

In *Love and Freindship,* Augustus is arrested for failing to pay his debts and is sent to Newgate. There were several debtors' prisons in London,[116] but Newgate was not one of them. Newgate was London's central prison, it housed criminals and those arrested or convicted of a capital crime. In 1783, public executions in London were moved from Tyburn Hill to Newgate, and were conducted outside the prison walls.

Jane wanted to record a critical event of her own life, D'Arcy's imprisonment in Newgate. He was held there through the month of November 1789, while the Bow Street magistrate made great efforts to find a witness with evidence to prosecute him for highway robbery, a capital crime. D'Arcy was taken back from Newgate to Bow Street on five occasions for public examinations, well publicised beforehand to attract people who might identify him.

The press carried the unusual offer of a full pardon to any highwayman prepared to appear against D'Arcy, but noone came forward to claim it.[117] D'Arcy, over six feet tall, dark haired and handsome, was the celebrity of the day, pursued by the paparazzi.

Jane Austen did not tell her parents she visited Newgate Prison. In *Love and Freindship*, Laura orders a carriage to take her to Newgate with Sophia, but Sophia refuses to go. Jane did record, *the unhappy situation of my imprisoned Husband. Alas, what would I not give to learn the fate of my Augustus! to know if he is still in Newgate, or if he is yet hung.*

A secret satisfaction　　　　*Emma*

In her daily life Jane Austen was forbidden to mention D'Arcy Wentworth. In *Love and Freindship* she recorded something of their story, and she continued to do so in her later novels. In *Pride & Prejudice*, she named him Fitzwilliam Darcy and stated he was a cousin of Earl Fitzwilliam.

In Jane Austen's day, it was improper for a young woman to address a man by his Christian name. Jane was not allowed to speak of D'Arcy Wentworth, but she had a great desire to say and to hear his name. In *Pride & Prejudice*, the story of their romance, by naming him Fitzwilliam Darcy, her characters were free to speak his name without reserve. Jane ensured her love for him and his name would resound across the years.

In *Love and Freindship* she recorded the length of time she and D'Arcy spent as man and wife: *7 weeks and a Day*, and included incidents from those few weeks in the narrative. Her description of *resting by the side of clear limpid stream to refresh our exhausted limbs,* tells us how she and D'Arcy had rambled through Scotland, outdoors, walking, living modestly, at times exhausted, cold, and even hungry.

In Letter 6th, Jane included a reference to D'Arcy in a joke about Edward Lindsay's arrival at Laura's *rustic Cot.* D'Arcy had left England for New South Wales, Jane had Edward find himself in South Wales, exclaiming, *tho' I flatter myself with being a tolerable proficient in Geography, I know not how it happened.*

Deceived in Friendship

In *Love and Freindship*, Laura refers constantly to her *freinds*, the word appears fifteen times in the story. Laura has known Isabel since she was eighteen, she is, *a real friend, my most intimate friend*, though from the outset the reader questions the sincerity of Isabel's friendship.

During their coach ride to Edinburgh, Laura relates to Isabel and her companions, every *misfortune which had befallen her since they parted.* Isabel gives Laura no comfort or sympathy, rather she wounds her with *unjustifiable Reproaches.*

Throughout *Love and Freindship,* we are conscious of Laura's poor judgement and misplaced enthusiasms. Her efforts are often futile, but it is her judgement of the character and the motives of people she encounters that are often most foolish and blind.

Arm in arm they tasted the sweets of friendship in unreserved conversation *Northanger Abbey*

Deprived of Isabel's friendship for three weeks, Laura meets Sophia, *the wife of Edward's friend, we flew into each other's arms and after having exchanged vows of mutual Freindship for the rest of our Lives, instantly unfolded to each other the most inward Secrets of our Hearts.* Laura declares Sophia *is one most truly worthy of the Name of friend.* The time she and Edward spent as guests of Sophia and Augustus were, *the happiest moments of my Life.*

Laura proves a true friend to Sophia. She packs and helps her to leave the house before the bailiffs arrive, she orders a carriage to take her to visit Augustus in Newgate, and has the carriage turn back when Sophia declares she could not endure seeing Augustus in such distress. She arranges their trip to Scotland, and after the death of their husbands, however impractical, she pays every *Attention to Sophia,*

At first sight, Laura pronounces Macdonald to be *a tender and simpathetic Freind,* but she decides her judgement was wrong – *for though he told us he was much concerned at our Misfortunes, yet they had neither drawn from him a single sigh, nor induced him to bestow one curse on our vindictive Stars.*

Laura takes a place inside the Stage-Coach to Edinburgh, hoping *to find some kind of pitying freind who would receive and comfort me in my Afflictions.* She fails to recognise Sir Edward's kindness to his sister Philippa and her wastrel husband, that he travels in their coach with his family, in order to *throw a little money into their Pockets.* Laura accepts his offer of four hundred pounds a year, *as the Widow of his Son,* but considers him unsympathetic, as his offer was not made on account of *her being the refined and Amiable Laura.*

Names, facts, every thing mentioned without ceremony   *Pride & Prejudice*

Jane Austen's *Love and Freindship* took ideas and situations from *Laura and Augustus,* a novel by Eliza Bromley, published in 1784. Central to *Laura and Augustus* is the love affair of Lieutenant Augustus Montague and Laura Levison, whose father refused to allow her to marry for love. The novel censures parents who force their children into arranged marriages. Jane appropriated the names of its hero and heroine, the tragic death of Augustus and the hysterical fainting and running wild that followed.

Jane gave Lord St Clair, who discovers his four grandchildren in a Scottish inn, a name closely connected to the Wentworth family. Arabella Holles, daughter of John Holles, 1st Earl of Clare (1564-1637), married Thomas Wentworth, 1st Earl of Strafford, in 1625. She was his second wife and the mother of his three elder children.

Macdonald of Macdonald Hall was another Wentworth connexion. Diana Bosville, daughter of Sir William Wentworth of Bretton, in Yorkshire's West Riding, married Sir Alexander Macdonald, 9th Baronet and 1st Lord Macdonald of Sleat (1745-1795), whose seat, Armadale, was on the Isle of Skye. Their eldest son, Alexander Wentworth Macdonald, born in 1773, was a contemporary of Jane Austen, he became 2nd Baron Macdonald in 1795.

Overturned in toiling up a long ascent   *Sanditon*

On 2 September 1789, Jane Austen and D'Arcy Wentworth attended a great garden party to honour the Prince of Wales, at *Wentworth Woodhouse,* Earl Fitzwilliam's seat in South Yorkshire.[118]

Shortly after leaving the party, the Prince's carriage was involved in an accident: *It was on the verge of the slope, and the carriage fell a considerable way, turned over twice and was shivered to pieces...His Highness was undermost in the first fall, and by the next roll of the carriage was brought uppermost.*[119]

Jane included a scene in *Love and Freindship* of the *overturning of a Gentleman's Phaeton. Those who but a few moments before had been in so elevated a situation as a fashionably high Phaeton, but who were now laid low and sprawling in the dust.*

Heyday! here's company, here's a carriage!   *Mansfield Park*

In Edinburgh, in September 1789, Jane and D'Arcy stayed directly below Edinburgh Castle, at the White Hart Inn. It was located in the bustling Grassmarket, where cattle, horses and grain were traded. Jane included a White Hart Inn in two of her novels, *The Watsons* and *Persuasion*.

She and D'Arcy took the opportunity to visit Stirling Castle, thirty-six miles away, to celebrate the anniversary of the coronation of Mary, Queen of Scots, 246 years earlier in September 1543. They travelled there, and back to Edinburgh, by coach.

In August 1814, twenty-five years later, Jane went by coach to London from Chawton to stay with her brother Henry. She assured Cassandra, it was a *very good Journey,* the coach had *a great load but was not crouded.* The cabin was not too full as two or three passengers were *Children, the others of a reasonable size; & they were all very quiet & civil.*

As well as those inside the coach, there were *4 in the Kitchen part*, at *the rear, and 15 at top.*[120] After leaving Chawton, they picked up several passengers, Jane knew most of them. A mile or so from Alton, at Holybourn, young Gibson got on, at Egham, nineteen miles from London, they picked up Percy Benn, on his way back to naval college at Woolwich. In short, she told Cassandra, *everybody either did come up by Yalden yesterday, or wanted to come up.*

When Jane arrived in London, her *Trunk & Basket had to be routed out from all the other Trunks & baskets in the World.* She recalled, *It put me in mind of my own Coach between Edinburgh and Sterling.*[121]

When her grand-nephew, William Austen-Leigh and great grand-nephew, Richard Austen-Leigh, published the letter in 1913, they added a footnote, stating firmly: *A visit of Jane to Scotland, of which no record is left in family tradition, is so improbable that we must imagine her to be referring to some joke, or possibly some forgotten tale of her own.*[122] It seems the Austen-Leighs had read neither *Love and Freindship* nor *Lesley Castle*.

Assured as his future inheritance – James expressed himself on the occasion with becoming gratitude   *Northanger Abbey*

Time, death and distance gradually separated the families of Jane Austen's brothers. James, her eldest brother, died in 1819, two years after Jane. His only son James Edward, ordained in 1823, served as the vicar of Bray, on the Thames in Berkshire, from 1852 to 1874. In 1837, he added Leigh to his name to become the heir of his great aunt Jane Leigh Perrot, widow of his namesake, Jane's mother's brother James. He received the blessing of a handsome inheritance, including the Leigh Perrot's house *Scarlets*, near Maidenhead in Berkshire.

James Leigh had married Jane Cholmeley in 1764, and later added Perrot to their names, to become the heir of his maternal great uncle, Thomas Perrot, who died childless. James Leigh Perrot and his wife had no children and James Edward Austen added the name Leigh, though not Perrot, to his own, to become their heir, as James Edward Austen Leigh.

Cassandra bequeathed *Volume the Third* to James Edward. Jane had given it to him and his half-sister Anna Lefroy to read, and with her encouragement, they tried their hand at continuing its two stories, *Evelyn* and *Kitty, or the Bower*. It seems that Jane had kept *Volume the Second* to herself, after Cassandra's death it passed to her brother Frank.

Frank lived twenty years after Cassandra, he died at Portsdown in 1865. His family did not share the same wealth and prominence as James Edward Austen Leigh. After the death at sea, off Burma in 1852, of the last of Jane's brothers, Charles Austen, Commander in Chief of the East India and China Station, James Edward took up the role of the senior member and spokesman for the Austen family.

James Edward considered the time had come to meet requests for biographical information about Jane Austen. He conferred with his sisters and various female cousins and in 1869, fifty-two years after her death, he published *A Memoir of Jane Austen*. Two years later he produced an enlarged second edition, including several unpublished manuscripts, including *The Mystery* from *Volume the First*.

Tell-tale compression of the pages   *Northanger Abbey*

The leaf following *Love and Freindship* was removed, torn out before Jane wrote her table of contents, though after she had numbered the pages. This left pages 65 and 66 missing from the volume. The stub of the missing leaf remains in the binding.

Produced a great alteration   *Sense & Sensibility*

At the end of *Love and Freindship*, Jane Austen wrote FINIS, and the date, June 13th 1790, but she continued to work on the story, she made, in all, ninety-six changes to the text.

18

Lesley Castle
an unfinished Novel in Letters

To whom this work is dedicated

Jane Austen dedicated *Lesley Castle* to her brother Henry Thomas Austen, fourth son of the Austen family, four years her senior. His kindness, encouragement and readiness to help her contributed in no small part to her happiness and to her success as a published author.

Jane showed Henry where she had recorded *Lesley Castle* in *Volume the Second*. He responded, writing below her dedication, a mock order to his banker to pay her a hundred guineas for her fine efforts.

Gathering her work together   *Pride & Prejudice*

Lesley Castle, like *Love and Freindship*, is a novel in a series of letters, though its structure is far more complex. Fourteen of the fifteen letters that make up *Love and Freindship* were written by Laura, Isabel wrote the first letter, Laura the rest. In *Lesley Castle* there are ten letters with five authors.

Margaret Lesley's four letters to her friend Charlotte Lutterell open and close the novel, and are central to the story. She writes the first three from *Lesley Castle*, her home, two miles from Perth, between January and March; and the last from Portman Square, in mid-April, *after a Journey of seven days* from Scotland.

In Margaret's first letter to Charlotte, she describes herself and her sister Matilda as *secluded from Mankind in Lesley Castle*, while their father is *fluttering about the Streets of London.* Their brother has gone abroad to heal the *Wounds of a broken Heart,* after his wife, *the Worthless Louisa left him, her child and reputation a few weeks ago in company with Danvers and dishonour.*

Margaret and Matilda are caring for their brother's two year-old daughter Louise, abandoned by her mother, and more recently by her father. Margaret's modest praise for Louise's achievements, *that she already knows the first two letters in the Alphabet, and never tears her frocks,* parodies the claims of a proud parent, and confirms that she is an attentive and sympathetic guardian.

Charlotte takes forty days to answer Margaret's first letter, with a *thousand excuses* for her *long delayed* reply. She has been preoccupied with catering for her sister Eloisa's wedding, that was cancelled, after the groom was thrown from his horse and killed. Charlotte is left to lament *the dreadful Waste in our provisions which this event must occasion, and in concerting some plan for getting rid of them.*

Charlotte ends her letter with important news for Margaret and Matilda, *it is confidently reported, your Father is going to be married.* She undertakes to find out more, she will write to her *freind Susan Fitzgerald, for information.* A late postscript to her letter, encloses Susan's reply. Sir George has remarried, Susan Fitzgerald is the new Lady Lesley.

This news causes Margaret and Matilda great disquiet. How will a step-mother affect their *Consequence*? *Matilda would no longer sit at the head of her Father's table;* their financial security? *the probable Diminution of our Fortunes; and the ownership of those Jewels which once adorned our Mother, and which Sir George had always promised us.*

Margaret tells Charlotte, *we both wish very much to know whether Lady Lesley is handsome and what is your opinion of her...as you honour her with the appellation of your friend, we flatter ourselves that she must be amiable.*

Charlotte is still preoccupied with disposing of the uneaten wedding feast. She replies two weeks later, she is in Bristol with her sister Eloisa, where *the air of Bristol-Downs, healthy as it is, has not been able to drive poor Henry from her remembrance.* She assures Margaret her pantry is *nearly cleared.* She has brought with her: *a cold Pigeon-pie, a cold turkey, a cold tongue, and half a dozen jellies.* She left orders with her *Servants, to eat as hard as they possibly could, and to call in a couple of Chairwomen to assist them.*

Charlotte answers Margaret's questions with an exact description of Lady Lesley's *bodily and Mental charms. She is short, and extremely well-made; is naturally pale, but rouges a great deal; has fine eyes and fine teeth...and is altogether very pretty.*

Charlotte is sorry to say that Margaret and Matilda's fears: *concerning your father's extravagance, your own fortunes, your Mother's Jewels and your Sister's consequence are but too well founded...But as so melancholy a subject must necessarily extremely distress you, I will no longer dwell on it.*

In the post, with Charlotte's letter, Margaret receives a letter from her father, he is in Edinburgh, on his way to Lesley Castle with Lady Lesley. They arrive with Lady Lesley's brother William Fitzgerald.

Charlotte receives a report on their visit from Margaret and from Lady Lesley. Margaret's letter is quite circumspect, although she tells Charlotte she does not agree with her that her step-mother is *altogether so pretty. She has not a bad face, but there is something so extremely unmajestic in her little diminutive figure, as to render her in comparison with the elegant height of Matilda and Myself, an insignificant Dwarf.*

Lady Lesley's letter to Charlotte is filled with *Disappointment and Surprise.* She dislikes *Lesley Castle,* it is *dismal old* and *Weather-beaten;* she is displeased with her two step-daughters, *two great, tall, out of the way, over-grown Girls, just of a proper size to inhabit a Castle almost as Large in comparison as themselves,* and *she detests Children,* their niece is, *a little humoured Brat.*

Lady Susan is most concerned that her brother William entertains a *partiality for Matilda Lesley.* There is nothing she hates *so much as a tall Woman: but however there is no accounting for some men's taste.* She decides it would be *a good-natured action* to let him know *Matilda is entirely dependent on her Father, who will neither have his own inclination nor my permission to give her anything at present.*

Finding herself alone with William *in one of the horrid old rooms of this Castle,* Lady Susan tries to draw him out about his interest in Matilda, and soon finds herself in an argument. While she finds the Miss Lesleys *terribly plain* and *so horribly tall,* William defends them, declaring, *their figures are perfectly elegant; and as to their faces, their Eyes are beautifull.* He suggests to his sister, *perhaps they might dazzle you with their Lustre.*

At this, Lady Susan *left the room immediately... so vexed by William she could not summon Patience enough, to stay and give him that Advice respecting his Attachment to Matilda which had first induced me from pure Love to him to begin the conversation.*

Charlotte replies to Margaret from Bristol, greatly entertained that she and Lady Lesley are *both downright jealous of each others Beauty.* She is very impatient with her sister Eloisa, still grieving for the death of her fiancé Henry Hervey, *with undiminished Constancy, notwithstanding he has been dead more than six weeks.* Eloisa has not praised Charlotte's cooking, and in retaliation she has *formed a concerted a scheme of Revenge.* Her lack of understanding or compassion for Eloisa leads into the next two letters, between Eloisa and her new friend, Emma Marlowe.

Eloisa tells Mrs Marlowe she has found in her, *one of my own Sex to whom I might speak with less reserve than to any other person.* She warns her: *You must expect from me nothing but the melancholy effusions of a broken Heart which is ever reverting to the Happiness it once enjoyed and which ill supports its present Wretchedness.*

Mrs Marlowe replies from Grosvenor Street, near Earl Fitzwilliam's London home.[123] She hopes their correspondence will *provoke a Smile in the Sweet but Sorrowful Countenance of my Eloisa.*

The last letter in *Lesley Castle* is from Margaret Lesley, now in London, to Charlotte. She is enjoying the *Amusements of this vaunted City.* She has met Mrs Marlowe and her brother Cleveland, *a Young Man the most lovely of his Sex.* Though they have not yet spoken, Margaret is *certain that on him depends the future Happiness of my Life.* Her sister Matilda has also met a young man she finds interesting, Lady Lesley's brother, *Mr Fitzgerald who is a very amiable Young Man in the main.*

Her father Sir George, *is almost always at the Gaming-table.* Margaret laments, *Ah! My poor fortune where art thou by this time?* Lady Lesley *(highly rouged)* delights in wearing *Delightful Jewels.., My Mother's Jewels too!* Tensions appear to be rising within the family.

Margaret's brother is now in Italy, in Naples, where *has turned Roman –catholic.* His first marriage annulled, he has *married a Neapolitan Lady of great Rank and Fortune.* His first wife is there as well, she too has also turned *Roman-catholic, and is soon to be married to a Neapolitan Nobleman of great and Distinguished Merit.* He has invited his sisters to visit with his daughter, *little Louisa, whom both her Mother, Step-Mother, and himself are equally desirous of beholding.* Margaret tells Charlotte, *Lady Lesley advises us to go without loss of time.*

What is in general called a friend   *Lesley Castle*

Lesley Castle gives a number of perspectives on female friendship: between the two sets of sisters, Margaret and Matilda Lesley, and Charlotte and Eloisa Lutterell; between Charlotte and Susan Lesley, and in particular, between Margaret and Charlotte.

The reader realises early in the story that Margaret Lesley is not the best judge of her friend, Charlotte Lutterell. In her first letter to Charlotte, Margaret opens with the news that her brother is now single, his wife Louisa has left him. Charlotte takes nearly six weeks to reply, with news about Margaret's father remarrying. Margaret replies with questions and concerns about her new stepmother, but the large part of her letter returns to her brother, who has *entirely ceased to think of Louisa with any degree either of Pity or Affection.*

Charlotte replies very promptly, thanking Margaret for the account of her brother Lesley, *which has not the less entertained me for having often been repeated to me before.* She is aware of an unspoken agenda, and ends her letter with a clear statement that she is not interested in marriage, *other than superintending and directing the Dinner.*

In *Amelia Webster* in *Volume the First*, Matilda sent a similar message to her friend Amelia, that her *amiable brother* had returned *from abroad.* It seems that young women were expected to do what they could to widen the range of choice for young men in their family, and to alert their female friends to romantic opportunities.

As in *Love and Freindship*, Jane Austen dissects notions of friendship in *Lesley Castle.* Charlotte tells Margaret that Susan Fitzgerald, who becomes the new Lady Lesley, is her friend, that *she never reads any thing but the letters she receives from me, and never writes anything but her answers to them.*

Later, she is more candid about their relationship: *To tell you the truth, our friendship arose rather from Caprice on her side, than Esteem on mine. We spent two or three days together with a Lady in Berkshire with whom we both happened to be connected. During our visit, the Weather being remarkably bad, and our party particularly stupid, she was so good as to conceive a violent partiality for me, which very soon settled in a downright Friendship, and ended in an established correspondence. She is probably by this time as tired of me, as I am of her; but as she is too polite and I am too civil to say so, our letters are still as frequent and affectionate as ever, and our Attachment as firm and Sincere as when it first commenced.*

Charlotte's candour may well lead the reader to wonder how she might describe her friendship with Margaret Lesley to Lady Lesley.

To form that ground-work

It is Lady Susan Lesley, the worldly, manipulative character, who brings *Lesley Castle* to life. Though she is the author of only one letter, she is the subject of many exchanges in the six letters between Margaret Lesley and Charlotte Lutterell.

The new wife of a Scottish nobleman, she hates *everything Scotch;* his seat is *a dismal old Weather-beaten Castle,* his daughters, *terribly plain and horribly tall,* and his granddaughter, *a little humoured brat.* She is manipulative, and eager to exercise her newly acquired power over Sir George and his daughters.

Lady Lesley is displeased her brother William *entertains a partiality* for Matilda Lesley, and plots to break them up. She tells him Margaret is *entirely dependent on her Father,* and that she will not give her husband *permission to give* Margaret *anything at present.* William can *choose for himself, whether to conquer his passion, or Love and Despair.* Fortunately her scheme backfires.

In a scene with echoes of *Jack and Alice,* Lady Lesley tells her brother she finds the Miss Lesleys *so horridly pale.* When he retorts, *if they have but little colour, at least, it is all their own,* it is too much for her, she feels her character has been cruelly aspersed, for *how often I have protested against wearing Rouge.*

A new object of interest

In 1793-94, Jane Austen reused the name *Lady Susan* in a new work, a complete novel in forty-one letters, she revised it in 1805, but never submitted it for publication. In 1871, her nephew, James Edward Austen-Leigh gave it the title, *Lady Susan.*

Lady Susan Lesley pales beside the energy and duplicity of her namesake, Lady Susan Vernon, independent, amoral, flirtatious, and desperate, *she finds delicious gratification in making the whole family miserable.*

Where Lady Susan Lesley was *short and naturally pale.* Lady Susan

Vernon *is delicately fair, with fine grey eyes and dark eyelashes; and from her appearance one would not suppose her more than five and twenty, though she must in fact be ten years older.*

Lady Lesley merely *detests children,* Lady Susan calls her own daughter Frederica, *horrid; a child without talent or education and a little devil,* she neglects and bullies her relentlessly, and pressures her to marry wealthy Sir James Martin, the *greatest simpleton on earth.*

Lady Susan Vernon manipulates her late husband's family, she has a married lover, Manwaring, and sets out to seduce her sister in law's brother, Reginald De Courcy. In the end, after her deceptions are exposed, she marries the simpleton, Sir James Martin.

My father's opinion of me does me the greatest honor   Pride & Prejudice

In *Lesley Castle,* Jane Austen gave Baron Lesley her father's name, George, and describes him, *Fluttering about the Streets of London.* Margaret tells Charlotte: *Sir George is 57 and still remains the Beau, the flighty stripling, the gay Lad, and sprightly Youngster.*

The description would have amused those around the Steventon dinner table. George Austen was fifty-seven when he took Jane and Cassandra to stay with Anne Lefroy in Cork Street in April 1788.

During her stay, Jane Austen's romance with D'Arcy Wentworth blossomed. Eight years later, staying in the same house in Cork Street, she sent an ironic note to Cassandra: *here I am once more in this Scene of Dissipation & vice, and I begin already to find my Morals corrupted.*[124] We can hear her sarcasm, her mockery of the Austen family criticism of her, and her romance with D'Arcy.

Suffering as a girl of fourteen, of strong personality & not high spirits must suffer at such a time   Persuasion

Critics have commented on the change of tone and mood in Letters the Eighth and Ninth, between Eloisa Lutterell and Mrs Marlowe. One observation, that, *the dominant effect is no longer that of satirical comedy but of serious and sincere feeling,*[125] catches the truth. The two letters describe Jane Austen's state of mind, confined at home in Steventon, after she was persuaded to forsake D'Arcy.

Through Charlotte's description of her irritation with her sister Eloisa, her *scheme of Revenge,* and the exchange between Eloisa and Mrs Marlowe in Letter the Eighth and the Ninth, Jane set down a record of the discord and tension that had arisen between her and Cassandra, and the comfort she found in her friendship with Anne Lefroy. Like Eloisa, Jane was her father's favourite, *she preferred Histories,* of the two Austen sisters, she was the better scholar, and she took great pleasure in playing the keyboard, a fortepiano.

Anne Lefroy, Jane's long standing friend and neighbour, reached out to her during this bleak period. She invited her to visit the rectory at Ashe as often as she wished, to spend time with the children, who loved her. It was in Ashe rectory that Jane and D'Arcy Wentworth met for the last time; she recorded their meeting in *Persuasion*:

He walked into the drawing-room at the cottage, where were only herself and the little invalid... She was obliged to kneel down by the sofa, and remain there to satisfy her patient; and thus they continued a few minutes, when, to her very great satisfaction, she heard some other person crossing the little vestibule.

Another minute brought another addition. The younger boy, a remarkable stout, forward child, of two years old, having got the door opened for him by some one without, made his determined appearance among them, and went straight to the sofa to see what was going on, and put in his claim to anything good that might be giving away..

He began to fasten himself upon her, as she knelt, in such a way that, busy as she was about Charles, she could not shake him off. She spoke to him, ordered, entreated, and insisted in vain. Once she did contrive to push him away, but the boy had the greater pleasure in getting upon her back again directly.

"Walter," said she, "get down this moment. You are extremely troublesome. I am very angry with you."

In another moment, however, she found herself in the state of being released from him; some one was taking him from her, though he had bent down her head so much, that his little sturdy hands were unfastened from around her neck, and he was resolutely borne away, before she knew that Captain Wentworth had done it... it required a long application of solitude and reflection to recover her.[126]

Years later, after Anne Lefroy's death, Jane Austen wrote a poem of praise to her, describing how she sought *to comfort, heal, enlighten, cheer.* She thanked her for, *bestowing Life, and Light, and Hope on me.*[127]

There are secrets in all families, you know *Emma*

In *Lesley Castle,* Jane appears to allude to another hidden Austen romance. In three of her four letters to Charlotte, Margaret writes about her brother's travails, how he needs to recover from the disappointment of his wife Louisa, leaving him for another man. *Lesley is at present but five and twenty, and has already given himself up to melancholy and Despair,* he is going abroad to recover.

Jane's eldest brother James went abroad in early October 1786, and spent nearly a year in Europe. George Austen may have been persuaded to finance James' Grand Tour to match that of his younger brother Edward, who was already in Switzerland, supported by the Knight family. Or was it to distract James from a broken heart at the end of an affair?

In 1785, aged twenty, James was infatuated with nineteen year old Lady Catherine Powlett, daughter of Admiral Harry Powlett, the sixth Duke of Bolton. James dedicated a romantic sonnet to her, filled with compliments and classical allusions to her beauty and his love.

The following year, George Austen leased the rectory to Anne Lefroy's brother, Egerton Brydges, and his new wife Elizabeth Byrche. Charlotte Brydges, Egerton's young sister, James' age, accompanied them, and soon replaced Lady Catherine in his affections. James addressed a series of passionate poems to her, including a sonnet ending with the couplet:

Teach me not then to bear a load of pain
But teach me Sweet Enchantress how to die.[128]

Matilda tells Charlotte that her brother met the faithless Louisa Burton *at the age of two and twenty.* James Austen was twenty-two in 1787, perhaps it was Charlotte Brydges who broke his young heart.

James' romantic adventures have been omitted from Austen family histories. Jane may have sought to redress the balance in *Lesley Castle*, and later in *Northanger Abbey*, mindful it was James who had insisted their father put an end to her relationship with D'Arcy Wentworth.

James' romance with Charlotte Brydges was the basis of the story of James and Isabella in *Northanger Abbey.* In it, Jane turned a satirical eye on her own youthful naivety, and on James and his Oxford friends, their gadding about, womanising and crass stupidity. Her heroine, Catherine Morland, is blatantly manipulated by her brother James and his lover Isabella, to act as a cover for their romantic assignations. When eventually she refuses to oblige them, James makes a loaded observation: *you were not used to be so hard to persuade.*

In 1803, Jane Austen sold the original manuscript of *Northanger Abbey,* then called *Susan,* to Crosby & Co. By 1816, it had still not been published, so she bought it back and put it aside, perhaps to avoid rousing James' ire. He had been angered by *Sense & Sensibility,* and she expected a similar response from him to her revelations in *Pride and Prejudice.*[129] *Northanger Abbey* was published after Jane's death, at the initiative of her brother Henry.

Jane's story of young Lesley leaving his two year old child in the care of his sisters, predicted events that occurred five years after *Lesley Castle* was written. In March 1792, James married Anne Mathew, and their only child, Anna, was born in 1793. After Anne Mathew died in May 1795, two year-old Anna, lived mainly at the Steventon Rectory, cared for by Jane and Cassandra, until James remarried in 1797.

In 1801, after James took over from his father as rector of Steventon, Jane wrote to her sister: *the whole World is in a conspiracy to enrich one part of our family at the expence of another.*[130] It was the theme she burnished and refined in the opening chapters of *Sense & Sensibility.*

The destruction of Jane's correspondence and gaps in her published letters may have been meant to hide more than one family scandal.

Conjecturing as to the date   *Pride & Prejudice*

Lesley Castle is the second story in *Volume the Second*, after *Love and Freindship*, dated June 13th 1790, and followed by *The History of England*, finished on *Saturday Nov. 26th 1791*, indicating *Lesley Castle* was written between June 1790 and November 1791.

The History of England was added to *Volume the Second* after *Lesley Castle*. Jane wrote the text, her sister Cassandra illustrated it. Jane wrote *finis* at the end and dated it.

The ten letters of *Lesley Castle* are dated from 3 January to 13 April. At some later date, the year "1792," was added to the first letter," suggesting impossibly, that *Lesley Castle* was written after *The History of England*.

Why should they not go on to Scotland   *Pride & Prejudice*

Jane's comic impressions of Scotland in *Lesley Castle* read like one of her lively letters home – *I wish.. you could but behold these Scotch giants; I am sure they would frighten you out of your wits.. In the first place they are so horribly tall!...I never can think such tremendous knock-me-down figures in the least degree elegant, and as for their eyes, they are so tall that I could never strain my neck enough to look at them.*

As well as the capital, Edinburgh, and Stirling, we know that Jane Austen and D'Arcy Wentworth visited Aberdeen,[131] and Perth, Scotland's medieval capital. D'Arcy was a surgeon, he was interested in Aberdeen's two universities, Kings College, founded in 1495 and Marischal College, in 1593, where physicians had been trained for almost two hundred years. A number of D'Arcy's contemporaries, surgeons in the Royal Navy, had received their training in Aberdeen.

In Aberdeen, Jane and D'Arcy met members of the Leslie family.[132] Jane knew their family seat, *Leslie Castle*, twenty-six miles from Aberdeen,[133] though it is not the castle she describes in *Lesley Castle*.

Jane Austen's *Lesley Castle*, the seat of her fictional Lesley family, is near Perth, a hundred and eleven miles from Aberdeen, her description of its location is precise and accurate: *I continue secluded from Mankind in our old and Mouldering Castle, which is situated two miles from Perth on a bold projecting rock, and commands an extensive view of the Town and its delightful Environs..You can form no idea sufficiently hideous, of its dungeon like form. It is actually perched on a Rock to appearance so totally inaccessible, that I expected to have been pulled up by a rope.*

The castle still stands, in the precise location Jane Austen described, two miles from Perth on a cliff overlooking the Tay River and the environs of the city. Today, it is known as *Kinnoull Tower,* and is surrounded by Kinnoull Hill Woodland Park.

Thomas Hay, 9th Earl of Kinnoull (1710-1787), built the castle on his estate, not as a residence or a defence, but as a folly. On his Grand Tour, the Earl admired the many castles built on promontories overlooking the Rhine. He decided to build a similar structure on his land near Perth, as a landmark, sited on a rocky cliff, overlooking the Tay River, to be seen from a distance, and visible from the city.[134]

It is easy to believe Jane and D'Arcy went to Perth, climbed Kinnoull Hill and even stayed there for several nights, on their ramble through Scotland in late 1789.[135]

Love and Freindship and *Lesley Castle* provide evidence that contradicts the Austen family assertion that Jane Austen never went to Scotland. Jane wrote *Love and Freindship* in June 1790, and *Lesley Castle* later that year, confirming she had visited Scotland before those dates.

In *Love and Freindship*, Jane Austen's descriptions of her travels in Scotland; in *Lesley Castle*, her observations of the Scots and her accurate description of a very minor castle, on Kinnoull Hill, two miles from Perth, one not mentioned in any contemporary guide or publication, give a convincing account of their visit to Scotland in 1789.

Produced a great alteration   *Sense & Sensibility*

Jane Austen continued to revise and amend *Lesley Castle*. Over the following years, in all, one hundred and two corrections were made to the text, though it is clear not all of them were hers.

In *Letter the Third*, Margaret Lesley wrote that her brother had an *Estate near Aberdeen,* where she and Matilda *often spent several weeks together with them.* After his marriage began to collapse, *Our visits therefore to the N. were now less frequent.* The story became confused after *"the N."* (the North) was later crossed out, and *Dunbeath* written above it.[136] Dunbeath is nowhere near Aberdeen, it is a village in the Highlands, one hundred and eighty four miles away.

It is not clear who deleted "the N." in *Letter the Third* and replaced it with "Dunbeath," nor who added the year 1792 to *Letter the First*. It may require a more rigorous scientific analysis of the manuscript and its handwriting to answer these and other questions. It does appear though, that these alterations were intended to confuse the story of her visit to Scotland, that Jane Austen recorded in *Lesley Castle*.

19

The History of England
from the reign of Henry the 4th
to the death of Charles the 1st

By a partial, prejudiced, and
ignorant Historian

To whom this work is dedicated　　　　　　　　　　　　*The History of England*

Jane Austen dedicated *The History of England* to her sister Cassandra, who collaborated with her in its production. Jane had invited Cassandra to join in the fun of producing a spoof *History*. In her *Volume the Second*, under the name of each monarch, Jane left a third of the page blank for Cassandra to illustrate the text with a little medallion-like portrait of each king, queen or consort she had described.

Jane's history of English monarchs from 1399 to 1649, pokes fun at the history taught in the schoolroom, groaning with significant dates, important people, irrefutable facts. It bubbles with schoolboy humour, it is mock serious, funny and disrespectful, with an occasional rude joke.

For much of the year, the Steventon rectory was home to several adolescent boys, George Austen's students. Jane clearly enjoyed their company. As daughters of the headmaster, she and Cassandra might sometimes have had an upper hand, there was doubtless a lively current of teasing and flirtation in the house.[137] In 1783, and again in 1785, Reverend Austen sent his two daughters away to boarding school.

Perhaps he considered it would be of benefit to the education of his students as well as his daughters, to separate them.

Their education has been such as will not disgrace their appearance in the world *Juvenilia*

George Austen was responsible for the education of his sons, and in their early years, for his daughters. In 1773, his eldest son James was eight, George, next, was seven, and his third son Edward was six. They would have been home-schooled around the dining table, learning their numbers and letters, reading, drawing, and the rest.

In 1773, two years before Jane was born, George Austen set up a small private school in the Steventon rectory, offering, by word of mouth, a small number of places for boarders, in addition to those for his sons. He took boarders in their mid-teens, most of whom aspired to go up to Oxford to study for the Anglican priesthood. A number of his students were sons of clergymen, others were from humbler social origins.

His curriculum prepared them to sit for the entry examinations to Oxford University colleges and to study for their matriculation. Oxford had a largely classical examination syllabus, requiring knowledge of Latin, of the Gospels in Greek, of the foundations of the Anglican faith: the Thirty-Nine Articles and the study of Anglican moral philosophy. Reverend Austen taught the academic components of ordination examinations and schooled his students in rhetoric, preparing them to speak effectively in public.

In its first few years, from 1773 to 1777, in addition to his sons James and Edward, Reverend Austen had just one boarder. By 1779, the rectory school had five boarders, and Henry Austen, now eight, joined them. That year, James left for St John's, Oxford, and Edward moved to Kent to live with Catherine and Thomas Knight.

George's two youngest sons, Frank and Charles spent several years in the rectory school before they entered the Royal Naval College in Portsmouth, at age twelve.

Cassandra and Jane were not admitted, they most likely learnt their letters and numbers from their mother, with their younger brothers. In 1783, George Austen sent his daughters away to Mrs Cawley, in Oxford, to be schooled, and took two more boarders into his rectory school. In 1785, when he sent them to the Abbey House School, he still had seven boarders, from 1787 to 1790, he had just one.

In July 1788, Henry Austen left Steventon for Oxford, joining his brother James at St John's. In 1791, the number of boarders studying at the rectory rose to three, and remained at three until 1795.[138]

By 1791, when Jane wrote *The History of England*, she and Cassandra were the last of the Austen children remaining at home, their six brothers were all out in the world. The three teenage students living in the rectory, were all around her own age.

The eldest, Deacon Morrell (1775-1854) was sixteen, the son of James Morrell of Wallingford, a business partner of Oxford's town clerk, Thomas Walker, and the solicitor for Oxford University; he was fifty miles from home.

Richard Buller (1776-1806) was the son of Reverend Dr William Buller, then Canon of Winchester Cathedral, fifteen miles from Steventon. During his thirty years in Winchester Dr Buller he secured a number of positions in both Winchester and Exeter cathedrals, and acquired the livings of seven parishes.

In 1791, Richard Buller, aged fifteen, was in his second year at the rectory school, he was sickly, a boy who needed special attention. Dr Buller paid more than twice the usual fee for his board and tuition[139] and he had his own room in the rectory. The following December, 1792, Dr Buller was appointed Bishop of Exeter and moved to Exeter, 155 miles from Steventon. He held the position until his death in 1797.

William Stephen Goodenough, (1776-1843) the son of Stephen Goodenough, Gentleman, of Winterborne Stoke, Wiltshire, came from the southern edge of the Salisbury Plain, three miles west of Stonehenge, thirty-three miles from Steventon. He was fifteen, and like Morrell, in his first year at the rectory school.

Morrell and Goodenough shared a bedroom at the rectory. During their first weeks they were woken at night by the harsh grating sound of the weathercock turning on its post in the rectory garden. Mrs Austen responded to their complaints with a verse addressed to Reverend Austen, titled, *The humble petition of Rd. Buller and W. Goodenough:*

Dear Sir, we beseech & intreat & request
You'd remove a sad nuisance that breaks our night's rest
That creaking old weathercock over our heads
Will scarcely permit us to sleep in our beds.
It whines & it groans & makes such a noise
That it greatly disturbs two unfortunate boys
Who hope you will not be displeased when they say
If they don't sleep by night they can't study by day.

Dinner at the rectory was served around five in the afternoon. On a late afternoon in September 1791, dark, cold and wet, the Austen parents, their two daughters and three students would have been seated at table. Perhaps the students were grumbling about studying history, the burden of having to learn an interminable stream of monarchs and dates.

Her own share in the story   *Emma*

If Jane suggested she could write a history of England with *very few dates*, the students would have cheered, her history was sure to be a good read! Those who had glanced at Oliver Goldsmith's *History of England from the Earliest Times*[140] in Reverend Austen's library, would have enjoyed her pert, at times irritated comments in the margins. She had a ready-made audience for her next project.

A few years later, Jane had Catherine Morland, the young heroine of *Northanger Abbey,* comment on the study of history: *History, real solemn history, I cannot be interested in...I read it a little as a duty, but it tells me nothing that does not either vex or weary me. The quarrels of popes and kings, with wars or pestilences, in every page; the men all so good for nothing, and hardly any women at all — it is very tiresome...*

Her father, she says, is fond of history; *and I have two brothers who do not dislike it...If people like to read their books, it is all very well, but to be at so much trouble in filling great volumes, which, as I used to think, nobody would willingly ever look into, to be labouring only for the torment of little boys and girls, always struck me as a hard fate.*[141]

Jane Austen's *History of England* is a very singular entry in her *Juvenilia*. It is unashamedly non-fiction, filled with insights into her views on range of subjects, including education and history.

When *Volume the Second* of her *Juvenilia* was released in 1922, *The History of England* opened a window for readers to hear Jane Austen's youthful voice, her laughter and opinions. It transformed the widely held view of her as a pious spinster, and revealed something of her life, confined in the rectory, in a remote, rural parish in Hampshire.

Unlike her earlier comic stories, *The History of England* was not a comic piece read at table and transcribed later into her journal. It was a specific project, planned and delivered at the end of term for her father's students to enjoy. The result was not unlike a miniature book, or an in-house magazine, akin to *The Loiterer*, edited by James and Henry, at Oxford, the previous year.

Cassandra, co-opted to provide illustrations, found printed engravings of long dead sovereigns in her father's library, and other sources of inspiration within the rectory.[142] Reverend Austen would have encouraged the project, delighted to see Jane's enthusiasm and energy revived, and its cheering effect on his students.

I am fond of history   *Northanger Abbey*

It is evident Jane Austen knew and relished English history. She took Goldsmith's *History of England* as a touchstone, making numerous allusions to his text as she sent it up with anecdotes, digressions, and strident personal opinions. Jane showed no disrespect to Goldsmith, nor the other historians she referenced: John Whitaker, William Gilpin, and William Shakespeare, though her narrator declared his tragedies, *not worth reading.*

Jane Austen took a schoolboy's voice for her narrator, and he confidently takes up the role of author, authority and critic, and sets off at a cracking pace, assuming that his Readers were *as well acquainted with the particulars of this King's reign as I am myself. It will therefore be saving* them *the task of reading again what they have read before, and* myself *the trouble of writing what I do not perfectly recollect by giving only a slight sketch of the principal Events which marked his reign.*

Jane declared her intention was: *only to vent my Spleen* against *and shew my Hatred* to *all those people whose parties or principles do not suit with mine, and not to give information.* Occasionally she gives reasons: that she is inclined to support Richard the Third because *he was a* York, and though Henry the 8th's *Crimes and Cruelties were too numerous to be mentioned,* his *only merit was not being quite so bad as his daughter Elizabeth.* In the end, she confesses that: *the recital of any Events (except what I make myself) is uninteresting to me.*

We are told Henry IV *made a long speech,* and the Prince of Wales, *a still longer. Things being thus settled between them the King died.* She refers her *Reader to Shakespear's Plays* for more detail on Henry IV, and for those who do not know all about the Wars of the Roses, suggests they *had better read some other History.*

In thirteen pithy, humorous pieces Jane reported, in seriatum, on the kings and queens who ruled England over two hundred and fifty years, from the coronation of Henry IV in 1399 to the beheading of Charles I in 1649. In each piece she whipped through a few selected facts and minor footnotes to the life of each monarch.

A faithful portrait undoubtedly   *Pride & Prejudice*

Heading each entry with the monarch's name, Jane left the next third of the page for her sister to fill. Cassandra drew a circle in the centre, perhaps with a compass or coin. Inside this frame she painted a tiny cameo portrait in watercolour, of each monarch except Edward the 5th. Jane noted he had *lived so little a while that no body had time to draw his picture.* Cassandra added a thirteenth cameo of Mary Queen of Scots, placed cheek by jowl with that of Elizabeth I.

Her tiny portraits of the Lancaster, York and Stuart kings all face outward, towards the edge of the page. In contrast, the Tudors are disorderly. Henry VII and Mary I face the reader, Henry VIII and Edward VI look inward towards the spine of the book, and Elizabeth I and Mary Queen of Scots look rather grimly towards each other, with Elizabeth drawn on a noticeably smaller scale than Mary. Cassandra signed her portraits: *C.E.Austen pinx,* C.E.Austen painted it!

And woman, lovely woman reigns alone *Emma*

Jane's *History* remedied the failure to include *hardly any women at all,* that she deplored in *History, real solemn history.* She included twenty-four women in the lives of her thirteen monarchs, and gave them thirty-five mentions. Many of them were on the losing side of history: Joan of Arc, Lady Jane Grey, most of Henry VIII's wives, and above them all, Mary Queen of Scots. She records their achievements, their failings and her feelings for them, such as Margaret of Anjou, wife of Henry the 6th, a *Woman whose distresses and Misfortunes were so great as almost to make me who hate her, pity her.*

Her entry on Henry the 7th was an opportunity to introduce his more interesting great granddaughter, *Lady Jane Grey, who tho' inferior to her lovely Cousin the Queen of Scots, was yet an amiable young Woman and famous for reading Greek while other people were hunting.* She returned to her with Edward the 6th, Lady Jane's father-in-law, devoting nearly a half of his entry to her history.

Jane Austen built up to the story of her heroine, Mary Queen of Scots, through her entries on Henry the 7th, Mary Tudor, and Elizabeth. Positioned in the entry for Queen Elizabeth, she is given twice as much space as Elizabeth, who was responsible for sending *this amiable woman to an untimely, unmerited, and scandalous Death.*

William Gilpin wrote, *Mary had those bewitching charms, which always raised her friends.*[143] Jane Austen stated, that in her day, Mary, Queen of Scots had only one friend, she now had four: *This bewitching Princess whose only friend was then the Duke of Norfolk and whose only friends are now Mr Whittaker,*[144] *Mrs. Lefroy,*[145] *Mrs. Knight*[146] *and myself.*

She described Elizabeth as wicked, a Queen who *committed such extensive Mischeif,* she was *the destroyer of all comfort, the deceitful Betrayer of trust reposed in her, and the Murderess of her Cousin.* Her view of Elizabeth that was quite at odds with the pride her mother's Leigh family took in their connexion to the *mighty Queen,* which Mary Leigh, a cousin of Mrs Austen, had recorded in verse:

When great Elizabeth ruled this realm,
(And a mighty Queen was she)
To be proclaim'd at St Paul's she rode,
Behind Sir Thomas Leigh.[147]

In the final entry in her *History,* Jane introduces Charles the 1st by way of his connection to Mary Queen of Scots: *This amiable Monarch seems born to have suffered Misfortunes equal to those of his lovely Grandmother; Misfortunes which he could not deserve since he was her descendant.* Charles the 1st gets Jane's support in one word, *He was a STUART.*

Jane Austen's mother's family were Stuart supporters during the Civil War. Their noble ancestor, Sir William Leigh was imprisoned for his loyalty to Charles the 1st:

But it was not the custom of the Leighs to flinch
From their sovereign in times of need.
So William lost both house and land,
And did everything but bleed.[148]

Jane castigated the leading *Villains* of the time, Cromwell, Fairfax, Hampden and Pym as *the original Causers of all the disturbances, Distresses and Civil Wars in which England for many years was embroiled.*

Midway through this last entry, the narrator confesses: *my principal reason for undertaking the History of England being to prove the innocence of the Queen of Scotland, which I flatter myself with having effectually done, and to abuse Elizabeth, tho' I am rather fearful of having fallen short in the latter part of my Scheme.*

Conjecturing as to the date

Jane finished *The History of England* on 26 November 1791, two and a half weeks before she turned sixteen. It had been a cold, wet and stormy autumn, in November the country around Steventon had record rain, 8.16 inches.[149] The residents of Steventon rectory would have spent most of the month indoors. It was almost end of term, four weeks till Christmas, a time for pranks and muck-ups.

When dinner is over

Jane would have presented her youthful, comic spoof after dinner was cleared away, with Cassandra, the three students, Buller, Morrell and Goodenough, and her father, in a warm room lit by candles and firelight. Jane rises to her feet, no longer a student or the youngest family member present, she is the tutor, a historian, launching a new history of England to her audience, for their edification and enjoyment. It would have been a memorable evening, full of laughter and repartee, with jokes and quips they would all remember, years later.

Gathering her work together

Jane Austen wrote *The History of England* nearly two years after D'Arcy Wentworth's departure. For her readers, it offers the reassurance she had regained something of her equilibrium. In *Love and Freindship* she described the brief interlude of freedom and adventure she had with D'Arcy, and her breakdown after he had gone: *I, raving in a frantic and incoherent manner...wildly exclaiming...raving thus madly.*

In *Lesley Castle*, she described her state of mind, *a tall, out of the way, over-grown girl,* confined at home in Steventon, *a dismal old Weather-beaten Castle,* relying on her correspondence with friends to unburden her despair. *You must expect from me nothing but the melancholy effusions of a broken Heart which is ever reverting to the Happiness it once enjoyed and which ill supports the present Wretchedness.*

What a surprise and delight to hear Jane Austen's laughter once more, to hear her shaping up to the leading historians of her day, measuring herself against those familiar to every school child who has been taught the panorama of English history.

All those arrangements for the future *Persuasion*

What became of the three students Jane entertained with *The History of England* at their end of term "muck-up day" dinner in 1791?

Just at the present he may be undecided *Sense & Sensibility*

Deacon Morrell returned to the rectory the following year, he sat and passed his entry examinations for Oxford, and in July 1792, aged seventeen, went up to Christ Church. He was called to the bar at Lincoln's Inn in 1796, and he graduated as Master of Arts from Oxford in 1799. Ordained a deacon in December 1801, and a priest a year later in December 1802, Morrell *had been bred to the Church*, he used the title, Reverend, but he did not join the clergy. In 1818, he contributed £25.00 to the *Society for Promoting the Enlargement and Building, and Repairing of Churches and Chapels*. Jane mentioned him in a letter to Cassandra in 1809, eighteen years after he left Steventon, she must have followed his progress.[150]

In 1812, on the death of his uncle, Robert Baker, Reverend Morrell inherited Moulsford Manor in Berkshire. By 1840, it appears from the tithe award, that he owned most of the village of Moulsford. He lived in London, in Sackville Street, off Piccadilly, and died unmarried in 1854, aged seventy nine.

The gentlemen in brown velvet & the ladies in blue satin *Sense & Sensibility*

Morrell's place in the rectory school was taken by Francis Newnham, from a family of mercers. He was a grandson of Nathaniel Newnham, a mercer, wealthy merchant, a director of the East India Company and Member of the House of Commons from 1780 to 1790, for London, and from 1793 to 1796, for Ludgershall.

The Worshipful Company of Mercers, one of the great livery companies of London, could trace its history back to 1172, it received its letters patent from Richard II in 1393. During the reign of Edward III, 1327 to 1377, mercers dealt mainly in woollen cloth; by the time of Henry VI, they were dealing mostly in silks and velvets.

Thomas Newnham, Francis' father, was a member of the Company of Mercers, and a wealthy sugar grocer in Watling Street, near St Paul's. During the 1760's, Newnham & Co supplied large quantities of Ivory Black, a fine black pigment used for making ink, as well as sugar, spices and dried fruits to George Washington at Mount Vernon in Virginia.[151]

Francis Newnham remained at Steventon for three years, until 1795. He went up to Oxford, to Worcester College, where he graduated as a Bachelor of Law. In 1801, he was admitted as a new freeman to the Company of Mercers. In 1803, he was ordained a Deacon by the Bishop of London, in 1805, made a priest by the Bishop of Exeter, and in 1811, he was appointed curate of East Horsley in Surrey.

In 1829, Reverend Newnham, under the title *Mercer-Citizen of London*, published a dramatic poem, *The Pleasures of Anarchy*. It caused a reviewer at the *London Literary Gazette* to opine: *This volume enjoys the distinction of being the greatest and most unqualified nonsense which we have ever read.*[152]

I had a most affectionate letter from Buller   Letters

Richard Buller remained at Steventon until 1795. After five years study with George Austen, at age nineteen he went up to Oxford, to his father's alma mater, Oriel College, where he gained a BA in 1798 and an MA in 1801. Made a deacon in 1798, in 1799, Buller was appointed vicar of Colyton in Devon. He was ordained a priest in 1800, the year he married Anne Marshall, and was made curate of Stoke Canon in east

Devon. In 1801, he was appointed domestic chaplain to Elizabeth Wentworth, Countess Strafford, widow of Frederick Wentworth, the 3rd Earl.

Buller remained in friendly contact with the Austen family. He wrote to Jane late in 1800, shortly after his marriage. She told Cassandra, *he is very pressing in his invitation to us all to come & see him at Colyton.*[153] Jane, Cassandra and their parents did so the following year. In April 1805 he called to see them in Bath, he was there to take the waters. Jane was pessimistic, telling Cassandra, *I am afraid it must be too late for these waters to do him any good, she added, his appearance is exactly that of a confirmed decline.* Richard Buller died at Colyton in December 1806, aged thirty, leaving his wife, a son and a daughter.[154]

Forever quarrelling with Steward and Tenants concerning Tythes

Kitty, or the Bower

William Stephen Goodenough went up to Oxford, to George Austen's alma mater, St John's, in 1795, after four years at Steventon. He gained an MA in 1799 and in October that year was ordained a deacon and appointed the curate of Yate, in Gloucestershire. The rector, Richard John Hay, moved to Chipping Sodbury, and Goodenough, ordained a priest in December 1800, was made rector of Yate in July 1801.[155] He remained the rector there until his death in 1843, aged sixty-seven.

The income of the parish appears to have been modest, perhaps due to the strong presence of non-conformists, who objected to paying tithes. Goodenough took legal action against Toby Walker Sturge, a Quaker gentleman of Yate, who had refused to pay his tithes for over twenty years, from 1795 to 1817.[156]

After Buller, Goodenough and Newnham left for Oxford in 1795, George Austen took no further students, after twenty-two years he closed the rectory school. There were fewer domestic chores and mouths to feed, of the eight Austen children only his two daughters remained at home. With extra room in the rectory, perhaps Jane enjoyed a little more privacy.

The names of people that fill up my time   *Mansfield Park*

The History of England displays Jane Austen's knowledge and interest in history and genealogy, particularly of the British nobility. She had found a fellow enthusiast for genealogy in the younger brother of her friend Anne Lefroy, Egerton Brydges, her father's tenant in the Deane Rectory, for several years after 1786.

Egerton Brydges was educated at the King's School, Canterbury, Queens College, Cambridge, and the Middle Temple. He was called to the bar in November 1787, but never practiced as a barrister. Instead he chose a literary life in Hampshire, near his sister in the Ashe rectory. In 1786, he published his first volume of poetry, and he worked for years, updating and augmenting *Collins' Peerage of England, Genealogical, Biographical and Historical,* published in 1735. Egerton's revised, twelve volume version published in 1812, has proved to be a magnificent resource for today's family history researchers.

His passion for genealogy roused Jane's interest. He was pleased to share his knowledge and findings. In their conversations, and his well worn copy of Collins' peerage, Jane encountered the names of many Wentworth connexions she included in her writing: sons, daughters, cousins once, twice and thrice removed, she knew their names, their biographies and connections to the family she could not acknowledge.

This connexion between the families   *Emma*

Jane Austen ended her *History of England* with the reign of Charles I, the king who, in April 1641, yielded to pressure from Parliament and signed the death warrant for Thomas Wentworth, 1st Earl of Strafford, beheaded on Tower Hill a month later. Jane included Strafford among the King's *stedfast* supporters, *Archbishop Laud, Earl of Strafford, Viscount Faulkland and the Duke of Ormond.* She passed over his fate and that of the King, who walked through the snow to his own execution eight years later.

D'Arcy Wentworth was a kinsman of the Earl of Strafford. In *Persuasion,* Jane raised that connection in relation to her character Captain

Wentworth, and had Sir Walter Elliott, an unreliable witness, deny it: *Mr. Wentworth was nobody, I remember; quite unconnected; nothing to do with the Strafford family. One wonders how the names of many of our nobility become so common.*[157]

Jane Austen was also connected to the Strafford family. Her mother was a descendant of Rowland Leigh, the eldest son of Sir Thomas Leigh, Lord Mayor of London from 1558 to 1559, who led the coronation procession of Elizabeth I on 15 January 1559. Rowland's younger brother, Sir Thomas Leigh of Stoneleigh was succeeded by his grandson Thomas, 1st Baron Leigh, in turn succeeded by his grandson, 2nd Baron Leigh. Anne Wentworth, the eldest daughter of Thomas Wentworth, 1st Earl of Strafford, married Edward Watson, 2nd Baron Rockingham. Their daughter Eleanor married Thomas, 2nd Baron Leigh of Stoneleigh.

Jane Austen's grandfather, William Leigh, married Mary Lord. Her sister, Elizabeth Lord, known to the Austen family as 'Aunt Wentworth', was married to General Sir Thomas Wentworth. After his death in 1747, Elizabeth went to live with her sister Mary, at *Adlestrop House* in Gloucestershire, the Leigh family home since 1553.

Jane would have been aware of parallels between the lives of historian, Oliver Goldsmith and D'Arcy Wentworth. Both men, born in Ireland, found survival in London financially difficult. Goldsmith, born in County Roscommon in 1730, the son of a curate, attended Trinity College, Dublin, then studied medicine at Edinburgh and Leiden universities. Rather than live in London in abject poverty, as an assistant apothecary or physician, he decided to be a hack writer.

Like D'Arcy, Goldsmith had applied unsuccessfully for a post in the East India Company, as a physician at Coromandel. He seems to have had few regrets, aware of *the fatigues of sea and dangers of war and the still greater dangers of the climate.*[158]

A Collection
of Letters

Jane Austen dedicated *A Collection of Letters*, five in all, to her cousin Jane Cooper. After a series of perfunctory, mock-serious dedications with obligatory flattery and obsequious sign-offs: by an *obedient humble servant*, her dedication to Jane Cooper takes one's breath away.

She dedicated *A Collection of Letters* with a rolling, playful flourish of alliteration on the letter C, leaping from the page with intelligence, wit and warmth. It tells us a great deal about her feelings for Jane Cooper:

To Miss Cooper
Cousin
Conscious of the Charming Character which in every Country, and every Clime in Christendom is Cried, concerning you, With Caution and Care I commend to your Charitable Criticism this Clever Collection of Curious Comments, which have been Carefully Culled, Collected and Classed by your Comical Cousin The Author

Jane Cooper and Jane Austen were first cousins, their mothers were sisters, the two daughters of Reverend Thomas Leigh and his wife, Jane, née Walker.

Reverend Thomas Leigh, born in 1696, was a Fellow of All Souls College, Oxford. In 1731, he was made rector of Harpsden, a parish under the patronage of the College.[159] In 1732, he resigned his Fellowship to marry Jane Walker. They lived at Harpsden, where they raised two sons and two daughters, Jane, born in 1736 and Cassandra in 1739. Thomas Leigh died at Harpsden in 1764.

That year, shortly after his death, Cassandra, his younger daughter, twenty-five, married Reverend George Austen. Four years later, in 1768, after her mother's death, Jane, now thirty-three, married Reverend Dr Edward Cooper, of nearby Henley.

Dr Cooper (1728-1792), eight years her senior, was the son of Gislingham Cooper, a London banker. He went up to Oxford at age fifteen, to Queens College, where he graduated Bachelor of Law. In 1747, he moved to All Souls College, where he attained doctorates in both Law and Civil Law. He was ordained at Oxford in 1752, and twelve years later, in 1764, was appointed rector of Buckland Saint Mary, in Somerset.

After their marriage in 1768, he and Jane lived at Southcote, near Reading, and later at Bath. Dr Cooper was appointed canon of Holcombe to Wells Cathedral in 1770, the year their son Edward was born. The following year, their daughter Jane was born, and he was appointed canon of Hill Deverill in Wiltshire.

Give my love
to Jane!

In the Spring of 1783, when she was twelve, Jane Cooper was sent to Oxford to board and study with her aunt, her father's younger sister, Ann Cawley, a widow, whose husband, Ralph Cawley, was the Principal of Brasenose College, Oxford from 1770 until his death in 1777. The Austens sent Cassandra, ten, and Jane, seven, to join her under Mrs Cawley's care.

In summer 1783, without warning, Mrs Cawley moved to Southampton, taking the children. There was an outbreak of typhus in the town, most likely carried by returning troops. When Jane Austen contracted the *putrid fever*, it was Jane Cooper who wrote urgently to tell their parents where they were and what had happened. Their mothers arrived to rescue them. Jane was seriously ill for some time but she recovered, Mrs Cooper caught the infection and died within three weeks.

In 1785, the three girls were together at school once again at Abbey House School in Reading. Jane Cooper was fourteen, Cassandra, twelve and Jane, nine. Jane looked up to her older cousin with great respect, for her guidance and approval.

At the end of August 1786, Edward Cooper and Edward Austen were in Reading together. The two handsome young men took the three girls out to dine at the Bear Inn. It was here Jane Austen first met D'Arcy Wentworth; Jane Cooper was with her.

George Austen took Jane out of school midway through the Michaelmas term. She looked forward to Christmas, when George's elder sister, her aunt Philadelphia, was coming to stay at Steventon with her daughter, Countess Eliza de Feuillide, and Eliza's baby son Hastings.

Jane and Edward Cooper came at New Year to join the celebrations, and take part in the family theatricals. Eliza took the lead roles, as Isabella in *The Wonder – A Woman Keeps a Secret*, and as Constantia in *The Chances*,[160] with a carried-on part for baby Hastings, as the mystery child. Eliza referred to Jane Cooper as: *one of our Theatrical Troop*.[161]

At Christmas 1788, two years later, Jane Cooper, now seventeen, took the lead opposite Henry Austen in two farces, as Lady Bab in *High Life below Stairs* by James Townley, and as Roxalana in *The Sultan, or a Peep into the Seraglio* by Isaac Bickerstaff.[162] Roxalana, a free-born woman enslaved by the Sultan, challenges him: *let your window-bars be taken down; let the doors of the seraglio be thrown open*. In *Henry and Eliza*, Jane included a reference Jane Cooper's fine performance: *She looked at the Window, but it was barred with iron.*

In summer 1792, the Coopers went on holiday to the Isle of Wight, where Jane, now twenty-one, met Captain Thomas Williams, Commander of 28-gun *HMS Lizard*. He was thirty-one, he had gone to sea aged seven, on *HMS Peggy*, under the command of his father, Captain William Williams. During the sixteen years before he met Jane Cooper, he saw active service in the American Revolutionary War.

That summer on the Isle of Wight, Captain Williams and Jane Cooper fell in love, they became engaged, and set the date for their wedding. Eliza Feuillide said he was a *happy man,* noting, *his present Fortune is but small, but he has expectations of future preferment.*[163]

On 27 August 1792, Shortly after the Coopers returned home to

Sonning, Jane's father, Dr Cooper, died suddenly. Jane put her wedding plans on hold, and after his funeral, she went to Steventon, to stay with the Austens for a period of mourning.

Later that year, she made new arrangements for their marriage. It would now take place at Saint Nicholas Church in Steventon in December. Cassandra's fiancé Tom, Reverend Thomas Fowle, a former student of George Austen, would conduct the service, with her cousins Cassandra and Jane as witnesses.

Sir Thomas was fully resolved to be a real and consistent patron   *Mansfield Park*

After their wedding at Steventon in December 1792, Captain and Mrs Williams returned to the Isle of Wight. While her husband resumed command of *HMS Lizard* and her crew of two hundred; Jane set about making her new home on the island.

In September 1794, Captain Williams took command of a 32 gun frigate *HMS Daedalus*, operating in the North Sea. Charles Austen, now fifteen, left the Royal Naval Academy at Portsmouth to join him as a midshipman on the *Daedalus*, berthed in Cork, in south west Ireland.

Captain Williams became Charles's patron, responsible for his training and his progress in the Navy, *the Captain's name... occurs again and again in the record of Charles' advancement over the next two decades.*[164]

In quest of two needlefuls of thread   *Mansfield Park*

At home in Steventon, it appears Jane had a fair degree of responsibility for Charles, four years her junior. More than likely, it was she who suggested to Captain Williams, through her cousin Jane, that he take Charles on as a midshipman, to complete his training. During his period under Captain Williams, she followed his progress diligently, corresponding with him and passing his news to the rest of the family.

Early in 1799, she told Cassandra, *when you come home you will have some shirts to make up for Charles.*[165] He needed a constant supply, and by the end of the following year, Jane was sending shirts to him, *by half dozens.*[166]

The very French frigate I wanted   *Persuasion*

In December 1794, Captain Williams commended for his service on the *Daedalus*, was given command of the 32 gun *HMS Unicorn*. Charles Austen went with him.

At 3.00am on the morning of 8 June 1796, Williams, took the *Unicorn*, along with another frigate *Santa Margaritta*, between Scilly and the Old Head of Kinsale. There he spotted three French frigates: *Tribune*, 40 guns and 330 men, *Tamise*, 36 guns, 360 men and a smaller ship of 24 guns.

The French made all the sail they could, Captain Williams chased *Tribune*, the largest and fastest of the three. By eleven o'clock *a running fight began, the Unicorn firing at the Tribune,* with both ships under press of sail, running before the wind into St George's Channel.[167]

At half past ten that night after having pursued Tribune 210 miles, Unicorn pulled alongside her antagonist, gave three cheers and commenced close action, which continued with great impetuosity on both sides for 35 minutes. When the smoke cleared and the enemy was seen attempting a masterly manoeuvre to gain the wind, Unicorn renewed the attack, the enemy's ship was completely dismantled, all further resistance appeared ineffectual and she surrendered.[168]

The press reported that, five days later, on 13 June, *that gallant officer* brought the *Unicorn* and the *Tribune* into the Cove of Cork. *The Tribune is in a very shattered state about the masts and rigging; the Unicorn not much less so, her main top-mast shot through, though, fortunately, it stood during the fight.*[169]

The wonders of his presentation and knighthood   *Pride & Prejudice*

On 13 July 1796, at St James's Palace, Captain Williams, received a knighthood from King George III, for his services on the *Unicorn*.[170]

That September, Lady Jane Williams came to stay at Steventon. Jane was away, at *Rowling* in Kent, visiting her brother Edward and his wife. She sent a message to her through Cassandra, teasing her about Sir Thomas's new title, presuming he was off on a leisurely cruise: So – *His royal Highness Sir Thomas Williams has at length sailed -; the Papers say "on a Cruize." But I hope they are gone to Cork, or I shall have written in vain. Give my love to Jane.*[171]

Jane Austen's joking familiarity is filled with affection and friendship, in this, the last mention in her surviving letters of her beloved cousin.

A singular accident   *Pride & Prejudice*

Ten months later, on 9 August 1798, Lady Jane Williams was killed in a carriage accident at Newport on the Isle of Wight. A runaway draft horse crashed into the light gig she was driving, overturning it.

Every proof of cousinly notice   *Persuasion*

Jane Austen continued to follow Sir Thomas' progress, she kept a cousinly eye on his happiness and his career. The *Endymion* was deployed for three years off the coast of Ireland and on convoy to the island of St Helena. Through Charles' regular letters, she could map their course, their encounters and skirmishes.

In November 1800, Jane wrote to Martha Lloyd: *it is reported in Portsmouth that Sir T. Williams is going to be married – It has been reported indeed twenty times before, but Charles is inclined to give some credit to it now, as they hardly ever see him on board & he looks very much like a Lover.*[172]

A week later she had more detail for Cassandra: *the young lady whom it is suspected that Sir Thomas is to marry, is Miss Emma Wabshaw; she lives somewhere between Southampton and Winchester, is handsome, accomplished, amiable, & everything but rich. He is certainly finishing his house in a great hurry.*

In December 1800, Jane wrote: *Mrs Wapshire is a widow, with several sons and daughters, a good fortune, & a house in Salisbury; where Miss Wapshire has been for many years a distinguished beauty. She is now seven or eight & twenty, & tho still handsome less handsome than she has been. – This promises better, than the bloom of seventeen; & in addition to this, they say she has always been remarkable for the propriety of her behaviour, distinguishing her far above the general class of Town Misses, & rendering her of course very unpopular among them.*[173]

Later that month, Sir Thomas, now in his late thirties, married Miss Wapshire, and they moved into their new house, *Brooklands*, near Southampton.

At Lisbon, last Spring

Persuasion

Two months later, in February 1801, the *Endymion* spent three days in Lisbon. She returned to Portsmouth with a royal passenger, Prince Augustus Frederick, sixth son of George III. Charles Austen came home with plenty of tales to tell. Jane could report: *they were well satisfied with their Royal passenger whom they found fat, jolly and affable, who talks of Ly. Augusta as his wife & seems much attached to her.*[174]

Prince Augustus had met Lady Augusta Murray while travelling in Italy, they married in secret in Rome, in April 1793. In December that year, they married again in London, discreetly, at St Georges in Hanover Square. They married without the King's approval, as required by their *Royal Marriage Act*, and though they later had two children, the marriage was never recognised.[175]

So effectually promoted *Emma*

In 1803, Captain Williams took command of *HMS Vanguard*, a 74 gun, third rate[176] ship of the line, deployed off Cadiz and in the Baltic Sea. In 1804, he moved to *HMS Neptune*, a 98 gun second rate ship of the line. Charles Austen was promoted later that year to Commander, for his active service in a series of operations. After ten years serving under Captain Williams, he left for Bermuda, deployed on patrols of the North American eastern seaboard.

In 1805, Captain Williams was put in charge of a unit of Sea Fencibles at Gosport. The Sea Fencibles, a naval home guard, made up mainly of volunteers, was formed during the Napoleonic Wars to help protect Britain's coastline against a French invasion.

The kindest welcome among her new friends *Northanger Abbey*

On 7 January 1807, Jane wrote to Cassandra from Southampton, where the Austen women had moved after Reverend Austen's death. Captain Foote dined with them, and she reported, *He gives us all the most cordial invitation to his house in the country, saying just what the Williams ought to say to make us welcome. Of them we have seen nothing since you left us, and we hear that they are gone to Bath again, to be out of the way of further alterations to Brooklands.*

In February 1807, Sir Thomas did call with Captain Brown, in charge of a group of Sea Fencibles under his command. The following month he called on the Austens once more, with his second wife.

In the Trafalgar action *Persuasion*

Later that year he again took command of the *Neptune*. In his absence she had been refitted, spent time on blockades and joined Lord Nelson's fleet at Trafalgar, where she had fought in the thick of the battle, with ten of her crew killed and thirty-four wounded.

Gentlemen of the Navy *Persuasion*

In January 1809, Jane noted Sir Thomas had returned to Southampton, after Rear Admiral Alexander Cochrane assumed command of the *Neptune*, to use as his flagship in the West Indies: *the Admiral, whoever he might be,*[177] *took a fancy to the Neptune, & having only a worn-out 74 to offer in lieu of it, Sir Tho. Declined such a command, & is come home Passenger. Lucky Man! to have so fair an opportunity of escape.*[178]

In 1809, Sir Thomas, now Rear Admiral, sailed with the Channel Fleet and to Lisbon in command of *HMS Venerable* and *HMS Hannibal*. In 1811, he returned to England, he took command of *HMS Royal George* and was made Commander in Chief of the Nore, responsible for protecting the entrance to the port of London and merchant traffic along the east coast of Britain.[179]

Quite ready to retire *Mansfield Park*

Vice-Admiral Sir Thomas Williams retired in 1814, to Burwood House, near Weybridge, Surrey. His final contribution to the Navy was the establishment of the *Royal Female School for the Daughters of Naval and Marine Officers.*

The second Lady Williams died at Brighton on 17 December 1824, seven years after Jane Austen. Four months later, in April 1825, Sir Thomas, now sixty-three, married a third time, to Miss Mary Anne Mallory, of Warwickshire. From 1833 to 1836 he was Commander in Chief of Portsmouth. He died in his eightieth year, on 10 October 1841. It was said he twice remarried because he had such a happy first marriage.

A Collection of Letters was Jane Austen's wedding gift to her cousin Jane Cooper, dedicated and presented to her shortly before her wedding day, 11 December 1792.

Reading the pieces in her *Juvenilia* Jane dedicated to her, we recognise the depth of their relationship, Jane Cooper's importance to her, and the trust and intimacy that existed between them.

20

Letter the First –
From a Mother to her freind

Letter the First is a spoof of the protocols of *coming out*. The correspondent, *A- F-*, is a mother introducing her two daughters into society. Her letter describes the intricacies of "coming-out", the formal introduction of a young girl into society, that allows her to join adult company at balls, assemblies and other social events.

This was a letter to supply matter for much reflection   *Mansfield Park*

In her letter to *her freind, Mrs A-F-*, sets out her plans to launch her two daughters, Augusta, seventeen, and Margaret, *scarcely a twelvemonth younger*. She will proceed by degrees, over a week, *as it would be awkward for them to enter too wide a circle on the very first day.*

Today, Sunday, they *drink tea with Mrs Cope and her Daughter, on Monday Mr Stanly's family will drink tea with them,* on Tuesday they *shall pay Morning-Visits,* on Wednesday they *dine at Westbrook,* on Thursday, *have Company at home,* on Friday they attend *a private Concert at Sir John Wynne's,* and on Saturday *they expect Miss Dawson to call in the Morning.*

Her plan for her daughters' coming out is so lengthy, colourless and tedious it is difficult to imagine how any young girl could endure it. Her week-long program, she declares, *will complete my Daughters Introduction into Life. How they will bear so much dissipation I cannot imagine; of their Spirits I have no fear, I only dread for their health.*

After they return from their first engagement with Mrs Cope and her daughter, Mrs A-F- announces, the *mighty affair is now happily over, and my Girls are out.* The reader wonders, if they are *out*, what point is there in labouring through the rest of the week's schedule.

Mrs A-F- reports to her friend that before they set off, *the Sweet Creatures trembled with fear and Expectation.* She told them: *the moment is now arrived when I am to reap the rewards of all my Anxieties and Labours towards you during your Education.* She warns them against being *swayed by the Follies and Vices of others.*

They assure her, they will ever remember her *Advice with Gratitude and follow it with Attention.* They are *prepared to find a World full of things to amaze and to shock them, but trust their behaviour would never give their mother reason to repent the Watchful Care with which she had presided over their infancy and formed their Minds.*

With this assurance, their mother believes she has *nothing to fear,* she *can cheerfully conduct* them *to Mrs Cope's without a fear of* them *being seduced by her Example, or contaminated by her Follies.* When they arrive at the door, *poor Augusta could scarcely breathe, while Margaret was all Life and Rapture.*

The comic effect of this letter is built on the disjunct between the mother's earnest and over-protective approach to her daughters' coming out, and the reader's response to their situation.

To the reader, Mrs A-F is exaggerating her daughters' naivety, and over-stating their reliance on her guidance and opinions. Margaret and Augusta must have given some thought to the young men they might meet, or even dance with, once they are out.

Their mother relaxes at last, as they enter Mrs Cope's parlour, observing with delight *the impression my Children made on them, her two sweet, elegant-looking Girls with an ease in their Manners and Address which could not fail of pleasing.*

Jane Cooper had no experience of a mother supervising her coming out. Her mother died nine years earlier, when she was eleven. On the surface Jane has written her a story of an overprotective mother guiding her daughters into society. The backstory, Jane Cooper knows, is of the cover up, the great deceit Jane Austen has been required to maintain since her return home, to revert to the role of a naïve, *sweet girl* not yet *conversant with the world.*

Her own share in the story
Emma

The layers of irony and exaggeration expose the back story to this letter, its thinly veiled reference to Mrs Austen, Cassandra and Jane. In real life, both daughters have already been *Introduced into Life* and love.

Cassandra was newly engaged, her fiancé Reverend Tom Fowle was almost one of the family. He had been friends with Cassandra and Jane since they were children. Tom was the second of four sons of Reverend Thomas Fowle, vicar of Kintbury, and a first cousin of Mary and Martha Lloyd. From age fourteen to eighteen, he was a pupil of George Austen at the rectory school.

In July 1783, Tom went up St John's College, Oxford. At around the same time, Cassandra and Jane, and Jane Cooper, went to Oxford to live and study with Mrs Ann Cawley. Nine years later, in late 1792, Tom Fowle and Cassandra became engaged. He was staying at Steventon, Jane Cooper was there too, and Tom officiated at her wedding on 11 December that year, to Captain Thomas Williams.

While Cassandra's newly engaged status was acknowledged and approved by the Austen family. Jane's ill-fated romance with D'Arcy Wentworth was a closed book. It was now three years since she was *all Life and Rapture,* and could truthfully declare, *the long expected Moment is now arrived and we shall soon be in the World.* Her family's stance, among those who knew the story, was that Jane was *swayed by the Follies and Vices of others.*

The backstory of *Letter the First,* hidden in plain sight, was the charade of artless, ingenuous innocence that Jane was expected to maintain in society, after she returned home to Steventon. As she reached the end of the letter, Jane could not resist slipping a momentary lapse into the mother's spiel, when she acknowledges her *two sweet, elegant looking Girls were somewhat abashed from the peculiarity of their Situation.*

It was the peculiarity of her situation Jane wanted to place on record in this letter; and she entrusted that record to her beloved cousin, Jane Cooper. She can end the letter on an upbeat, truthful, optimistic note, that she has returned *in raptures with the World, its Inhabitants, and Manners.*

21

Letter the Second – From a Young Lady crossed in Love to her freind

It is nearing Christmas when Sophia writes to her friend Belle. She is staying with her uncle and cousins, recovering from a broken heart. Sophia has had other lovers, Neville, Fitzowen, two different Crawfords, *for all of whom she once felt the most lasting affection that ever warmed a Woman's heart.* She was not aware of having any greater attachment to Edward Willoughby, but losing him wounded her more deeply than ever before. She asks Belle why *this last disappointment hangs so heavily on her Spirits... why I still sigh when I think of the faithless Edward, or why I weep when I behold his Bride?*

In hopes of relieving Sophia's Melancholy, her hosts *have invited several of their friends* for Christmas. She tells Belle, *Lady Bridget Dashwood and her sister-in-Law Miss Jane are expected on Friday. This is most kindly meant by my Uncle and Cousins; but what can the presence of a dozen indifferent people do to me; but weary and distress me.*

On Friday evening, Sophia returns to her letter, to tell Belle about a bewitching conversation she had with Miss Jane. She has been *acquainted with her for above fifteen Years, Yet I never before observed how lovely she is. She is now about 35, and in spite of sickness, Sorrow and Time is more blooming than I ever saw a Girl of 17.*

At first, Sophia found it hard to speak to her, she found herself *confused, distressed* and *bewildered*. To alleviate her embarrassment, Jane offers to *turn the Conversation,* asking her, *Do you ride as much as you used to do?*

Sophia replies, she is advised to ride by her Physician, she mentions the *delightful Rides* nearby, her *Charming horse* and her fondness for *Amusement.* Quite recovered from her *Confusion,* she concludes, *in short I ride a great deal.*

Miss Jane responds, *"Ride where you may, Be Candid where You can."* With unexpected candour, she confides in Sophia, – *'I rode once, but it was many years ago.'* She spoke this in so low and tremulous voice, that I was silent-. Struck with the manner of speaking I could make no reply. *'I have not ridden,...since I was married.'* I was never so surprised – *'Married ma'am!'* I repeated. *'You may well wear that look of astonishment, said she, since what I have said must appear improbable to you – Yet nothing is more true than that I once was married.'*

When Sophia asks, *Then why are you called Miss Jane?* she replies, *'I married, my Sophia without the consent or knowledge of my father...'*

Miss Jane's story becomes more overwrought and affecting. *After a most happy union of seven years,* her husband Captain Henry Dashwood died in the American War. Soon after, their three children, *two sweet Boys and a Girl,* living with Miss Jane and her father, *fell sick and died.* She had told her father, and everyone else, they were *the Children of a Brother (tho' I had ever been an only Child).*

She asks Sophia to imagine her *feelings, when as an Aunt I attended my Children to their early Grave.* Then, just weeks later, her father died, *poor Good old Man, happily ignorant to the last hour of my Marriage.*

Sophia asks Miss Jane, why, after her husband's death, she didn't admit to having married, and take her husband's name. Miss Jane replies that she could not bring herself to do it, *she could never hear* the name of Dashwood *without emotion.* And *Conscious of having no right* to her father's name, she *dropt all thoughts of either* name. Since her father's death, she has *made a point of bearing only her Christian* name.

The story of her marriage is known only to her companion, Lady Bridget, and now, to Sophia: *Lady Bridget and yourself are the only persons who are in the knowledge of my having ever been either Wife or Mother.*

Sophia thanks Miss Jane for diverting her with so *entertaining a story.* She asks if she is *done,* but Miss Jane has one more detail to add, an explanation of her friendship with Lady Bridget Dashwood, widow of Henry Dashwood's elder brother.

The two brothers died around the same time, their widows had never met, but they were *determined to live together. We wrote to one another on the same subject by the same post, so exactly did our feelings and our Actions coincide.* From that time they have *lived together in the greatest affection.*

Sophia asks, *is that all? I hope you have not done.*
Miss Jane replies: *Indeed I have; and did you ever hear a Story more pathetic?*
Sophia tells her, *it pleases me so much, for when one is unhappy nothing is so delightful to one's Sensations as to hear of equal Misery.*
Ah! But my Sophia why <u>are you</u> unhappy? asks Miss Jane.
Sophia asks, hadn't she heard of Willoughby's marriage.
Miss Jane asks why she is so affected by <u>his</u> *perfidy, when she bore so well that of many young Men before?*
Ah! Madam, Sophia replies, *I was used to it then, but when Willoughby broke his Engagements I had not been disappointed for half a year.*
Poor Girl! Said Miss Jane. The letter and story end there.

Her own share in the story
Emma

In *Letter the Second*, through the disappointment of Sophia and the trauma of Miss Jane, Jane Austen recorded something of her feelings at losing D'Arcy Wentworth and of carrying the burden of her secrets. Now seventeen, in this letter, she imagines herself at thirty-five, still burdened with her memories, but hoping that: *in spite of sickness, Sorrow and Time she might be more blooming than I ever saw a Girl of 17.*

JANE AUSTEN HAD A LIFE!

Both Sophia and Miss Jane have suffered the distress of losing the man they loved. Sophia's *friends are all alarmed* for her. *They fear her declining health; they lament her want of Spirits*. Sophia names four men she had once loved *just as sincerely*, but never before had she felt this deep distress. After the end of her affair with Willoughby, she is distraught, on the verge of a breakdown. A woman of experience, she anticipates Lady Susan Vernon, in the short novel *Lady Susan* met Jane Austen wrote the following year, 1793.

Gathering her work together
Pride & Prejudice

In *Letter the Second*, Jane Austen set Sophia and Miss Jane in counterpoint to each other, having each reflect a different side of her temperament and her feelings. Sophia provides the repetitive drone with her, *are you done?*

Jane Austen used this contrivance later, most effectively between Elinor and Marianne Dashwood in *Sense & Sensibility*, and Elizabeth and Jane Bennet in *Pride & Prejudice*. After reading *Sense & Sensibility*, her brother, James Austen, described Elinor and Marianne as two aspects of Jane herself:

On such Subjects no wonder that she shou'd write well
In whom so united those Qualities dwell..
Fair Elinor's Self in that Mind is exprest,
And the Feelings of Marianne live in that Brest[180]

Perhaps with her mention of Sophia's four love interests, Jane was remembering her own *admirers*, some, former students of the rectory school. She alluded to them in her earliest surviving letters, Charles Powlett, who wanted to give her a kiss, John Willing Warren, who gave her *indubitable proof of his indifference* by delivering a gift to her *without a Sigh, Mr Heartley & all his estate,* and *all my other Admirers into the bargain.*[181] Perhaps she was recalling the time when she was seen as, *the prettiest, silliest, most affected, husband-hunting butterfly.*

In this letter, Jane Austen was exploring a way of recording the most important event in her life, and the truth of her feelings. In 1795, she wrote the first draft of a first full length novel, *Elinor & Marianne*, revised in 1810 and published in 1811, as *Sense & Sensibility*.

Jane Austen told the story of her breakdown after D'Arcy Wentworth disappeared from her life, in great detail in *Sense & Sensibility*. Forbidden to use the name *Wentworth*, she named him *Willoughby*, sometimes referring to him simply as *W*. She used the surname Dashwood, from *Letter the Second*, for sisters, Elinor and Marianne, and their family.

Letter the Second is an astonishing revelation, in it Jane Austen revealed aspects of her story she most wanted to put on record. Through Miss Jane, she described the burden of her family secrets, of being forbidden to reveal her true self and her real feelings.

She had *married without the consent or knowledge of her father,* making it necessary to *keep the Secret from every one.* She anticipates that when her father dies, she will maintain her secrets, and she will not use her married name, Wentworth.

Twelve years after her father's death, Jane Austen used the name Wentworth for the hero of *Persuasion*. Written in the last year of her life, it was her imagined story of D'Arcy Wentworth's return to her. She hid the finished manuscript away in her writing box, kept secret from her family and her publisher.[182]

Tell-tale compression of the pages

Northanger Abbey

In the original manuscript of *Volume the Second*, three leaves, or six pages, were removed towards the end of *Letter the Second*, after the words: *We wrote to one another on the same subject by the same post, so exactly.* The stubs of these leaves are still visible in the manuscript. One leaf was cut out before Jane Austen numbered the pages, and two leaves removed afterwards.[183]

JANE AUSTEN HAD A LIFE!

She completed the sentence on the following page, the narrative flattens out, it returns to Sophia, who is pleased to hear the story of someone else's misery, puzzled at her own disappointment and unhappiness. Jane ended the letter within a few lines.

The missing pages may go some way to explain why Letter the Second reads unevenly, more like an early draft. It fails as either a piece of comic writing or as a credible story. Miss Jane's claim, for example, that her father believed her three children were really her brother's children, when she had no brother, comes across as confused rather than amusing.

Despite these disconnects, Miss Jane's emotions ring true, her distress is unfeigned. Sophia's response: *how infinitely I am obliged to you for so entertaining a Story! You cannot think how it has diverted me! But have you quite done?* is jarring.

Miss Jane asks Sophia: *did you ever hear a story more pathetic?* With her reply: *it pleases me so much, for when one is unhappy nothing is so delightful to one's Sensations as to hear of equal Misery,* the reader has her measure. Sophia is so self centred she did not hear or could not respond to the depth of Miss Jane's heartbreak. We could assume that Jane Austen had experienced similar glib responses, from listeners to her story: *how entertaining, have you done?*

To form that ground-work
Pride & Prejudice

Letter the Second, From a Young Lady crossed in Love to her friend, provides evidence to refute the claim that the love of Jane Austen's life was Tom Lefroy. It was at least three years after she wrote this story that he entered her life, in late 1795.

This letter verifies the depth of Jane Austen's trust in Jane Cooper. She was confident she could record for her cousin the truth about her relationship with D'Arcy Wentworth, her sense of loss, her despair, and her fears for her future.

22

Letter the Third – From a young Lady in distress'd Circumstances to her freind

The author of *Letter the Third*, Maria Williams, is a young woman, living with her widowed mother. It seems she has recently *come out* into society, having made her *appearance in the World*, she is duly invited with other young people to social events in the district. Maria's mother *never goes out* and they have no carriage. This leaves Maria to walk to and from these events or to rely on lifts from others.

A few days ago, she was invited to a private ball given by Mr Ashburnham. Her mother *entrusted* her *to the care of Lady Greville*, who was attending the ball with her two daughters. At nine o'clock, on their way there, Lady Greville, a woman of some importance and status in the district, calls for Maria in her carriage with her daughters, and will deliver her home afterwards.

Before Maria has stepped inside the carriage, Lady Greville has begun to denigrate, undermine and humiliate her, taking every opportunity to remind Maria that she and her mother lack the wealth and social position her Ladyship and her daughters enjoy.

Every neighbourhood should have a great lady Sanditon

Lady Greville invites Maria to sit beside her, facing forwards, an honour Maria knows from prior experience *as conferring a great obligation* on her. It soon becomes clear she is obliged to suffer a constant stream of barbs from Lady Greville, without complaint, and so she does, *with as much indifference as I could assume.*

Lady Greville starts with a compliment: *you seem very smart tonight... have you got a new Gown on?* This rapidly turns into an accusation of extravagance, that her gown is one Maria and her mother could ill afford: *I only hope your Mother may not have distressed herself to set **you** off...In my opinion your old striped gown would have been quite fine enough for its wearer.*

You know I always speak my mind, she tells Maria. *It is not my way to find fault with people because they are poor, for I always think that they are more to be despised and pitied than blamed for it, especially if they cannot help it...But I suppose you intend to make your fortune tonight -:Well the sooner the better; and I wish you success.*

Her Ladyship asks innocuously: *Was your Mother gone to bed before you left her?* Her intention is to point out to her daughters that Maria's family is too poor to afford candles. *Candles cost money, and Mrs Williams is too wise to be extravagant.* She asks Maria what her mother had for supper, *Bread and Cheese, I suppose.* She can assure her daughters that they are *always provided* with better than that.

Lady Greville is enjoying herself at the expense of Maria. Her elder daughter laughs *excessively, as she constantly does at her mother's wit.* The younger, Ellen, does not join her mothers' sport. Later during supper, she stays with Maria, while her sister joins their mother's party.

Lady Greville's malice continues at the Ball. Seeing Maria standing alone, she assumes she has not been asked to dance. She calls out, loud enough to be heard by all the old Ladies: *Hey day, Miss Maria! What cannot you get a partner? Poor young Lady! I am afraid your new Gown was put on for nothing. But do not despair; perhaps you may get a hop before the Evening is over.*

Maria has indeed been asked, and is soon dancing with *the most agreeable partner in the room,* the *heir to a very large Estate.* Maria notes Her Ladyship looks displeased when she sees them together, and realises, *she was determined to mortify me.*

Loud enough to be heard by half the people in the room, Lady Greville attacks the reputation of Maria's grandfather, declaring he had worked in *some low way,* and *died insolvent.* Next she targets her late father, asking Maria, was he not *poor as a Rat,* had he been in debtor's prison? Maria angers her with her polite answers, rebutting each of her claims. Lady Greville gives her <u>such</u> a look, and turns *away in a great passion.*

Maria writes to *her freind,* that she was *half delighted with myself for my impertinence, and half afraid of being too saucy.*

Conscious superiority rather than any solicitude to oblige   *Mansfield Park*

The following day, Maria and her mother are at dinner, when Lady Greville's coach pulls up outside. Her Ladyship sends in a servant to call Maria to *make haste and come immediately* to the coach door. She is reluctant to respond to such an *impertinent message,* but her mother says, *Go Maria,* and she does. She is *obliged to stand* beside the coach, *though the Wind was extremely high and very cold.*

Lady Greville tells Maria she *may dine with them the day after tomorrow,* an order rather than an invitation, followed by detailed instructions designed to belittle and humiliate her. She is to walk there, Her Ladyship *shant send the Carriage,* as there is *no occasion for* Maria *being very fine. If it rains* Maria *may take an umbrella.* Maria writes to her friend: *I could hardly help laughing at hearing her give me leave to keep myself dry.*

Her Ladyship instructs Maria not to come <u>before</u> the time, five o'clock, and to be on *time, for I shant wait.* She is to tell her maid to come for her at night, as *there will be no Moon – and you will have an horrid walk home.*

When Ellen calls from the carriage, *I am afraid you find it very cold Maria,* Lady Greville agrees, saying she *can hardly bear the window down.* She turns on Maria again: *you are used to be blown about by the wind Miss Maria, that is what has made your Complexion so ruddy and coarse. You young Ladies who cannot often ride in a Carriage never mind what weather you trudge in, or how the wind shews your legs. I would not have my Girls stand out of doors as you do in such a day as this. But some sort of people have no feelings either of cold or Delicacy.*

Lady Greville sends her compliments to Maria's mother, and observing that Maria's *dinner will be cold,* orders her coachman, *Drive on, And away she went,* Maria wrote to her freind, *leaving me in a great passion with her as she always does.*

Maria is indeed, *a young Lady in distress'd Circumstances.* Her mother will do nothing to defend or help her, she *insists on my accepting every invitation of Lady Greville, or you may be certain that I would never enter her House, or her Coach, with the disagreeable certainty I always have of being abused for my poverty while I am in them.* Lady Greville will continue to take every possible opportunity to abuse and humiliate her. Her *distress'd Circumstances* will persist, nothing she can do or say will alter them. We can only hope she will retain her spirit.

Mortifying & humiliating
Sense & Sensibility

With characters such as Lady Greville, and Lady Williams in *Jack and Alice,* Jane Austen exposed those women who use their social status and power to humiliate and belittle younger, less advantaged woman. In *Pride & Prejudice* she presented Lady Catherine De Bourgh, whose bitchiness and viciousness outdid both Ladies Greville and Williams, but who meets her match in the heroine, Elizabeth Bennet.

The names of people that fill up my time
Mansfield Park

Jane Austen's contemporary, Lady Henrietta Greville was the second wife of George Greville, 2nd Earl of Warwick, formerly Henrietta Vernon, daughter of the Hon Richard Vernon and Lady Evelyn Leveson-Gower. They wed in Gower House, Whitehall, the home of her uncle, Granville Leveson Gower, 2nd Earl Gower. Jane Austen used the names, Vernon, Evelyn and Gower, in several of her stories.

23

Letter the Fourth – From a young Lady rather impertinent to her freind

This is the shortest of the five letters in *A Collection of Letters*. The writer tells her *freind* Mary, that she and her mother had dined the day before at Mr Evelyn's. There she had met his cousin, Miss Grenville, who she found *engaging*, with *something peculiarly interesting in her manner and voice*. She was filled with a great *curiosity to know the history of her Life, who were her parents, where she came from, and what had befallen her.* She was convinced that something has befallen Miss Grenville. Perhaps she suspects it is a failed romance.

After dinner, while the rest of the party were *playing at Cards, engaged in a whispering Conversation* or had fallen asleep, the writer takes the opportunity to strike up a *Conversation* with Miss Grenville.

She begins by asking how long she has been in Essex. Miss Grenville's answer is short and succinct, she resists being quizzed: *I arrived on Tuesday.*

To draw her out, the writer asks a leading question, *You came from Derbyshire?* Miss Grenville replies, *No Ma'am –! appearing surprised at my question, from Suffolk.*

Having extracted a definitive answer from her, this *young lady rather impertinent* crows to her friend Mary. *You will think this a good dash of mine my dear Mary, but you know that I am not wanting for impudence when I have any end in view.* Clearly, she had asked the question knowing Miss Grenville did not come from Derbyshire.

She asks more questions. Miss Grenville answers them, she has loosened up a little, but her answers are still short and non-committal, without detail or an opinion that might encourage her interrogator.

The writer persists with her questions, Miss Grenville's vague answers only cause this rather impertinent young lady to long to know more. Her *Curiosity was so much raised, that she was resolved at any rate to satisfy it.* She questions Miss Grenville about her feelings at leaving Suffolk, had it led to the loss of her *dearest Friends?* When Miss Greville replies that she passed *many happy years there,* her questioner offers the hope that she *never spent any unhappy ones there.*

Miss Grenville gives a clichéd reply, *Perfect Felicity is not the property of Mortals,* then lets slip an unfortunate confidence: *Some Misfortunes I have certainly met with – What Misfortunes dear Ma,am,* asks the young Lady rather impertinently, *burning with impatience to know every thing,* with *no doubt but that any sufferings* she *may have experienced could arise only from the cruelties of Relations or the Errors of Friends.*

She moves in: *You seem unhappy my dear Miss Grenville – Is it in my power to soften your Misfortunes.* Suggesting that Miss Grenville probably needs advice from someone of superior *Age and Judgement,* she declares: *I am that person, and I now challenge you to accept the offer I make you of my Confidence and Freindship, in return to which I shall only ask for yours.*

Miss Greville's reply is quite definite: *You are extremely obliging Ma'am – said She – and I am highly flattered by your attention to me –. But I am in no difficulty, no doubt, no uncertainty of situation in which any Advice can be wanted. Whenever I am however continued she brightening into a complaisant smile, I shall know where to apply.*

A good deal mortified by such a repulse, but not dissuaded, the rather Impertinent young Lady decides to change tack: *I found that by the appearance of Sentiment and Freindship nothing was to be gained and determined therefore to renew my Attacks by Questions and Suppositions.*

Finally, in response to a question about her parents, Miss Grenville replies, *They are neither of them alive, Ma'am.* This stops her interrogator in her tracks: *This was an answer I did not expect – I was quite silenced, and never felt so awkward in my life.*

Meditations on the contents of the letter   Sense & Sensibility

With *Letter the Fourth,* Jane Austen presented Jane Cooper with a conversation she had likely experienced during her stay at Steventon, after her father's death. She would have met people in the district who asked similar questions, busy bodies and women who felt she could do with their advice.

A great secret & known only to half the neighbourhood   Letters

At the same time, Jane Austen was highlighting her own experience, over the three years since her return to Steventon in December 1789. It was a tiny settlement, at the close of the eighteenth century it comprised a mere thirty-three families; Deane, nearby, had twenty-four. Jane would have fielded similar, seemingly innocuous questions from neighbours, acquaintances and women at large, probing about the *sufferings she may have experienced, the cruelties of Relations or the Errors of Friends.*

Forbidden by her father to tell where she had been, to explain her *loss of bloom* or the source of her depression and unhappiness, she would have learnt to recognise those women who approached her with an *end in view*, eager for a juicy detail or for any gossip to report.

In *Letter the Fourth*, Jane calls them out as *impertinent*. She distilled their inquiries into a seemingly polite, but relentless barrage, with asides that exposed their tactics. She could not disguise her delight in Jane

Cooper's power to silence and embarrass them, with an answer they did not expect, one that had little value as gossip.

Jane would have caught Jane Cooper's tone of voice in Miss Grenville's responses, and perhaps as well, the tone of a particular *young Lady*, known to them both, who they deemed particularly *impertinent*.

Gathering her work together *Pride & Prejudice*

Like the heroines in two of Jane Austen's earlier stories, *Jack and Alice* and *Love and Freindship*, the writer of this letter has *a great curiosity to know* every thing about Miss Grenville, *the history of her Life, who were her parents, where she came from, and what had befallen her.*

Jane scrutinises the letter-writer's empty need to know more, her refusal to countenance the obvious, that Miss Grenville does not want to confide in her. From *the rather impertinent* young Lady's asides, it is clear she is not offering *Confidence and Freindship*. Anything she can glean through her probing is grist for her mill, a fresh item of gossip, to be flaunted and broadcast around the district.

Tell-tale compression of the pages *Northanger Abbey*

One leaf, making two pages, was torn out between the second and third pages of Letter the Fourth, in the *Volume the Second* manuscript. The cut occurred in the first paragraph of the letter, after *Dr Drayton, Miss Grenville and*. This leaf was torn out before Jane numbered the pages, she had ensured the sentence flowed easily onto the next page.

24

Letter the Fifth – From a Young Lady very much in love to her Freind

The last letter in *A Collection of Letters*, illustrates the pitfalls that can await a young woman who has *come out* into society and is now in a position to meet and appraise eligible young suitors. Letter the Fifth scrutinizes the role that older, female family members could assume in match-making, how they might exert their authority and influence over an inexperienced young woman, in order to persuade and steer her towards the young man they have selected for her.

The author is a young heiress, Henrietta Halton, courted by the seemingly besotted young Mr Musgrove, whose cause is championed by his cousin, Lady Scudamore.

Henrietta Halton tells *her friend,* Matilda, she is *more in love every day.* She sends her a copy of a letter she has received from London, from Tom Musgrove, her *most ardent admirer.* It appears they had seen each other a month earlier at his cousin Lady Scudamore's house, though they do not seem to have met or spoken there.

Musgrove writes to Henrietta, in a chaotic stream of pronouns: *The sight of you was like the sight of a wonderful fine Thing. I started – I gazed at her with Admiration – She appeared every moment more Charming,* and the unfortunate Musgrave became a Captive to your Charms before I had time to look about me.

He assures her he has an *improvable Estate* and *my own house which tho' an excellent one is at present somewhat out of repair and a Heart which trembles while it signs itself your most ardent Admirer.*

Henrietta considers his letter a *masterpeice of Writing. Such Sense, Such Sentiment, Such purity of Thought, Such flow of language and such unfeigned Love in one Sheet.*

She copies Matilda into her reply to *dearest Musgrave,* filled with cloying sweetness and palpitating fervour. *I quite die to see you...we are so much in love that we cannot live asunder. Oh! my dear Musgrave you cannot think how impatiently I wait for the death of my Uncle and Aunt – If they will not die soon, I believe I shall run mad, for I get more in love with you every day of my Life.*

It seems at this point, that Jane Austen has returned to her gleeful mockery of popular novels of sensibility and sentiment, with their facile, affected voices and deliberate working up of sentiment. But, having introduced the young couple, she shifts her focus to Lady Scudamore and Henrietta, exposing her Ladyship's determination to direct Henrietta's heart, mind and quite likely her fortune, towards young Musgrove.

Lady Scudamore tells Henrietta, Musgrove *is distractedly in love* with her, *he was in love with you from the first moment he beheld you... I give you Joy of your conquest...for my Cousin is a charming young fellow, has seen a great deal of the World, and writes the best Love-letters I ever read.*

Henrietta tells Matilda that, *excessively pleased with her conquest, she thought it was proper to give herself a few Airs.* "This is all very pretty Lady Scudamore, but you know that we young Ladies who are Heiresses must not throw ourselves away upon Men who have no fortune at all.*

Lady Scudamore assures her: *Mr Musgrove is so far from being poor that he has an estate of Several hundreds an year which is capable of great*

Improvement, and an excellent House, though at present it is not quite in repair.

Henrietta replies, she has *no reason to find fault with him for admiring her, tho' perhaps I may not marry him for all that Lady Scudamore.*

Lady Scudamore moves in on her: *if I am not greatly mistaken You are at this very moment unknown to yourself, cherishing a most tender affection for him...every look, every word betrays it...come my dear Henrietta, consider me as a friend, and be sincere with me – Do you not prefer Mr Musgrove to any man of your acquaintance?...Every word you say more deeply convinces me that your Minds are actuated by the invisible power of sympathy, for your opinions and Sentiments so exactly coincide.*

Lady Scudamore presses on, reporting Musgrave had declared his love for Henrietta,
"Yes I'm in love I feel it now
And Henrietta Halton has undone me-"

From her account Musgrove is a young man filled with the sentiment and suffering of the delicate soul, a hero worthy of the novel of sensibility. *Convinced* he has *little Chance of winning* Henrietta, he wants *the exquisite Gratification of dieing for her, of falling victim to her charms... When I am dead...Let me be carried and lain at her feet, and perhaps she may not disdain to drop a pitying tear on my poor remains.*

Henrietta interrupts, she asks Lady Scudamore to *say no more on this affecting Subject. I cannot bear it.* Not wishing to wound *the sweet Sensibility* of Henrietta's *Soul* too deeply, her Ladyship agrees, *I will be silent.* But after a moment, Henrietta replies, *"Pray go on,"* and she does so, reporting in detail the work of some hours that it took her to convince Musgrove that Henrietta *had really a preference for him.*

From that point, her Ladyship reports: *his transports, his Raptures, his Extacies are beyond my power to describe.*

Henrietta seems to enjoy her conversation with Lady Scudamore, she replies politely, with interest, seemingly flattered to be the recipient of his love at first sight. She appears gratified to hear Mr Musgrove would be happy to die for her love, for his dead body to lie at her feet so that he could feel her tear drops falling on his *poor remains*. Her sensibility is evident, impressed by the vision of *hapless Musgrave* lying dead at her feet, she praises his *"exalted mind."*

The reader though, has listened to her Ladyship insinuating herself: *Come my dear Henrietta, consider me as a freind, and be sincere with me;* and noted how Musgrove's letter echoes several of her key phrases: *his improvable Estate* and his *excellent House, though at present not quite in repair.* Her careful description of his assets has been repeated several times. With just a whiff of suspicion that Lady Scudamore may have ghost-written Musgrove's *masterpeice of Writing,* the reader is more and more conscious of a trap being laid for Henrietta.

It is a surprise and a delight to reach the farcical last paragraph of her letter, following the ecstasy of exquisite love, the tears falling on the lover's corpse, with making pies: *What a noble Creature he is! Oh, Matilda what a fortunate one I am....My Aunt is calling me to come and make the pies.*

The divine Henrietta Halton, appears to have escaped unscathed, for the moment. Having obtained a wealth of material for a full report on her romantic conquest to *her Friend,* she happily turns her mind to more practical matters. The reader, relieved, concludes this is a *Young Lady very much in love* with the prospect of love, and wishes her well.

Names, facts, every thing mentioned   *Pride & Prejudice*

Jane Austen used the surname Musgrove again in *Persuasion,* she included three generations of the Musgroves of Uppercross Hall in Somerset in the story, with one named *Henrietta.* Henrietta Musgrove and her elder sister Louisa, vie for the attentions of Captain Wentworth, who is staying at nearby Kellynch.

Austen used a variant, *Musgrave,* in *The Watsons,* for Tom Musgrave, friend of Lord Osborne and *the smartest and most fashionable man of the two. In the town of D. in Surrey, he trifles with their affections, and transfers his attentions from one girl to another, he never means anything serious.* Emma Watson, the heroine, finds him *very vain, very conceited, absurdly anxious for distinction and absolutely contemptible in some of the measures he takes for being so.*

It is most likely that Jane Austen took the name Scudamore from the Knight family physician, Dr Edward Scudamore, who was one of a family of doctors who practiced in Canterbury, nine miles from Godmersham.

I will read you their names directly, here they are in my pocket-book

Northanger Abbey

D'Arcy Wentworth's *Medical Notebook* refers to Sir Charles Scudamore, of the same Canterbury family, for his knowledge of gout.[184] Sir Charles published *A Treatise on the Nature and Cure of Gout* in 1816, dedicated to Matthew Baillie, a London physician whose *Morbid Anatomy of Some of the Most Important Parts of the Human Body* (1793) was the first systematic study of pathology. Baillie also treated young Hastings de Feuillide and later Henry Austen, for phthisis, a chronic prolonged chest infection.

D'Arcy Wentworth studied in London with several eminent surgeons. He walked the wards at St Bartholomew's under Percivall Pott, one of the founders of orthopaedics, the first to associate the incidence of a cancer with exposure within a specific occupation, and to identify its likely cause as an environmental carcinogen

In 1775, Pott had documented the high incidence of testicular cancer in chimney-sweepers: *which has not been publicly noticed. The fate of these people is singularly hard: in their early infancy they are most frequently treated with great brutality and they are almost starved with hunger an cold. They are then thrust up narrow, and sometimes hot, chimneys where they are bruised, burned and almost suffocated; and when they get to puberty become peculiarly liable to a most noisome, painful and fatal disease.*[185]

D'Arcy was in London during the time of great progress in medical knowledge and practice, particularly among surgeons. He regularly observed dissections in the anatomy theatre of the Company of Surgeons, and attended John Hunter's Sunday evening medical levees. Years later, he recalled his teachers in his *Medical Notebook: John Hunter, born February 14th (my own birthday) Hunterian Oration instituted by Sir E. Home and Dr Baillie ($500 each). J.H. began as a pupil at St Bartholomew's in 1748, thirty years Pott's junior.*

In New South Wales, where D'Arcy practiced, his patients were convicts, emancipists and the poor. To keep abreast of advances in medicine, he subscribed to a number of medical journals, and he recorded their most useful advice in his *Medical Notebook*.

The *Medical Notebook* contains nearly four hundred entries, detailing symptoms, diseases, complaints and their recommended treatment. He recorded the source of each entry, the journal in which it appeared, and the names of over three hundred contemporary physicians and surgeons who recommended particular procedures. He carried it in his medical bag for reference, as an *aide memoire,* and to assist in training staff at the hospitals where he practiced, many of whom were convicts.

Scraps

Six weeks after Jane Cooper and Thomas Williams were married, there was another cause for celebration amongst the Austens. On 23 January 1793, the first child of the new generation was born. At *Rowling* in east Kent, Jane's third brother, Edward, and his wife Elizabeth Bridges had a daughter, Fanny Catherine.

Jane Austen dedicated five short pieces to her first *neice*, she named this little collection *Scraps* and she closed *Volume the Second* with them.

In her dedication to Fanny, Jane, just seventeen, assumed the tone of an elderly aunt, saying, as she was *prevented by the great distance between Rowling and Steventon from superintending her Education*, she considered it her *particular Duty* to address her *neice* on paper, with her *Opinions and Admonitions on the conduct of Young Women*.

The choicest gift

Persuasion

The five pieces Jane Austen dedicated to Edward's daughter, offer insights into her relationship with him. Edward was eight years older than Jane. The year she turned eight, he was sent to live with the Knight family in Kent, a hundred and twenty five miles from Steventon.

At the end of August 1786, he and his cousin Edward Cooper came to Reading for the annual races on Bulmershe Heath. They took Jane, Cassandra and Jane Cooper for dinner at the *Bear Inn*. Jane was introduced D'Arcy Wentworth there, by her brother Edward.

Later that year, Edward set off on his Grand Tour, returning two years later to Kent. On 27 December 1791, he married Elizabeth Bridges, third of the six daughters of Baron Sir Brook Bridges and his wife Fanny, of *Goodnestone Park,* in Kent. Jane gave them, *The Three Sisters*, as a wedding gift.

Jane wrote regularly to her brothers Henry, Frank and Charles, but she did not have the same familial relationship with Edward. The stories she sent him, are very particular. She seems to have used these occasions to display, even to confront him, with the strength of her intelligence, determination, and her refusal to be cowed.

More than three years after Fanny was born, in early September 1796, Jane visited them at *Rowling*, the house near the Bridges' family home, where they lived for the first seven years of their marriage.

Jane wrote happy letters home from *Rowling*, where she was *very busy making Edward's shirts, and proud to say she was the neatest worker of the party.*[186] During the fortnight she spent there, her brothers Henry and Frank also came to stay, it was a sociable family holiday. They had *dreadful Hot weather;* she told Cassandra, *it keeps one in a continual state of Inelegance.*[187]

In the autumn of 1797, Edward and Elizabeth and their four children moved to *Godmersham*, the Knight family estate. Jane wrote to Cassandra from there on 24 August 1805, *they were very civil to me, as they always are.* She enjoyed playing with Edward's nine children, particularly *Battledore & Shuttlecock* with William, seven.[188]

Thrown aside at Godmersham   *Verse*

Three years later, in June 1808, Jane was staying in London with Henry and Eliza. James and Mary arrived from Steventon, with three year old Caroline, and nine year old James Edward. They were on their way to *Godmersham*, and Jane joined them,

James went on an earlier coach; Jane travelled with Mary and the children, and reached *Godmersham* at six in the evening. As they approached, she saw James and Edward *walking before the house*. Edward did not come to greet her, and next day, he asked her, unambiguously, when she planned to leave.

The slight had been most determined *Mansfield Park*

Jane wrote to Cassandra: *Edward will be going about the same time to Alton.. and I shall probably be his companion to that place, and get on afterwards somehow or other. I should have preferred a rather longer stay here certainly, but there is no prospect of any later conveyance for me..I shall at any rate be glad not to be obliged to be an encumbrance on those who have brought me here..I need scarcely beg you to keep all this to yourself.* [189]

Jane recorded her feelings in Northanger Abbey: *so grossly uncivil; hurrying her away without any reference to her own convenience, or allowing her even the appearance of choice as to the time or mode of her travelling..What could this mean but an intentional affront? By some means or other she must have had the misfortune to offend him.* [190]

Any former supposed slight *Mansfield Park*

While at *Godmersham*, she told Cassandra she had written to thank Mrs Knight, Edward's stepmother, for her usual gift of money, *I wrote without much effort; for I was rich – and the Rich are always respectable, whatever be their stile of writing.* [191]

During her stay Jane offered to help with the children. She hoped, *when Louisa is gone, who sometimes hears the little girls read, I will try to be accepted in her stead,* [192] but she was not invited to take Louisa Bridges' place.

In the stories she gave to Edward and his family in 1793 and 1796. Jane

Austen gave her characters the names of three of the Bridges sisters, Sophia, Elizabeth and Louisa,

Nearly sixty years later, Jane's niece Anna Lefroy observed that Elizabeth and her family were wary of Jane's quick wit and intelligence. *A little talent went a long way with the Goodneston Bridgeses of that period, & <u>much</u> must have gone a long way too far.*[193]

Nothing but a thorough change of sentiment could account for it
Sense & Sensibility

Sense and Sensibility the first of Jane Austen's novels to be published, came out at the end of October 1811. Although it was published anonymously, her brothers appear to have discussed it amongst themselves. She had received criticism from James, Edward and Charles. In 1813, Henry sent Edward and Charles advance copies of *Pride and Prejudice.* Jane commented, they were *just the two Sets which I was least eager for the disposal of.*[194]

By September 1813, Jane's success seems to have gained Edward's respect. She had two novels in print, *Sense & Sensibility* and *Pride & Prejudice*, with second editions of both due out the following month. On 14 September, Jane accompanied Edward and his three eldest daughters to London from Chawton, and went on to Godmersham with them, where she stayed until November.

She wrote to Cassandra, *I have not been here these four years so I am sure the event deserves to be talked of before & behind as well as in the middle.*[195]

Eighteen months later she wrote to James youngest daughter Caroline, with more than a touch of irony – *we four sweet Brothers & Sisters dine today at the Great House. Is not that quite natural?* [196]

25

The female philosopher – a Letter

The female philosopher is a letter from Arabella Smythe to Louisa Clarke, to tell her Mr Millar and two of his daughters, Julia and Charlotte, had called the day before, *on their way to Bath*. Arabella knew the eldest daughter, Julia, was a friend of Louisa. Mr Millar was an old and valued friend of Arabella's father, though they had not seen each other for *nearly twenty years*.

The two fathers meet with a *social shake and Cordial Kiss*, Mr Millar observes that *many events had befallen each*, since they last met. Julia promptly takes up his comment, with *most sensible reflections on the many changes in their situation which so long a period had occasioned*.

Louisa had mentioned to Arabella that Julia was *remarkably handsome*, Arabella declares both girls *extremely pretty*, Charlotte, sixteen, has *a pleasing plumpness*, an expressive face, *sometimes of softness the most bewitching, and at others of Vivacity the most striking*. Her *conversation during the half hour they set with us, was replete with humourous Sallies, Bonmots and repartee.*

It seems that *the lovely* Julia's musings dominated the visit. Arabella carefully reports every turn of this *female philosopher's sensible reflections, short digressions* and *illustrations*. Her monologue, made up almost entirely of clichés, generalities and moral platitudes, culminates in a soliloquy on *the instability of human pleasures* and the imperfection of *all earthly Joys.*

Julia is interrupted by the arrival of their Carriage. *The amiable Moralist with her Father and Sister was obliged to depart, but not without a promise of spending five or six months with us on their return.* Arabella's politeness appears strained, plainly, she has no desire to see the Millars again.

Suddenly her letter changes direction, as she turns her attention to Louisa. *We of course mentioned You,* she assures her, and *ample Justice was done to your Merits by all.* Taking aim, she attacks Louisa's looks, her character, *her vanity, her pride and her folly.* Ending with a turn of the knife she tells Louisa her friends the Millars had joined in the attack, *to my opinion every one added weight by the concurrence of their own.*

She ends, *your affecte. Arabella Smythe,* the *affecte,* an abbreviation of *affectionate,* was a perfunctory form of sign-off, but after her attack on Louisa it seems wildly out of place.

There was something in the name .... *Emma*

In her title, *The female philosopher,* Jane Austen joined two contrary ideas together in an oxymoron, for ironic effect. In the eighteenth century, as in ancient Greece, philosophy was the domain of men, who questioned, formulated and argued fundamental questions about life and morality. The title is sarcastic, ridiculing Julia Millar's efforts to address questions of life and morality, giving her trite commonplaces the inflated status of philosophy.

In Samuel Johnson's Dictionary, published in 1755, he used a quotation from Shakespeare's *Romeo & Juliet* to illustrate his primary definition of philosophy as, *Knowledge natural or moral*:
Hang up philosophy;
Unless philosophy can make a Juliet,
Displant a town, reverse a prince's doom,
It helps not.

Julia's *Sentiments of Morality*, are little more than banal clichés. She would be advised to take Shakespeare's advice, *Hang up philosophy...It helps not.*

Arabella's comment, *the amiable Julia uttered Sentiments of Morality worthy of a heart like her own*, appears to refer to the opening lines of Adam Smith's *The Theory of Moral Sentiments*[197] describing *pity or compassion as the emotion we feel for the misery of others.* He notes: *this sentiment like all the other original passions of human nature, is by no means confined to the virtuous or the humane. The greatest ruffian, the most hardened violator of the laws of society, is not altogether without it.*

Jane Austen included a prominent Wentworth name in *The female philosopher*. Thomas Wentworth 1st Earl of Stafford's second wife was Arabella Holles, their second daughter was also named Arabella.

Gathering her work together
Pride & Prejudice

Arabella's letter to Louisa appears at first to be a report of the visit from her friends. Her tone hardens as she notes Mr Millar's *very just* observations give *occasion to the lovely* Julia's *sensible reflections.*

Arabella's summary of Julia's philosophical musings becomes increasingly sarcastic and dismissive. At the end, she turns on Louisa in a shocking conclusion, with undisguised contempt and hatred.

The reader is startled by the intensity of the unexplained and unresolved anger that erupts at the end of the letter. At first, Louisa's predicament seems not unlike that of a contemporary young woman, confronted with an abusive text message. Arabella gives no clear details of Louisa's failings, though the evidence is there, laid out in the story.

A rap foretold a visitor
Sense & Sensibility

Mr Millar and his daughters call unexpectedly on the Smythes. Arabella welcomes them, they were calling, ostensibly, for Mr Millar to make contact with her father. Charlotte lightened their entrance with her entertaining humour, Mr Millar referred to the *many events that had befallen each* of the fathers, then hands over to the *lovely Julia*, to deliver her *Sentiments of Morality*.

Arabella listens to Julia's *reflections on the many changes* that had occurred over the years; to her moralising on *the advantages of some* of these changes and *the disadvantages of others*; on *the instability of human pleasures*, and *the uncertainty of their duration*, concluding that, *all earthly Joys must be imperfect*.

Arabella realises that Julia's moralising is aimed directly at her, that the Millars, father and daughters, have called, basking in their moral superiority, to gawk at her.

She realises it was Louisa's gossip to Julia Millar that is behind their visit. Arabella responds with an attack on Louisa's credibility, calling her peevish, envious and spiteful. She wants to sow doubt in the minds of the Millars about Louisa's motivation, and the truth of her chatter and prattle.

Next day, probably after a sleepless night, Arabella writes to Louisa Clarke, telling her the Millars had called. Louisa would have read on eagerly, wondering what had led Arabella to connect her with their visit. Arabella makes her wait, more than three quarters of the letter is taken up by her account of their half hour together.

Then abruptly, Louisa's suspense is over, *we of course we mentioned you*, says Arabella. She reports *the ample justice done to her Merits by all:* her *Peevishness, Envy and Spite*, her *very trifling Understanding* and *pretensions to Beauty, her vanity, her pride and her folly*. Arabella's final revenge is to tell Louisa the Millars had all agreed: *And to my opinion every one added weight by the concurrence of their own*.

Gossips! – Tiresome wretches! *Emma*

In *The female philosopher*, Jane Austen was venting her own anger and frustration. From Christmas 1789, when she returned to Steventon with D'Arcy, and remained there without him, she had to deal with innuendo and gossip. Her anger and indignation burn through the story, particularly at those who sought her out, to take the moral high ground, to denigrate her – the parson's daughter, and through her, her father.

The expectation of an unpleasant event *Sense & Sensibility*

In January 1813, *Pride & Prejudice*, Jane's story of her romance with D'Arcy Wentworth, was published, with its hero named Mr Darcy. Her father had died eight years earlier, now she was anxious about her brothers. How would they react?

To her relief, Cassandra wrote to say James had not objected. Jane replied: *the caution observed at Steventon with regard to possession of the book is an agreeable surprise to me, & I heartily wish it may be the means of saving you from everything unpleasant, but you must be prepared for the Neighbourhood being perhaps already informed of there being such a Work in the World, & in the Chawton World! Dummer will do that you know.*[198]

Dummer was the village nearest *Kempshott*, the house where twenty-five years earlier D'Arcy Wentworth had stayed with William Wickham.

In *Pride and Prejudice*, Jane gave *Kempshott* the name *Netherfield*. She described how, in July 1788, she walked there after heavy storms, to visit D'Arcy: *The distance is nothing when one has a motive; only three miles...I shall be back by dinner.*

The female philosopher was the first of five pieces Jane Austen sent her brother Edward, dedicated to his daughter Fanny. Elizabeth Bridges, his wife, was the third of six Bridges sisters. It was no coincidence the fifth Bridges sister was named Louisa. Jane wanted Edward to know how angry she was that his sister-in-law had been diverting her friends with gossip about her; that she knew it would have been Elizabeth who told Louisa her story.

Modesty, Sense & Dignity are happily blended   *A female philosopher*

Louisa Bridges was two years younger than Jane Austen, in 1793, the year Fanny Austen was born, she was sixteen. Fanny was also Louisa's first niece; her second, Sophia Deedes, daughter of her second eldest sister, also Sophia, was born just eight days after Fanny. Later that year, a third niece, another Fanny, was born to her eldest sister, Fanny Cage.

Jane received occasional news of her sisters-in-law's sister, Louisa. She saw her on the rare occasions she visited Edward and his family, though it seems they rarely spoke. She mentioned her in letters to Cassandra, always circumspect, with a certain unspecified sarcasm.[199] Louisa was overweight, Jane alludes to this when she describes Julia as having *a form which at once presents you with Grace, Elegance and Symmetry.*

Three years after *The female philosopher*, Jane noted: *Louisa's figure is very much improved; she is as stout again as she was. Her face, from what I could see of it one evening, appeared not at all altered.* Twelve years later, Louisa was now thirty-one, Jane commented: *I was agreeably surprised to find Louisa Bridges still here. She looks remarkably well (legacies are very wholesome diet) and is just what she always was.*

Louisa never married, she and two of her sisters, Marianne and Harriet, lived with their widowed mother, Fanny, Lady Bridges, until her death in 1825. Louisa Bridges died in 1856, four years after Edward, thirty-nine years after Jane Austen. Her copy of *Emma* still survives.

26

The First Act of a Comedy

The *First Act of a Comedy*, set in the *Lion Inn* at Hounslow, comprises four scenes. In the first, the Hostess, manager of the inn, directs her staff, Maria, Cook and Charles, to attend to the inn's patrons, giving us an introduction to the setting, and an overview of the characters in the play.

In Scene Two, in the inn's public *Moon* room, we meet *their Honours,* the important guests, Popgun and his favourite daughter Pistoletta. She asks how far it is to London, he tells her they have seven miles to go. Popgun is taking her there to marry Strephon, to whom he plans to leave his *whole Estate.*

In Scene Three, Chloe enters, and announces she is going to London to be married to *Strephon.* Accompanied by her chorus, she bursts into song about what *fun, fun, fun* it will be to be married to him.

When Cook enters with a menu, Chloe orders *the leg of beef and the partridge,* and sings a comic song with the chorus,
I am going to have my dinner,
after which I shan't be thinner,
I wish I had here Strephon
For he would carve the partridge if it should be a tough one.

Scene Four opens inside the *Lion Inn*, Strephon enters with a postilion, who is waiting to be paid his fare of *eighteen pence,* for driving him the six miles from Staines to Hounslow. Strephon tells him he is on his way to London to marry Chloe.

Alas, my friend, Strephon apologises, he has only a forged guinea to support himself *in Town.* He offers to pawn an unaddressed letter he received from Chloe, as payment. The postilion accepts the offer, doubtless assuming Strephon will pay him later, eager to reclaim the letter from the woman he is to marry.

The First Act of a Comedy ends on this note. Strephon has arrived at the inn where two women are waiting, each of them expecting to be his bride. Jane Austen left the play unfinished, and the unfolding of the story to her reader's imagination.

Her own family & friends *Pride & Prejudice*

Jane's family circle would have recognised her references to *The Beggar's Opera,* the smash hit of 1728, by English poet and dramatist John Gay (1685-1732). Some would have noted her allusions to the poem *Strephon and Chloe,* written in 1734 by Anglo-Irish satirist Jonathan Swift.

John Gay and Jonathan Swift along with Alexander Pope, Thomas Parnell and John Arbuthnot were founding members of the informal *Scriblerus Club,* they collaborated in ridiculing pedantry, pretentious erudition and academic jargon.

John Gay premiered *The Beggar's Opera* at Lincoln Inn Fields Theatre, on 29 January 1728. The idea for the opera came from Jonathan Swift, twelve years earlier he had asked Alexander Pope: *What think you of a Newgate pastoral among the thieves and whores there?*

Gay's opera contained sixty-nine short songs with satirical lyrics set to popular tunes, Scottish ballads, French folk tunes, and two melodies of George Frederic Handel, the popular composer of the day. In the opera, the heroine, Polly Peachum, secretly marries a famous highwayman, Macheath. Her parents oppose the match and plot to have him murdered.

Jane made a droll reference in *The First Act of a Comedy* to Jonathan Swift's poem, *Strephon and Chloe*, in which, after marvelling at Chloe's beauty: *So beautiful a nymph appears but once in twenty thousand years...* he observes: *You'd swear that such divine a creature felt no necessities of nature.* Swift exposes such romantic, unrealistic descriptions of Chloe, with descriptions of her sweaty armpits, smelly toes, her *frouzy steams, noisome whiffs and sweaty streams.*

After Chloe's song about *fun, fun, fun,* she deals with the more mundane matter of food. She reads the Lion Inn's bill of fare: *2 Ducks, a leg of beef, a stinking partridge, and a tart,* and orders a very filling dinner, declaring: *I am going to have my dinner after which I shan't be thinner.*

While Swift's Chloe was ordered by her father to marry Strephon, Jane Austen created a possible love triangle, adding Pistoletta, a second bride for Strephon.

The names of people that fill up my time *Mansfield Park*

Like Swift, Jane Austen used names from traditional pastoral romances for her putative lovers, Strephon and Chloe. In a second century Greek romance, *Daphnis & Chloe,* Chloe was abandoned by her parents at birth. Left exposed on a mountain to die, she was rescued by a shepherd and reared as a shepherdess.

Strephon was a traditional name for a rustic lover. Sir Philip Sidney's *Arcadia*, written in the 1580s, opens with a lament by Strephon for his lost love. Henry Fielding, in his 1749 novel, *The History of Tom Jones, a Foundling,* referred to Strephon and Phyllis as *two doves, or two wood pigeons* who retire *into some pleasant solitary grove, to enjoy the delightful conversation of Love.*

The names Popgun and Pistoletta evoke characters from traditional puppet shows, such as Pulcinella in sixteenth century Italian *commedia dell'arte*, or in the English puppet theatre, Punch and Judy.

Pistoleta (1185-1228), was the nickname of a medieval troubadour of Provence, a singer and a *jongleur*, who carried the news and stories from place to place, and love songs from a suitor to his beloved. Pistoleta also suggests a small handgun, the pistol, first made in Italy, in Pistoia, during the late fifteenth century.

Paired with her father Popgun, Jane's Pistoletta, sounds like a little pistol, daughter of a pistol, a small surprise weapon that makes a popping noise, but perhaps is not a deadly weapon.

Jane's Popgun is fooling himself, taking Pistoletta, his favourite child, to London to marry Strephon. Strephon is not interested in her, nor she in him. Popgun, is so convinced of Strephon's value as a son-in-law, he is offering him a dowry of his *whole Estate*, a long-term financial incentive, regardless of Pistoletta's wishes, or the needs of his other children. Strephon arrives from Staines, a town on the Thames that Jane uses as a pun, to suggest he has soiled his history and reputation.

There was something in the name *Emma*

Lavinia Fenton (1708-1760), the first actress to play Polly in *The Beggars Opera*, achieved fame and great popularity in the role. At the end of the first production, in April 1728, she decamped with Charles Powlett, 3rd Duke of Bolton (1685-1754). They had three sons, Charles, Percy and Horatio Armand, and married in 1751, after the death of the Duke's first wife.

Percy's son Charles lived with his uncle, Reverend Charles Powlett at *Hackwood Park*, the Duke of Bolton's estate in Hampshire, a mile south of Basingstoke. In 1787, the young Charles Powlett was made curate of Winslade, ten miles from Steventon. He was the rector of Winslade from 1789 to 1794 and from 1796 to 1811, a neighbour, fellow clergyman and friend of the Austens.

Jane included a minor character, Charles, in *The First Act of a Comedy*. Her family would have recognised her reference to Charles Powlett, and his family association with the heroine of the *The Beggar's Opera*.

They would not have forgotten James Austen's passionate interest in Lady Catherine Powlett, youngest daughter of the 6th Duke of Bolton.

In 1787, she married her cousin, Viscount Barnard, son of the 2nd Earl of Darlington, whose grandmother, Lady Grace Fitzroy, was a granddaughter of King Charles II, by his mistress, Barbara Villiers.

In a letter to Cassandra in 1796, Jane, then twenty, mentioned *the kiss which C. Powlett wanted to give me.*[200] Nearly three years later she attended a dance he gave, *to the great disturbance of all his neighbours, of course, who, you know, take a most lively interest in the state of his finances, and live in hopes of his soon being ruined.*[201]

The dance was to celebrate Reverend Charles Powlett's second wedding anniversary. Jane described his wife, Anne Temple, as, *everything that the Neighbourhood could wish her, silly & cross as well as extravagant.*[202]

Five years later, James Austen invited the Powletts to dinner at the Deane rectory. He asked Jane and Martha Lloyd to join them, which Jane noted, *we did not fail to do. Mrs Powlett, she wrote to Cassandra, was at once expensively & nakedly dress'd; we have had the satisfaction of estimating her Lace & her Muslin; & she said too little to afford us much other amusement.*[203]

Conjecturing as to the date

Pride & Prejudice

Jane Austen celebrated the birth of Fanny Catherine, on 23 January 1793, with the four *Scraps.* Perhaps anticipating her birth, Jane had put together the stories in advance. *The first Act of a Comedy* and *A Tour through Wales* have a light heartedness and insouciance that set them apart from the first and third Scraps, *The female philosopher* and *A Letter from a Young Lady.*

Jane did not record Scraps in *Volume the Second* until 2 June 1793. Brian Southam noted that in the manuscript of *Volume the Second, The first Act of a Comedy* is written in a "calligraphic hand" while the other *Scraps* appear rushed and scribbled.[204] *The first Act of a Comedy* may have been drafted on loose sheets of paper to read at table in the rectory, sometime before Fanny's birth. Perhaps Jane selected it with *A Tour through Wales*, to soften the two more serious and aggressive *Scraps* that accompanied them.

Her own share in the story *Emma*

The First Act of a Comedy appears trivial and innocuous, but its backstory was actually a powerful and significant comment on the most irreparable and destructive parental decision in Jane Austen's life. Under pressure from her father she had acquiesced and abandoned her relationship with D'Arcy Wentworth.

In John Gay's *Beggars Opera,* Polly married a highwayman, Macheath, her parents disapprove of the match, and attempt to have him killed. Jane's father persuaded her to abandon D'Arcy after learning he had been charged with highway robbery, leaving D'Arcy to travel to the other side of the world without her.

Jane undercut her references to idyllic pastoral romances with the hard realities of infanticide, duped fathers and forced marriages. We do not imagine the Second Act will result in an uncomplicated happy marriage, but we will never know.

27

A Letter from a Young Lady, whose feelings being too Strong for her Judgement led her into the commission of Errors which her Heart disapproved.

Anna Parker's letter to her beloved *Ellinor* opens with her lament: *many have been the cares and vicissitudes of my past life.* She offers no explanation for her troubles, but the reader has been told, in the title of her letter, that it was her *feelings being too Strong for her Judgement that led her into the commission of Errors of which her Heart disapproved.*

Meditations on the contents of the letter   *Sense & Sensibility*

Anna feels bitterness about her past life, but takes full responsibility for her *cares and vicissitudes.* She states, *on a close examination of my conduct, I am convinced that I have strictly deserved them.*

She gives a devastating list of her crimes and misdemeanours: *I murdered my father at a very early period of my Life, I have since murdered my Mother, and I am now going to murder my Sister. I have changed my religion so often that at present I have not an idea of any left. I have been a perjured witness in every public trial for the last twelve years; and I have forged my own will. In short there is scarcely a crime that I have not committed –*

Anna declares, *I am now going to reform.* She has decided to marry Colonel Martin in a few days. *There is something Singular in our Courtship,* she tells Ellinor, and gives her *an account of it.*

Colonel Martin has acquired his fortune by disinheriting his elder brother. He forged a new will from his father and served it in Court, but no one believed his claim that his was the *right Will.*

Anna describes how she met the Colonel, and came to be complicit in his crime. She *happened to be passing the door of the Court, and was beckoned in by the Judge.* The Judge is corrupt, he tells the Colonel that she is *a Lady ready to witness anything for the cause of Justice, and advised him to apply to me. The Affair was soon adjusted,* Anna and the Colonel swore to *its' being the right Will,* and his elder brother was obliged to *resign all his illgotten Wealth.*

The Colonel is now *immensely* rich, the beneficiary of the bulk of his father's fortune, *about eight Million.* Anna tells Ellinor that, *in gratitude he waited on me the next day with an offer of his hand.*

This was a letter to supply matter for much reflection   *Mansfield Park*

In this, one of the more revealing stories in her *Juvenilia,* Jane Austen offers insights into the climate of criticism, distrust and humiliation that swirled around her, after the end of her relationship with D'Arcy Wentworth.

In many ways it is a follow up to her first piece in *Scraps, A female philosopher.* As Anna's misdemeanours are amplified and exaggerated, we hear the anger, recriminations and accusations directed at Jane by her family, and amplified by gossips like Louisa Bridges: that she was guilty of unthinkable crimes, she had destroyed her family's reputation, ruined her own life and future, she was damaged goods, unmarriageable.

Like Anna Parker, Jane Austen had made *a close examination* of her *conduct* and her conscience. She acknowledges she had hurt her father deeply in *a very early period of* her *life,* but she offers no justification for her behaviour, she is not seeking redemption.

Virginia Woolf recognised Jane Austen was telling her own story through her writing. After reading *Volume the Second*, she observed: *Never, even at the emotional age of fifteen, did she round upon herself in shame.*[205]

The marriage Anna offers as proof she has reformed addresses Jane's family's desire to see her married. This is not a quiet marriage to a timid country parson, she proposes to marry in London, in full splendour, to a Colonel of the Horseguards. Her marriage will not be one based on love or respect, but between high flying partners in crime. Jane is declaring: "You say I am bad – you don't know just how bad I can be!"

This is a marriage designed to mock and deride her critics, and those broadcasting her story abroad. It will vindicate their accusations of Jane, their repudiation of her relationship with D'Arcy Wentworth. They can state with confidence that Colonel Martin is exactly the type of man Jane would choose, one worthy of her, given she has already mired herself in fraud, theft and perjury.

Her own share in the story
Emma

Jane unfolds the letter with a bold, dramatic flourish, like so many of her *Juvenilia* stories, beneath its surface, it has a dark backstory.

In late October 1789, Jane and D'Arcy returned to London from Scotland. They took lodgings in Clipstone Street, off Great Portland Street, under the name of Wilson.

Their lodgings were not long a secret
Pride & Prejudice

On the last day of October, a man called Jack Day, came to see D'Arcy. He was in great pain, he had a gunshot wound under his arm. D'Arcy examined the wound, he probed it, but the bullet was too deep. He fetched a surgeon to examine the injured man, and together they took him to the Middlesex Hospital for treatment.

The surgeon was convinced that the man had received his wound from a person situated below him, as if he had been on horseback, and fired at from a post-chaise.[206]   Whitehall Evening Post

Two gentlemen had been stopped by a man on Hounslow Heath, who attempted to rob them; but one of the gentlemen knocked the pistol, which he presented, out of his hand, and immediately fired and wounded the highwayman, who made his escape. A suspicion arose that this person might be the highwayman who had been wounded on Hounslow Heath. They procured the description of those who went in the coach to the hospital with the man, when the officers immediately recognised the person of the famous D'Arcy Wentworth.[207]   Gazetteer & New Daily Advertiser

Two officers were sent to the hospital...but found the man had contrived to escape out of the window of the ward in which he was lodged. They then met with a surgeon, who said he had been called in to dress the wounds of a man, who said he had received them from a highwayman.

The surgeon informed them that he had been called on to go to No. 23 Clipstone Street, which he did; but found that the man's wounds had been dressed by the person who now appears to be Wentworth, who being originally a surgeon, had probed the wounds, but could not extract the ball. The medical gentleman who had been called in advised the man to go to the Hospital, where Wentworth took him in a Hackney coach, and left him in the name of John Smith.

On receiving this information, the proper officers repaired to Clipstone Street, but neither Mr Wentworth, who went by the name of Wilson, nor the woman who passed for his wife, by the name of Wilson, were within. They waited a short time, when Mrs Wilson, whose real name appears to be Weaver, came in.

They of course secured her; but a great crowd being collected about the door, they thought it necessary to take Mrs Wilson, alias Mrs Taylor, alias Mrs Weaver, away with them, as they knew Wentworth would not come home is he saw any mob around the door.[208]   Whitehall Evening Post

Jane Austen appeared in the Bow Street Magistrates Court before

Nicolas Bond, who noted her youth. Jane, a month short of turning fourteen, gave her name as Taylor, her age as not yet one and twenty. She was released without charge.

D'Arcy Wentworth was held on suspicion throughout November 1789, awaiting a witness with evidence for a prosecution. The Bow-street magistrates made great efforts to find a witness to prosecute or to supply evidence for a charge of highway robbery. The press even carried the unusual offer of a full pardon to a highwayman prepared to appear against him.

Notice having been given to a great many persons robbed, that W, was to be brought up for examination.[209] *The office was extremely crowded with Gentlemen.*[210]

The Times

For the rest of November, at least once a week, five times in all, D'Arcy was returned to Bow-street for further examination. These were well publicised beforehand, to attract people who might identify him.

Post-chaise drivers whose passengers had been robbed attended, in order to know if they could identify the prisoner, which however, they could not do; they all declaring that they had not the least recollection of his person.

Several Stable Keepers also attended, of whom it was supposed the prisoner had hired horses on the particular days on which the highway robberies had been committed; but in this also proofs were wanting; all the Stable Keepers but one declaring they did not know his person, and the one that did know the prisoner, said he had not let him a horse to hire these two years.

A great concourse of people attended the hearings, including the Duke and Duchess of Cumberland, brother and sister in law of the King, and the Duke of Hamilton, Scotland's premier peer. The head-dress worn by the Duchess of Cumberland at the Old Bailey, was strongly attractive – the hat was black beaver, exhibiting in front an enormous bow of deep, pink satin ribbons.[211]

The Times

Jane expected every day to see D'Arcy again. She wrote him lively, funny letters, wanting him to be cheered. Alone in their lodgings, afraid, out of her depth, with his encouragement, she returned to her writing.

I must relieve myself by writing *Lady Susan*

It was here Jane Austen wrote the second and last of her three London novels, *Frederic and Elfrida, Jack and Alice* and *Henry and Eliza*, not simple tales, but detached, dark, fantastical in part, filled with an awareness of the unrelenting upturns and complications of the world.

Jane Austen's first entries in the first volume of her *Juvenilia* were her London stories, along with *Edgar and Emma*, written on an earlier occasion when she was anxiously waiting for D'Arcy's release.

Jane wrote her London novels without inhibitions, these are not innocent stories they are *strong, spirited Sketches, full of variety & Glow*, quite at odds with *the little bit (two Inches wide) of ivory on that she worked with so fine a Brush*, in her later years.[212]

Jack and Alice and *Henry and Eliza* brim over with determination, violence and liveliness. At times abrupt and boisterous, their heroines are independent, courageous young women who break with conventions and restrictions, who follow their hearts and watch them being broken.

Her London novels are filled with sexual knowingness, Charlotte in *Frederic and Elfrida*, whose earnest desire to oblige, to not make anyone miserable, persuades her within a very short time, to promise to *become the Wife* of two different men. After reflecting on her folly, she suicides, throwing herself into a deep stream.

The stories contain a wealth of violent episodes. In *Frederic and Elfrida*, Captain Roger threatens Rebecca's mother with a dagger, *that shall be steeped in your hearts blood*, if she does not agree to him marrying Rebecca. In *Jack and Alice*, Charles Adams sets a steel trap that breaks Lucy's leg when she tries to approach his house; Sukey Simpson tries to cut Lucy's throat and finally kills her with poison.

Henry and Eliza opens with landowners, Sir George and Lady Harcourt, *punishing the idleness of their Haymakers* with a cudgel, Lady Harcourt abandons her baby girl, exposing her to the weather beneath a Haycock. Eliza is *seized by the officers of the Dutchess* and conducted by them to a *snug little Newgate, barred with iron*.

At the end of *Henry and Eliza*, where Eliza *demolishes the Dutchess's Newgate and gains the Blessings of thousands*, we hear Jane's confidence that D'Arcy would be released, they would continue their life together, that she was never going back to Steventon and her mother.

Dwelling on some passages which proved that Jane had not written in spirits

Pride & Prejudice

It was from London, in mid-November 1789, as she waited for the Court to release D'Arcy from Newgate, that Jane wrote another spoof letter to her brother James, editor of *The Loiterer*, she signed this one Margaret Mitten.

Ms Mitten's letter ended: *I intend shortly paying you a visit to Oxford; where your publisher will direct me to your Rooms, and where I trust we shall quickly settle matters to our mutual satisfaction; for as I before told you, I am sure that it is destined by fate, that I am to be Mrs. Loiterer: in hopes of which I remain.*

Ms Mitten was coy about her age: *Such, Mr Loiterer, as I am, and in my thirty – but no matter my age, I am ready to become yours. Mr Loiterer,* the editor, James Austen, inserted a tongue-in-cheek reply below her letter, *I do not answer the description she has given in the smallest particular and that it is impossible for me to accept her intended kindness, as I have the misfortune to be a Fellow of a College.*

Jane had not written home for some time. She knew each issue of *The Loiterer* was eagerly received at the Steventon rectory. Ms Mitten's letter may in large part have been intended to assure her father all was well, which it certainly wasn't. It seems to have had the opposite effect. Did he read something more deeply, or was it her mock flirtatious, knowing tone that persuaded George Austen to leave Steventon to look for her?

Jane had given a misleading address, the Precincts, Canterbury, beside Canterbury Cathedral, where Anne Lefroy's mother, Mrs Jemima Brydges lived. After learning she was not in Canterbury, George Austen went to London, he searched for her, but did not find her.

Guilty of such an enormity at so early an age *Pride & Prejudice*

It was Cassandra who told George Austen that Jane had appeared before a magistrate. Jane's anger resounds through the closing words of the letter, as Anna renews her threat: *I am now going to murder my Sister.*

We know the sisters were reconciled. After Jane's death when her family burnt most of her private papers, Cassandra kept many letters Jane had written to her over the years. Though she took the scissors to bits of them she did keep a record of Jane's exasperation with her, when she wrote — *Do pray meet with someone belonging to yourself. I am quite weary of your knowing nobody.*[213]

In her last completed novel, *Persuasion*, Jane wrote of the opposition of her family to D'Arcy, and of Cassandra's disloyalty: *her father's ill-will... unsoftened by one kind word or look on the part of her sister...She was persuaded to believe the engagement a wrong thing: indiscreet, improper, hardly capable of success, and not deserving it.*[214]

28

A Tour through Wales –
In a Letter from a young Lady -

This last of three letters in *Scraps* is a comic nonsense tale. Elizabeth Johnson thanks Clara for her letter, and explains why her reply is so late. For the past month, she and her sister have been on a ramble through Wales, accompanying their mother. *We travelled on horseback by preference. My Mother rode upon our little poney and Fanny and I walked by her side or rather ran, for my Mother is so fond of riding fast that She galloped all the way. You may be sure that we were in a fine perspiration when we came to our place of resting.*

As she ran, Fanny made *a great Many Drawings of the Country.* Elizabeth tells Clara, they *are very beautiful,* though *perhaps not such exact resemblances as might be wished, from their being taken as she ran along.*

The two girls had each taken an extra pair of shoes, but, as Elizabeth tells Clara: *it would astonish you to see all the Shoes we wore out on our Tour ... we were obliged to have them both capped and heelpeiced as Carmarthen, and at last when they were quite gone, Mama was so kind as to lend us a pair of blue Sattin Slippers.*

Elizabeth and Fanny *hopped home from Hereford delightfully* wearing one slipper each. With this comical picture of the two sisters, hopping along on one foot, shod in a blue satin slipper, struggling to keep abreast of their mother, galloping along on horseback, *A Tour through Wales,* a miniature burlesque, ends – *delightfully.*

Of the five *Scraps* Jane Austen dedicated to her newborn neice Fanny, this is the one with appeal for a small child.

Her own share in the story
Emma

In *A Tour through Wales,* Jane Austen gave a comic glimpse of a mother's self-centred approach to mothering. While she enjoys the comfort of a horse and the joy of riding fast, her daughters must run along in her wake, struggling to keep up. Finally, footsore, their shoes ruined, their mother gives them a pair of her satin slippers, to share between them.

The scene has echoes of an Austen family story, of their parents' move from the rectory at Deane to the Steventon rectory in 1771. Mrs Austen made the journey of two and a bit miles: *on a feather bed placed upon some soft articles of furniture in the waggon which held their household goods.*[215] It seems Jane's mother was not someone who could cope with any discomfort!

The names of people that fill up my time
Mansfield Park

Carmarthen, where the three ramblers stop, and the two girls have their shoes repaired, *capped and heelpeiced,* is believed to be the oldest town in Wales, situated on the south coast, on the River Towy.

During the Wars of the Roses, Edmund Tudor took possession of Carmarthen Castle for the House of Lancaster. In August 1456, troops loyal to the House of York captured and imprisoned him there. Edmund died in Carmarthen Castle, most likely of plague, leaving his thirteen year-old widow, Lady Margaret Beaufort, seven months pregnant with their son. In 1485, he was crowned King Henry VII, first monarch of the House of Tudor. He would *have the happiness of being great-grandfather to one of the first Characters in the World, Mary Queen of Scots.*

29

A Tale

This tale about two brothers and the purchase of a small cottage in Pembrokeshire, in Wales, is a simple story that contains a little nonsense and some coincidences.

Robertus promises his younger brother Wilhelminus, that if he buys *a small house near the borders of an extensive Forest and about three Miles from the Sea,* he will furnish two rooms and a Closet for him. Wilhelminus gladly accepts his offer and spends some time looking for the right property.

One morning he sees an advertisement in the paper:
To be Lett. A neat cottage on the borders of an extensive Forest and about three Miles from the Sea. It is ready furnished except two rooms and a Closet.

Wilhelminus shows the advertisement to Robertus, who *sent him in his Carriage to take possession of the Cottage.* Wilhelminus travels three days and *Six Nights without Stopping,* to the forest, where he follows a track alongside it, *down a steep Hill over which ten Rivulets meandered, and reached the Cottage in half an hour.*

He knocked on the door, there was no answer so he lifted the latch and went inside. He found himself in a small unfurnished room, *he proceeded into a Closet equally bare,* went upstairs into an unfurnished room above, and realised he had seen through the entire house. It comprised just *two rooms and a Closet,* there was nothing *ready furnished.* He was pleased with it as it was, *as he would not be obliged to lay out any thing on furniture himself.*

He returned *to his Brother, who took him the next day to every Shop in Town,* and bought everything to furnish *the two rooms and the Closet.*

In a few days everything was completed, and Wilhelminus returned to take possession of his Cottage. Though the cottage was advertised for rent, we were told in the opening sentence that the Gentleman *bought a small Cottage in Pembrokeshire,* so we might guess that Wilhelminus completed his purchase in the few days, before returning to his cottage.

Robertus and his wife Cecilia accompanied him, along with her two sisters, Arabella and Marina, and a large number of servants. Robertus anticipates his whole party can be accommodated there. He had offered to furnish part of a cottage, never imagining it would comprise just *two rooms and the Closet.*

Wilhelminus had not told him the cottage could not accommodate the number of people in his party. The reason may have been his tender attachment to Cecilia's sister Marina.

The narrator observes, *Where an ordinary Genius might probably have been embarrassed at endeavouring to accommodate so large a party,* Wilhelminus, undaunted orders the immediate erection of *two Noble tents in an open spot in the Forest adjoining the house.*

His *noble Tents* are a *Couple of old blankets, each supported by four Sticks.* The narrator, with increasing irony, describes their *Construction as both simple and elegant, striking proof* of Wilhelminus' *Taste for Architecture* and his *happy ease in overcoming difficulties,* some of his *most striking Virtues.* The condescension in these final comments says a great deal.

We never learn if Robertus' party camped outside under the *noble Tents*. If they did, we can only trust it did not rain.

Conscious superiority rather than any solicitude to oblige   *Mansfield Park*

Jane Austen's *Tale* describes the relationship between two brothers, the elder wealthy, sociable and worldly, the younger, a loser. There is nothing unfriendly or malicious in their relationship, they appear to have come to a mutually acceptable arrangement.

Robertus offered Wilhelminus a financial incentive to leave Town and live somewhere remote from him, beside *an extensive Forest* near the sea. The cottage is a non-stop journey of three days and six nights from Town. Robertus can be confident his brother won't return too often to bother or embarrass him.

There was something in the name   *Emma*

The names Wilhelminus and Robertus read like nicknames schoolboys might give each other as they pile out of their Classics class, attaching Latin suffixes to each other's names. Wilhelminus is the Latinate version of William, Robertus the Latin for Robert.

Latin was still the language of the clergy, used in formal church documents and on the gravestones of the nobility and clergy. Jane may have seen the name Wilhelminus Lloyd in the Fowle's sunlit church of St Mary the Virgin at Kintbury, where he was rector from 1713 to 1719.

Robertus has a *–us* suffix indicating he is masculine. He is the elder brother, more motivated, wealthier, more sociable — he arrives *with a large number of Attendants,* and brings a group of friends with him to stay at the cottage.

The *minus* suffix indicates Wilhelminus is the younger of the two brothers. He lacks Robertus' confidence and his resources, he is less energetic and more solitary. He defers to Robertus and follows his directions to the letter, though he is *by no means displeased* with the tiny cottage, and will have nothing to pay for furniture.

Her own share in the story
Emma

Given the prickly nature of a number of the stories in *Scraps*, *A Tale* raises questions of its own. Was Jane describing the relationship between two of her own brothers in this story? Was Edward the likely model for Robertus? We gather from Jane's correspondence that he of all her brothers was wealthy, sociable and worldly, and possessed a degree of cynicism.

If Robertus was a snapshot of Edward, who was Wilhelminus, the younger brother, meant to represent? It could have been any one of his three younger brothers, Henry, Frank or Charles, though Frank's full name was Francis William Austen.

Preferring the country to every other place
Northanger Abbey

In *A Tale*, Jane Austen sends up a fashion of the time, the acquisition of a cottage in the country, near the sea.[216] In *Sense & Sensibility*, first drafted in 1795, two years after *Scraps*, she had Robert Ferrars, vain, *silly and a great coxcomb*, praise the comfort and elegance of a cottage: *For my own part," said he, "I am excessively fond of a cottage; there is always so much comfort, so much elegance about them. And I protest, if I had any money to spare, I should buy a little land and build one myself, within a short distance of London, where I might drive myself down at any time, and collect a few friends about me, and be happy. I advise every body who is going to build, to build a cottage.*[217]

Conjecturing as to the date
Pride & Prejudice

Jane Austen probably sent a copy of *Scraps* to Edward and Elizabeth shortly after Fanny Catherine was born at *Rowling*, on 23 January 1793. She recorded *Scraps* in *Volume the Second*, sometime later, on 2nd June 1793. Beneath *A Tale*, she signed off, *Finis, End of Second Volume.*

Her own family & friends

Fanny, Jane's first born niece lived in Kent, more than a hundred miles away. Jane followed her progress and communicated with her mostly by letter, often through Cassandra who stayed for long periods at *Rowlings*, and later at *Godmersham*, helping out with Edward and Elizabeth's rapidly growing family.

Fanny was five in 1798, when Jane asked Cassandra, *Pray give her a kiss from me.* On her sixth birthday Jane wished her, *many returns of this day & may she on every return enjoy as much pleasure as she is now receiving from her doll's beds.* Later that year Fanny asked for a printed letter, which she rather thought she would answer.[218]

At age twelve, Jane declared her to be *the happiest Being in the world.* At fifteen, Jane wrote to Cassandra at *Godmersham. I found her this summer – almost a sister & could not have supposed that a niece would ever have been so much to me. She is quite after one's own heart, give her my best love.* The day after Jane wrote this letter, Fanny's mother Elizabeth Austen died, after delivering her eleventh child. Fanny, the eldest, at fifteen, had to grow up quickly.[219]

At sixteen, Fanny offered Cassandra her opinion of Jane's writing. Jane, amused, replied: *I am gratified by her having pleasure in what I write but I wish the knowledge of my being exposed to her discerning criticism may not hurt my stile. I begin already to weigh my words & sentences more than I did & am looking about for a sentiment, an illustration or a metaphor in every corner of the room.*[220]

In February 1813, Fanny read *Pride and Prejudice*, and wrote to Jane to say she liked Darcy and Elizabeth. Cassandra passed a more exact truth to Jane, who declared it, *good enough.* Later that year Jane spent two days with Fanny in London, shopping, visiting the theatre, the dentist, choosing music to play and seeing art exhibitions, where they looked for portraits of Mrs Bingley, Miss and Mrs Darcy.

Later that year, at *Godmersham*, Jane declared, i*n this house there is a constant succession of small events, somebody is always coming or going.* She told Cassandra, *yesterday Fanny and I sat down to breakfast with six gentlemen to admire us.*[221]

In November 1814, Fanny, now twenty-one, wrote asking Jane's advice about true love. Jane, amazed and delighted, replied, asking her to keep their correspondence secret from Cassandra. *What strange creatures we are!... Dear Fanny, your mistake has been one that thousands of women fall into. He was the first young Man who attached himself to you. That was the charm, & most powerful it is.*[222]

A fortnight later, she wrote again, *Nothing can be compared to the misery of being bound without Love, bound to one, & preferring another. That is a punishment which you do not deserve.*[223]

Fanny took her advice. Three years later she wrote again for advice on resolving difficulties with a new lover. We can sense Jane's delight in her reply: *My dearest Fanny, you are inimitable, irresistible. You are the delight of my Life. Such Letters, such entertaining Letters as you have lately sent! – Such a description or your queer little heart! – such a lovely display of what Imagination does. – You are worth your weight in Gold, or even in new Silver Coinage. I cannot express to you what I have felt in reading your history of yourself, how full of Pity & Concern & Admiration & Amusement I have been.*

You are the paragon of all that is Silly & Sensible, common-place and eccentric, Sad & Lively, Provoking & Interesting. – Who can keep pace with the fluctuations of your Fancy, the Capprizios of your Taste, the Contradictions of your Feelings!..You can hardly think what a pleasure it is to me, to have such thorough pictures of your Heart.[224]

Jane's advice was clear, *You are not in love with him. You never have been really in love with him. Depend upon it the right Man will come at last... who will so completely attach you, that you will feel you never really loved before... Adieu my dearest Fanny. – Nothing could be more delicious than your Letter; & the assurance of your feeling relieved by writing it, made the pleasure perfect.*[225]

Jane did not live to see her words come true. In 1820, three years after her death, Fanny, now twenty-seven, married widower, Sir Edward Knatchbull, she became stepmother to his six children and she bore him nine more.

When her cousin James Edward Austen Leigh was writing his *Memoir of Jane Austen*, he asked his sisters and cousins for input. Fanny refused to share her letters from Jane with him.[226]

In 1869, the year his *Memoir* was published, Fanny wrote to her younger sister Marianne, countering James Edward's description of Jane, *to speak the truth* as she remembered it: *Jane,* she wrote, *was not so refined as she ought to have been from her talent...They were not rich and the people around them with whom they chiefly mixed, were not at all high bred, or in short anything more than mediocre & they of course tho' superior in mental powers & cultivation were on the same level as far as refinement goes... Aunt Jane was too clever not to put aside all possible signs of "common-ness" (if such an expression is allowable) & teach herself to be more refined.*

Both the Aunts were brought up in the most complete ignorance of the World & its ways (I mean as to fashion etc) & if it had not been for Papa's marriage which brought them into Kent... they would have been, tho' not less clever & agreeable in themselves, very much below par as to good Society & its ways.[227]

By 1869, Jane had been dead for more than fifty years, Fanny was now seventy-six. Her snobbery and disloyalty to Jane reveal something of the attitude of her mother, Elizabeth Bridges, one of the six Bridges sisters, who were a key part of the society of *Godmersham*. Jane had told Cassandra, *They were very civil to me, as they always are*, but Fanny confirmed what Jane knew - she was not welcome, she would never be accepted there.

Tell-tale compression of the pages
Northanger Abbey

After *Scraps*, five leaves were cut from the manuscript of *Volume the*

Second. Perhaps Jane Austen decided she had completed this volume and could use the remaining paper elsewhere. The stubs, at the end of the notebook, are still visible in the binding. In all, twenty-four pages were cut from *Volume the Second*.

Juvenilia,
Volume the Third

The third and last volume of Jane Austen's *Juvenilia*, a small quarto notebook with seventy leaves, a hundred and forty pages, is held with *Volume the Second*, in the British Library in London. George Austen, Jane's father, is believed to have written his endorsement in pencil on the inner front cover: *Effusions of Fancy by a very Young Lady consisting of Tales in a Style entirely new.*

Volume the Third contains just two stories, *Evelyn and Kitty, or the Bower.* They are less frenetic than many in the earlier volumes, but family authority is ever present, overshadowing young people; disapproving parents and guardians watch every move, determined to assert control over youthful spontaneity and desire.

Jane wrote the date, May 6th 1792, at the beginning of the volume, and dated her dedication of *Kitty, or the Bower*, August 1792. This was her last entry in *Volume the Third*, her interest in adding to the *Juvenilia* was waning, though after this date, she recorded ten more pieces in the earlier volumes.

A year later, it seems Jane Austen was eager to finish. After recording *A Collection of Letters*, six months had passed since she had added anything to *Volume the Second*. On June 2nd 1793, she added five short *Scraps* and declared it complete. On the same day, she returned to *Volume the First*, after an interval of nearly a year and a half, and transcribed *Detached Pieces*, dedicated to her niece, Jane Anna Elizabeth Austen, to celebrate her birth seven weeks earlier. Next day she recorded her only poem in the *Juvenilia, Ode to Pity, completing Volume the First*.

Cassandra Austen inherited the three volumes of Jane's *Juvenilia*, they remained together, in her care, for twenty eight years until her death in 1845. She left *Volume the First* to her youngest brother, Charles, *Volume the Second* to the second youngest, Frank, and *Volume the Third* to James Edward Austen-Leigh, only son of her eldest brother James, who had died in 1819, two years after Jane.

Volume the Third remained in the Austen-Leigh family until the late 1980s. After receiving permission from the family in 1949, R.W. Chapman transcribed, edited and published it in 1951. It was the last volume of the *Juvenilia* to be released, a hundred and fifty nine years after it was completed, one hundred and thirty four years after Jane Austen's death.

In 1953, *Volume the Third* was deposited in the British Museum. It was sold by Sotheby's in 1976 to the British Rail Pension Fund for £30,000, and sold in 1988, again by Sotheby's, to the British Library, for £120,000.[228]

30

Evelyn
a Novel

Jane Austen dedicated *Evelyn* to Miss Mary Lloyd (1771-1843), four years older than her, and youngest of the three Lloyd sisters, after Martha and Eliza.

In January 1792, the Lloyds left the Deane rectory, to make room for James Austen to move there with his bride Anne Mathew, after their marriage in March. They had found a suitable house to rent at Ibthorpe, in the parish of Hurstbourne Tarrant, thirty miles south of Steventon, across the North Wessex Downs.

Jane made Mary Lloyd a farewell present, a little sewing kit of *flowered silk*. Mary's son described it *as a very small bag*, inside it was *a little rolled up housewife, furnished with minikin needles and fine thread*. Jane had sewn *a tiny pocket* inside the housewife, *in the pocket she enclosed a slip of paper, on which, written as with a crow quill*, was a little verse to her friend:
This little bag, I hope, will prove
To be not vainly made;

For should you thread and needles want,
It will afford you aid.
And, as we are about to part,
'T will serve another end:
For, when you look upon this bag,
You'll recollect your friend.

Jane Austen probably wrote *Evelyn* around this time, and dedicated it to Mary, as part of her farewell. The story of finding a house in an attractive village, with its manicured orderly landscape, could refer to discussions had while the Lloyds were searching for a house to rent, before they vacated the rectory at Deane.

James Austen's wife Anne died suddenly in May 1795, leaving a two year old daughter Anna. By January 1796, Jane noted *the very great improvement which has lately taken place in James' dancing.*[229] In September 1796, she pondered, *which of the Marys will carry the day with my Brother James.*[230] A few months later, she had her answer, in January 1797, James and Mary returned to live in the Deane rectory.

Eliza de Feuillide reported: *James has chosen a second wife in the person of Miss Mary Lloyd, who is not either rich or handsome but very sensible & good humoured. Jane seems much pleased with the match, and it is natural she should, having long known & liked the Lady.*[231]

Conjecturing as to the date   *Pride & Prejudice*

Evelyn was the first story Jane Austen recorded in *Volume the Third*. She marked the date, May 6th 1792, on the Contents page.

There was something in the name   *Emma*

Jane Austen named this story a *Novel*, and the fictional village at its heart, *Evelyn*, in honour of John Evelyn (1620-1706) the Restoration garden designer, traveller, diarist, poet, pamphleteer, and member of the Royal Society, said by Samuel Pepys to be a *little conceited.*

Educated at Balliol College, Oxford, and the Middle Temple, at age twenty, on 12th May 1641, John Evelyn witnessed the beheading of D'Arcy Wentworth's kinsman, Thomas Wentworth, 1st Earl of Strafford: *I beheld on Tower-hill the fatal stroke which severed the wisest head in England from the shoulders of the Earl of Strafford, whose crime coming under the cognizance of no human law or statute, a new one was made, not to be a precedent, but his destruction. With what reluctancy the king signed the execution, he has sufficiently expressed: to which he imputes his own unjust suffering – to such exorbitancy were things arrived.*

Next year, Evelyn went abroad, to avoid the excesses of the Civil War. For five years, he explored France and Italy, becoming acquainted with many of their original scientific thinkers. He studied anatomy in Padua, where he purchased four anatomical preparations, displaying different systems within the human body, arteries, veins and nerves. In 1667, he presented them to the Royal Society.[232]

In 1652, Evelyn settled in Deptford, near the naval dockyard. There he *devoted most of his time to gardening, fruit and tree culture.* In 1660, he was one of the principal founders of the Royal Society.

In 1661, he published the first book to address the growing problem of air pollution in London, *The Inconvenience of the Aer & Smoake of London Dissipated*, in which he recommended removing certain trades, and planting a ring of fragrant trees around the city. In 1664, he published *Sylva, or a Discourse on Forest Trees;* by 1825, it had run through ten editions.

John Evelyn's diary, from 1640 to 1706, was published in 1818, seven years before that of his contemporary, Samuel Pepys. He described the execution of Charles I, the rise and death of Oliver Cromwell, the last great Plague of London, and the Great Fire of London in 1666. Both he and Christopher Wren submitted plans to Charles II, to rebuild London after the Great Fire. Evelyn had encouraged Wren to rebuild St Paul's, after the fire, with a cupola.

Generosity overstrained

Evelyn opens with a *Gentleman*, Mr Gower, arriving on horseback in the village of Evelyn, *in a retired part of the County of Sussex.* He puts up at the *little Alehouse,* and asks *the Landlady* if there is a house to let in the village.

The innkeeper, Mrs Willis, seems unwilling to answer him, but realising he is agitated, she offers him *the friendly balm of Comfort and Assistance.* Her offer *serves to make him the more warmly wish for a house in this sweet village. – What would I not give to be your Neighbour, to be blessed with your Acquaintance, and with the farther knowledge of your virtues!*

Mrs Willis, *an amiable Woman,* tells him there are no vacancies, *every house in this village, from the sweetness of the situation, & the purity of the Air, in which neither Misery, Illhealth, or Vice are ever wafted, is inhabited.*

After a pause, she directs him to a family, with a peculiar *Generosity of Disposition, who may be willing to oblige him with their house.* He approaches the house, and is *delighted with its situation,* and its *uncommonly striking* appearance, placed in the centre of highly ordered geometric landscape, with its trees, shrubs, gravel paths, and even the cows forming an integrated design.

Mr Gower rang the doorbell and was ushered upstairs to meet Mrs Webb, the lady of the house. She plies him with delicious food: *chocolate, venison pasty, sandwiches, a Basket of Fruit, Ices, a bason of Soup, Jellies and Cakes.* Telling him *"Believe me you are welcome to everything that is in my power to bestow,"* she hands him her purse, adding that her husband will bring him a hundred pounds.

Mr Gower, *put the purse in his pocket and accepted her offer of the hundred pounds, he tasted something of all the dishes she proffered, and pocketted the rest.* Mr and Mrs Webb next conducted him *into the dining parlour, where he eat a most excellent Dinner and partook of the most exquisite Wines.*

Mr Webb asks, *tell us what you wish more to receive.* Gower replies, *"Give* me then your house and Grounds; I ask for nothing else." "It is yours, exclaimed both at once; from this moment it is yours."

The Webbs prepare to leave the house, ring for a Carriage, have their *Young Ladies* called, and assure Mr Gower, *Best of men, we will not long intrude upon your time.* He replies, *You are welcome to stay this half hour.*

Mrs Webb introduces him to her two daughters, one seventeen. the other several years younger, telling them: *Our dear friend Mr Gower – He has been so good as to accept of this house, small as it is, & to promise to keep it for ever.*

Mr Gower suggests that *if they would complete their generosity by giving me their elder daughter with a handsome portion, I should have nothing more to wish for.*

Mr Webb responds: *Take our girl, take our Maria, and on her the difficult task must fall, of endeavouring to make some return to so much Benefiscence. Her fortune is but ten thousand pounds, almost too small a sum to be offered. This objection however being instantly removed by the generosity of Mr Gower, who declared himself satisfied with the sum mentioned.*

The Webbs and their younger daughter took their leave, next day Mr Gower and Maria were married.[233] *This amiable man now found himself perfectly happy; united to a very lovely and deserving young woman, with a handsome fortune, an elegant house, settled in the village of Evelyn, and by that means enabled to cultivate his acquaintance with Mrs Willis.*

Some months later, while Mr Gower and Maria were walking in the shrubbery, she offered him a rose from the garden, saying *"Pray take this charming rose."*

He was immediately reminded of his sister Rose. Her *heart had been engaged by the attentions and charms of a young Man whose high rank and expectations seemed to foretell objections from his Family to a match which would be highly desirable to theirs.*

The young man was required to return home to his *family seat in Sussex.*

His angry father learning he was determined to marry Rose, sent him *for a fortnight to the Isle of Wight...with the hope of overcoming his Constancy by Time and Absence in a foreign Country.* The young *Nobleman was not allowed to see his Rosa.. He prepared to bid a long adieu to England.. They set sail – A storm arose which baffled the arts of the Seamen. The vessel was wrecked on the coast of Calshot and every Soul on board perished.*

When Rose received the news, *she was affected by it, beyond the power of Expression.* Mr Gower, *the only son of a very large Family,* had been on his way to see the young man's Father, hoping to *soften her affliction by obtaining a picture of her unfortunate Lover. The pleasing events which befell him in Evelyn had for a while made him totally forget the object of his Journey.*

Mr Gower *bitterly repented his neglect...agitated by Greif, Apprehension and Shame* he wrote to Rosa, four months after he had left their home in Carlisle. His letter reflects his agitation, he tells Rose it would be unjust to accuse him of *Neglect and Forgetfulness,* but he blushes to *own the truth of her accusation.* He tells her not to *suppose* he *could for a moment forget her situation,* and that he *will forget her no longer.* He twice asks Rose if she is *still alive,* if she is, he will hasten as soon as possible to the Castle *of her unfortunate Lover.* He signs off with *every dutiful and affectionate wish,* from himself and Maria.

After an anxious wait, a reply arrived, *it came not from Rosa,* the thirteenth daughter, but from another sister. She tells Mr Gower that Rose *has been dead these six weeks,* that his *Silence* had *hastened her to her Grave.* She chides him for not saying where he has been since he left Carlisle, and for not accounting for his *tedious absence.* She signs off with compliments from them all to Maria, and begs to know who she is.

The news of his sister's death, which Mr Gower was *obliged to attribute to his own conduct,* caused him so violent a shock to his feelings, he was attacked by a fit of the gout. But with *the unremitting attentions* of Maria, he slowly recovered.

As soon as he was well enough, *Mr Gower mounted his horse, and rode to*

— *Castle*. He had abandoned his original plan to obtain a picture of Henry, to give to Rose. Now *he wished to find whether his Lordship softened by his Son's death, might have been brought to consent to the match, had both he and Rosa been alive.*

Late in the evening he arrives at the castle, situated on a woody eminence commanding a beautiful prospect of the Sea. Mr Gower found its situation greatly inferior to that of his own house, he thought it required a Paddock, like his own, to form a Contrast and enliven the structure. *The gloomy appearance of the old Castle, and the winding approach, struck him with terror.*

Mr Gower is received by Lord — *with all the politeness of a well bred man.* Mr Gower tells him that, for the satisfaction of his Family, he wishes to know whether the death of his son, Henry, and his own unfortunate sister, Rosa, *this unhappy Pair,* has affected Lord — sufficiently, for him to consent to their Marriage, if they were still alive.

His Lordship seemed lost in astonishment. Lady — could not support the mention of her Son, and left the room in tears; the rest of the Family remained attentively listening, almost persuaded Mr Gower was mad.

His Lordship replied, *this is a very odd question.* He told Mr Gower, he was *supposing an impossibility.* If he were to suppose them alive, it would destroy any *Motive for a change in his sentiments concerning the affair.* In short, even if they were alive he would still not consent to their marriage.

Mr Gower replied angrily, *My Lord, I see you are a most inflexible Man, and that not even the death of your Son can make you wish his future Life happy. He wished them all a good Night and immediately left the room... leaving the whole Company unanimous in their opinion of his being mad.*

He mounted *his horse* and as the *great Gates of the Castle shut him out, he felt a universal tremor through out his whole frame.* He rode *almost distracted with his fears, with no house within a quarter of a mile, and a Gloomy castle blackened by the deep shade of Walnuts and Pines, behind him,* shutting his eyes as he rode, until he *arrived at the Village.*

Her own share in the story *Emma*

The most lively and compelling portion of *Evelyn* is the scene of insistent and extraordinary gift giving by the Webbs. Was Jane Austen satirising her parents' desire to see her married, mocking their eagerness to encourage any suitor they thought respectable, suggesting they would invite even a complete stranger to take her?

Jane had allowed for a blush in the *cheeks of the lovely Miss Webb*, but her parents showed no interest in her wishes. Mr Webb gave away his money, his house, and his daughter — without her consent, to a stranger looking for a house to let. After handing her to him, the Webbs left, without any concern for her future.

Jane's mother had applauded her relationship with D'Arcy, and the prospect of their marriage. After Christmas 1789, when her father ruled their Scottish marriage was never to be mentioned, Jane came under increasing pressure to marry. Her parents, and friends such as Anne Lefroy introduced her to a stream of eligible young men, mostly members of the clergy.

Jane resisted these overtures, she considered herself indissolubly bound to D'Arcy Wentworth. After he sailed, she had scanned the newspapers for any mention of him, the *Neptune*, or of New South Wales. *She had only navy lists and newspapers for her authority.*[234] For years she had counted the days, waiting to see him again, *she felt the want of his society every day, almost every hour.*[235]

In *Evelyn*, Jane Austen described the absolute power of two fathers over their children. Their expectations, the power they wield within the family, and the way there is taken for granted, are all condemned in the story.

Admiration of landscape scenery has become a mere jargon *Sense & Sensibility*

The theme of men preoccupied with houses and landscape was one Austen had used in *A Tale*. She revisited it in *Mansfield Park*, and returned to it with greater emphasis in her last unfinished novel, *Sanditon*.

Both *A Tale* and *Evelyn* are stories about men who follow trajectories set by others, propelled by their demands. In the end, both Wilhelminus and Mr Gower are seen as fools, each finds himself in a greater muddle, of his own making. Jane Austen's attempts at comedy in both stories do not work, they simply fall flat.

Evelyn is a tragic burlesque, full of irony, exaggeration and other attempts at comedy. Jane Austen ridicules the preoccupation of the time with the aesthetics of landscape. She contrasts the effects on Mr Gower of the ordered modernity and overdesigned landscape around the Webb's house, with *the irregularity in the fall of ground around the Gloomy Castle, blackened by the deep shade of Walnut and Pines.*

Mr Gower is dull and acquisitive, he pockets everything the Webb family offers, including their daughter Maria, *he obtains a lovely and deserving young woman, with an handsome fortune, an elegant house, settled in the village of Evelyn, and by that means enabled to cultivate his acquaintance with Mrs Willis,* the landlady at the Alehouse.

Mrs Willis directed Mr Evelyn to the Webb's house after his appeal to her: *What would I not give to be your Neighbour, to be blessed with your Acquaintance, and with the farther knowledge of your virtues! Oh! with what pleasure would I form myself by such an example! Tell me then, best of Women, is there no possibility? – I cannot speak – you know my meaning-.* Jane Austen did not develop the subplot of Mr Evelyn's pursuit of Mrs Willis; it would have added a greater dimension and a certain coarseness to his character, perhaps hinting at it was sufficient.

The choicest gift
Persuasion

Margaret Doody[236] put forward a view that the *Juvenilia* questions *the new enlightened capitalism* of the eighteenth century. At the heart of *enlightened capitalism* was the work of Adam Smith, who defined the clear distinction between a gift and a transaction: *it is not from the benevolence of the butcher, the brewer, or the baker that we expect our dinner, but from their regard for their own interest.*

Shawn Normandin points out the young Jane Austen *depended upon gifts,* her *economic precariousness made her especially sensitive to problems of giving.* He asks if, *by imagining the gift, does she teach us that what usually passes for giving is self-serving hypocrisy? Or does she reveal the disingenuousness of the Enlightenment's separation of gift from exchange? This separation, taken literally, bequeaths the gift to madmen under a starry sky. He suggests that Evelyn: may be Western literature's keenest examination of the gift – because, not in spite of, its absurd frivolity.*[237]

Such a prodigious act of Generosity
Letters

Mrs Knight, the widow of Thomas Knight, who adopted Jane's brother Edward, was an early benefactor of Jane Austen. In a letter to Cassandra, Jane acknowledged her kindness, and recognised that her gift of money was also a Fee. Mrs Knight wanted Jane to visit her in Canterbury. *This morning brought me a letter from Mrs Knight, containing the usual Fee, & all the usual Kindness. She asks me to spend a day or two with her this week...& I believe I will go...Her very agreeable present will make my circumstances quite easy. I shall reserve half for my Pelisse...I sent my answer to Mrs Knight, my double acceptance of her note & her invitation.*[238]

Names, facts, every thing mentioned
Pride & Prejudice

If Jane used the name Webb to suggest a spider's web, Mrs Webb is the female spider, she is at the centre of circle, she lays the trap, welcoming Mr Gower: *Welcome best of Men – Welcome to this House, and to every thing it contains. She sends the servant to: tell your Master of the happiness I enjoy – invite him to partake of it.*

Jane Austen gave the hero of *Evelyn*, the name of a prominent and very wealthy Tory family, the Leveson-Gowers. John Leveson-Gower (1675-1709), made 1st Baron Gower in 1703. His son and grandson progressed further up the ranks of the English peerage. His son, John Leveson-Gower (1694-1754), 2nd Baron Gower, a prominent Tory politician, was made Viscount Trentham and 1st Earl Gower in 1746. His grandson, Granville Leveson-Gower (1721-1803) was made 1st Marquis of Stafford in 1786.

Granville Leveson-Gower who served the Parliament as Lord President and Lord Privy Seal, was said to have inherited a talent for *absorbing heiresses*. His first wife, Elizabeth Fazackerley, came with a dowry of £20,000. His second wife, Lady Louisa Egerton, with a dowry of £10,000. Through her, his son, George Granville Leveson-Gower, the future 1st Duke of Sutherland, gained control of the profits of the Bridgewater Canal. The eldest daughter of his third marriage, to Lady Susanna Stewart, Lady Georgiana Augusta Leveson-Gower, married William Eliot, 2nd Earl of St. Germans. Jane used his name for another unpleasant character in *Persuasion*.

Jane Austen's contemporary, George Granville Leveson-Gower (1758-1833), Viscount Trentham, one of the wealthiest men in Britain, married the 19th Countess of Sutherland, Elizabeth Sutherland.

In 1776, when Elizabeth was one year old, both her parents had died of putrid fever. She inherited an enormous holding of land in the Scottish Highlands, the largest landed property in private ownership in Europe. In 1772, the tacksmen managing the estate began clearing it of small tenants. Over the next seventy years thousands of crofters were relentlessly displaced, sometimes with great harshness, to be replaced by large-scale sheep farms.

In 1790, Viscount Trentham was appointed Ambassador to France, where he and his wife witnessed the turmoil that followed the French Revolution. After their return to England in 1792, Lady Sutherland was a prominent social figure in London.

In *Evelyn*, Jane Austen made a show of protecting the identity of the family of Rose Gower's lover, discreetly referring to his father as Lord -. From her description of the castle in Sussex, readers in her day would have easily identified it as Arundel Castle, seat of Charles Howard, 11th Duke of Norfolk, a Tory, and a friend and colleague of D'Arcy Wentworth's cousin, Earl Fitzwilliam.[239]

Arundel Castle, founded on Christmas Day 1067, has been the seat of the Howard family, the Earls of Arundel and Dukes of Norfolk, since William the Conqueror.

These details are an important subtext to *Evelyn*, not evident to today's readers. The Webbs went to enormous pains to ingratiate themselves with Mr Gower, doubtless assuming he was a member of the wealthy Leveson-Gower family. Their flattery and *Benefiscence*, were a comic exaggeration, their fawning response to the honour he did them, by his visit.

Readers in Jane's day would have known why Rose Gower's family saw her match with Henry Howard as *highly desirable*; and would have anticipated objections from his family. Dukes of Norfolk could trace their noble line and contribution to public life, back eight hundred years. The Gowers, though very wealthy, were *arrivistes*.

Mr Gower found the castle *ancient and gloomy, greatly inferior* to his own modern house in its landscaped *Paddock*. Once inside, *in a large party of superior Rank,* his manners fail him, he makes a fool of himself, storms out, agitated, and rides home to Evelyn, *alarmed* even by the twinkling of the stars.

A generosity so polite and so determined
Persuasion

Jane's description of the *peculiar Generosity of Disposition* of the Webb family, could owe something to the story of John Evelyn's encounter with Peter the Great, *the Czar Emperor of Muscovy.* The twenty-six year old Czar arrived in England on 11th January 1698 from Holland. He returned on 21st April 1698, on the *Royal Transport,* the fastest ship in the English fleet, a gift from King William, in return for his granting trading concessions in Russia to English tobacco merchants.

In England, Peter the Great visited Oxford, the Woolwich Arsenal, the Royal Observatory at Greenwich, the Royal Mint in the Tower of London, where Isaac Newton was the Warden, and the Royal Society. He wanted to learn about shipbuilding in England, and spent a lot of time on the Thames, where he learnt seamanship with Edmund Halley. He was quoted as saying he would far rather be an admiral in England than a Czar in Russia.[240]

The Czar met many notable scientists in a variety of fields and recruited a large number of them to undertake projects in Russia, to help progress his development of St Petersburg and the Russian Navy.

John Evelyn's house at Deptford was next door to the Royal Dock-yard. His diary entry for 6th February 1698 reads: *The Czar Emperor of Muscovy, having a mind to see the Building of Ships, hired my house at Says Court and made it his Court & palace.*

The Czar was accompanied by six trumpeters, three interpreters, four chamberlains, two clocksmiths, a cook, a priest, seventy soldiers, four dwarves and a pet monkey. Evelyn's housekeeper sent him an urgent report: *There is a house full of people, and right nasty.*

On 21 April 1698, Evelyn wrote: *The Czar of Muscovy went from my house towards Russia. An exceedingly sharp and cold season.* His house was in absolute disarray. He requested His Majesty's Surveyor, Sir Christopher Wren, and Mr London, his gardener, to assess *how miserably the Czar of Muscovy had left my house, after three months making it his Court.*

Wren's account of *Goods that is Lost, Broke, and Damage done to them,* included *3 wheelbarrows broke & Lost, Eight Fether beds, eight bolsters, twelve pair of blankets very much dirtied and spoyled.* There was a trail of broken chairs, dressers, shattered windows, torn and soiled curtains, carpets, sheets and pillows, and *twenty fine pictures very much tore and the Frames all broke.* Damage done to the fabric of the house included posts, tiles, locks and a *new Floore to a Bogg House.*

Evelyn's garden, his pride and joy, was ruined: *All the grass worke is out of order, and broke into holes by their leaping and shewing tricks upon it, the bowling green is in the same condition. All that ground that used to be cultivated for eatable plants is all overgroune with weeds and is not manured or cultivated, by reason the Czar would not suffer any men to worke when the season offered. The wall fruite and stander fruite trees are unpruned and unnailed, the gravel walks are all broke into holes and out of order.*

There was a hole through the wall at the bottom of the garden, made to give the Czar direct access to the King's Dock-Yard, *very convenient for his intended Business of conversing with our English Builders.*[241] Evelyn's greatest regret was the mischief done to his famous four hundred foot long, nine foot high holly hedge. He had believed it resistant to hedge-breakers, but one of the Czar's favourite recreations was to demolish the hedges by being trundled through them in a wheelbarrow.

31

Kitty, or the Bower

To whom this work is dedicated *The History of England*

Kitty, or the Bower was the third piece in her *Juvenilia* that Jane Austen dedicated to her sister Cassandra, two years her senior. In April 1789, three years earlier, she dedicated *The beautifull Cassandra* to her, a comic novel in twelve tiny chapters, of Cassandra's adventures on a day in London. In November 1791, Jane dedicated *The History of England* to her to thank her for illustrating the story with her watercolours.

Though *Kitty, or the Bower* ends *Volume the Third,* it was not the last piece in the Juvenilia Jane dedicated to her sister. Ten months after she finished this story, in June 1793, Jane completed the *Juvenilia* with a poem, *Ode to Pity*, which she dedicated to Cassandra, and placed at the end of *Volume the First.*

Conjecturing as to the date *Pride & Prejudice*

Jane Austen was sixteen in August 1792, when she recorded *Kitty, and the Bower*, the longest work in the *Juvenilia*, in *Volume the Third.* Her writing is more confident and mature, her readers find themselves in more familiar territory.

Gathering her work together

Kitty is a young woman, probably around Jane's age. She seems to have recently come out into society, she is invited to local balls and has the confidence to arrange for a carriage to take her there on her own.

Kitty was orphaned when very young, she has been reared by her maiden aunt, Mrs Percival. She has had a good education, she is familiar with *the Music of Italian Opera*, confident in Geography, well read in history, and enjoys reading novels. Her accomplishments certainly stand up well against those of her guest, Camilla, who *had been attended by the most capital Master for a period of twelve Years.*

Her aunt most likely employed a governess to teach Kitty at home. Her friends, Cecilia and Mary Wynne, were sent away to school, *since her earliest years,* they *were separated for the greatest part of the Year by the different Modes of their Education, but constantly together during the holidays of the Miss Wynnes.*

Mrs Percival has always scrutinised Kitty's conduct with great severity, her *jealous Caution* has frequently deprived Kitty of real pleasure: not being allowed to go to a Ball, *because an Officer was to be there,* or required to dance with the partner her aunt selects, rather than *one of her own Choice.*

Kitty found *constant releif* from all her *misfortunes* in *a fine shady Bower* at the end of a *walk in her Aunt's Garden,* which she had built years ago, with help from her friends Cecilia and Mary. There she found *Solitude and reflection. Her Bower alone could restore her to herself.*

Cecilia and Mary were *the daughters of the Clergyman of the Parish* of Chetwynde, Mr Wynne, who had died two years before, a few months after his wife. His death left his children *in great distress, reduced to a state of absolute dependence on some relations.*

Cecilia Wynne was *obliged to accept* an offer, *opposite to all her ideas of Propriety, so contrary to her Wishes, so repugnant to her feelings,* to go to the East Indies, where *she had now been married nearly a twelvemonth. Splendidly, yet unhappily married.*

Her younger sister Mary, *had been taken by another relation, the Dowager Lady Halifax as a companion to her daughters.* In the family, *all were her relations but she had no friend, and she wrote to Kitty usually in depressed spirits.*

The new rector of Chetwynde was Mr Dudley, his *Family unlike the Wynnes, were productive only of vexation and trouble to Mrs Percival and her Neice.* They could not *console Kitty for the loss of the Wynnes.*

Kitty's aunt was *most excessively fond of her, and miserable if she saw her for a moment out of spirits; Yet she lived in such constant apprehension of her marrying imprudently if she were allowed the opportunity of choosing, and was so dissatisfied with her behaviour when she saw her with Young men, for it was, from her natural disposition remarkably open and unreserved...* her aunt always thought her defective, and frequently complained of a want of Steadiness and perseverance in her occupations.*

There being young Men in almost every Family... prevented Mrs Percival joining much in the Society of her Neighbours and led her equally to avoid inviting her relations to spend any time in her House.

Mrs Percival had discouraged certain relatives from visiting, she had heard rumours about their son *that alarmed her.* He was *now on his travels,* and she had welcomed them with *great Earnestness* to visit *during the Summer.* Kitty had something *to look forward to, to relieve the dullness of a constant tete-a-tete with her Aunt.*

The day of their arrival so long expected, at length came. Mr and Mrs Stanley were people of Large Fortune and high Fashion. Their daughter Camilla, aged eighteen, *was elegant in appearance, rather handsome, and naturally not deficient in Abilities. After twelve years acquiring Accomplishments that were now to be displayed and in a few years entirely neglected, she had an Understanding unimproved by reading and a Mind totally devoid either of Taste or Judgement.* Kitty, though, *from her solitary Situation was ready to like anyone, she attached herself to Camilla from the first day of her arrival.*

By the end of the first day, Kitty could *scarcely resolve what to think of her new Acquaintance; She appeared to be shamefully ignorant as to the Geography of England, if she had understood her right, and equally devoid of Taste and Information. Kitty was however unwilling to decide hastily... she determined therefore to suspend all Judgement for some time.*

Kitty asked Camilla if she and her mother were acquainted with Lady Halifax. On learning they were, she asked if Camilla had ever seen a Miss Wynne with them. Camilla answered, *I know who you mean perfectly – she wears a blue hat.*

Kitty discovers that she and Camilla have very different views about the fate of the Wynne sisters. Camilla believes that *they are the luckiest Creatures in the World, that Sir George Fitzgibbon you know sent the eldest girl to India entirely at his own Expence, where they say she is most nobly married and the happiest Creature in the World.*

In her opinion, *Lady Halifax has taken care of the youngest and treats her as if she were her daughter; She does not go out into Public with her to be sure...nothing can be kinder to her than Lady Halifax is; she would have taken her to Cheltenham last year, if there had been room enough at the Lodgings, and therefore I don't think she can have anything to complain of.*

Kitty realises it is a subject on which they will never agree, she leaves the room and runs *out of the House to her dear Bower, where she could indulge in peace all her affectionate Anger against the relations of the Wynnes, which was greatly heightened by finding from Camilla that they were in general considered as having acted particularly well by them.*

Camilla comes to tell her the Dudleys have invited them to a Ball the following Thursday. *The Days passed gaily away* as they made their preparations, then slowed and lengthened as they counted down the hours.

On Thursday morning, Kitty woke with a *violent Toothake*. After trying *every remedy*, she was finally obliged *to reconcile herself not only to the pain of the Toothake, but to the loss of the Ball.*

At length, after the others departed, she was *better able to amuse herself than she had been the whole day before.* After writing a letter to Mary Wynne, she found *her toothake so much relieved, she began to entertain an idea of following her Friends to Mr Dudley's.* Within an hour she was *very well-dressed and in high Beauty,* and she sent her maid *in the same haste to order the Carriage. In a few Minutes she heard the Carriage drive up to the Door.*

As Kitty got ready to leave, the maid ran in to tell her a *Gentlemen in a Chaise and four had arrived, one of the handsomest young Men you would wish to see.* Though he did not give his name, she fancied his business was with Kitty, he sent her *his Compliments,* and said *he should be very happy to wait on her.*

Kitty ran downstairs with great impatience, the *Stranger, laying aside the Newspaper,* greeted her by name, and asked after Mrs Percival and the Stanleys. Noticing Kitty was *dressed for a Ball,* he asked her, *what kind Angel in compassion to me, has excluded you from it?*

Kitty, extremely confused, asked him if his business was with the Stanleys. *I merely know them by sight,* he answered, *very distant relations; only my Father and Mother; Nothing more. I assure you.*

Realising he was Camilla's brother, Kitty told him she was *going to a Dance at a Neighbour's,* and he asked if he could accompany her. He was dusty from travelling, he needed to powder his hair and change his shoes. Kitty had him shown to his father's dressing room, expecting him to return in ten minutes. H took half an hour, the clock struck ten before he was ready, *the rest of the party had gone by eight.*

Their entrance attracted *the attention of every body in the room. Mrs Percival, colouring with anger and Astonishment, rose from her seat. She had a most unfortunate opportunity of seeing her Neice whom she had supposed in bed, or amusing herself as the height of gaiety with a book, enter the room most elegantly dressed, with a smile on her Countenance, and a glow of mingled Cheerfulness & Confusion on her Cheeks, attended by a young Man uncommonly handsome, and who without any of her Confusion, appeared to have all her vivacity.*

Kitty received *a very severe lecture from her Aunt on the imprudence of her behaviour,* in arriving so late to the Ball, in having come *in the same Carriage with Edward Stanley,* and entering the room with him. *Kitty longed to say she had not thought it civil to make Mr Stanley walk, but she dared not trifle with her aunt.*

When Edward Stanley asked her *to begin the next Dance* she *immediately gave him her hand, and joyfully left her Seat.* Her *Conduct was highly resented by several young Ladies present,* including Camilla, though Kitty *remained insensible of having given any one Offence, and therefore unable either to offer an apology, or make a reparation; her whole attention was occupied by the happiness she enjoyed in dancing with the most elegant young Man in the room, and every one else was equally unregarded. The Evening indeed to her passed off delightfully.*

Camilla was very sulky during their Coach ride home,: *Well, I must say this, that I never was at a stupider Ball in my Life!...To have a person come in the middle of the Evening and take everybody's place is what I am not used to, and tho' I do not care a pin about it myself, I assure you I shall not easily forgive or forget it.* Kitty followed with *a very submissive apology... with such unaffected Sweetness, that it was almost impossible for Camilla to retain her anger.* Mrs Percival, though, *continued silent and Gloomy.*

Next morning *she seized the very first opportunity* to tell Mr Stanley *it was a rule with her never to admit a young Man into her house as a visitor for any length of time.* She asked him to desire his *Son to leave Chetwynde, or I cannot be answerable for what might happen between him and my Neice...I must own that Kitty is one of the most impudent Girls that ever existed. I assure you Sir, that I have seen her sit and laugh with a young Man whom she has not seen above half a dozen times. Her behaviour indeed is scandalous, and therefore I beg you will send your Son away immediately, or everything will be at sixes and sevens.*

Mr Stanley *went immediately to Edward and strongly pointed out the necessity of him leaving Chetwynde the next day, since his word was already engaged for it.*

His son however appeared struck only by the ridiculous apprehensions of Kitty's aunt, *and highly delighted at having occasioned them himself, seemed engrossed alone in thinking how he might increase them...Mr Stanley could get no determinate answer from him.*

His Son though by no means disposed to marry, or otherwise attached to Miss Percival than as a good natured Girl who seemed pleased with him, took infinite pleasure in alarming the jealous fears of her Aunt by his attentions to her...

Her Neice whose imagination was lively, and whose Disposition romantic, who was already extremely pleased with him, and of course desirous that he might be so with her, as is little to be wondered at...

As for Mrs Percival, she was in tortures the whole Day...her impatience to have them separated conquered every idea of propriety & Goodbreeding... she could not help asking him after Dinner, in her eagerness to have him gone, at what time he meant to set out. Edward answered her very flippantly without committing himself to a time.

Mrs Percival: immediately began a long harangue on the shocking behaviour of modern young Men, & the wonderful Alteration that had taken place in them, since her time, which she illustrated with many instructive anecdotes of the Decorum & Modesty which had marked the Characters of those whom she had known, when she had been young. This however did not prevent his walking in the Garden with her Neice, without any other companion for nearly an hour in the course of the Evening.

When Edward looked up and saw her Aunt approaching, *he suddenly seized hold of Kitty's hand... pressed it passionately to his lips, and ran out of the arbour.* Her Aunt began her harangue: *Well; this is beyond anything I could have supposed. Profligate as I knew you to be, I was not prepared for such a sight.*

Kitty replied, *Mr Stanley's behaviour has given me as much surprise as it has done to You, and I can only suppose that it was the effect of his high spirits.* She suggested it was late and her Aunt should be inside. Mrs Percival, fearing *she may have caught a dreadful cold,* went in and up to bed.

When Edward came in, he admitted to Kitty, *his intentions had been to frighten her Aunt by pretending an affection for her.* Kitty was greatly disappointed at him making such *Sport.*

They passed the evening agreeably, *and such was the power of his Address, and the Brilliancy of his eyes, that when they parted for the Night, tho' Kitty had but a few hours before totally given up the idea, yet she felt almost convinced again that he was in love with her.*

Kitty *went to bed in high Spirits, determined to study his character, and watch his Behaviour still more next day.* But next morning her maid tells her, he was *already gone,* he had *ordered a Carriage the evening before,* and left that morning a *little after eight.*

Kitty blushed *with anger at her own folly, this is the affection for me of which I was so certain. Oh! what a silly thing is a Woman! How vain, how unreasonable! ...Yet I should like to have seen him before he went, for perhaps it may be many Years before we meet again.*

Camilla came to her room with a message from Edward: *He desired me when we all met at Breakfast to give ..his Love to you, for you was a nice Girl he said, and he only wished it were in his power to be more with you. You were just the girl to suit him, because you were so lively and good-natured, and he wished with all his heart that you might not be married before he came back, for there was nothing he liked better than being here. Oh! you have no idea the fine things he said about you...*

But he is gone – Gone perhaps for Years – Obliged to tear himself from what he most loves...In what anguish he must have left the house! Unable to see me, or to bid me adieu, while I senseless wretch, was daring to sleep. This, then explains his leaving us at such a time of day. He could not trust himself to see me. Charming young Man! How much you must have suffered!... Kitty went in high spirits to her Aunt's apartment, without giving a Moment's recollection on the vanity of Young Women, or the unaccountable conduct of Young Men.

Her own family & friends

Pride & Prejudice

In *Kitty, or the Bower,* we learn of two sisters, the Miss Wynnes, we never meet them, they had been Kitty's friends *since her earliest years.* Jane Austen based their stories on the history of two of her aunts, George Austen's sisters, Philadelphia and Leonora Austen. Perhaps she wished to honour their memories, Philadelphia had died of breast cancer, just six months before, on 26 February 1792, aged sixty-one, Leonora died nine years earlier, in February 1783, aged fifty-one.

This pathetic piece of family history

Persuasion

Jane was affected by the story of her father's childhood, how he and his sisters were orphaned, then *dispersed* and *left in great distress, reduced to a state of absolute dependence on some relations, who though very opulent and very nearly connected with them, had with difficulty been prevailed on to contribute anything towards their Support.*

Her grandmother

Emma

Her father's mother, Rebecca Austen, had died in 1732, leaving her husband, William, a surgeon at Tonbridge, with four children to care for – their newborn daughter Leonora, George, aged one, Philadelphia two, and eleven year old William Hampson Walter, Rebecca's son from her first marriage.

Till her grandfather's death

Pride & Prejudice

William Austen managed alone for four years. In 1736 he remarried, his second wife, Susanna Kelk, was twelve years his senior. The following year he died, aged thirty-six. His will, made before he married Susannah, left his estate to be divided equally between his three children, and named his brothers, Francis and Stephen, as executors. Susanna, now forty-eight, remained in the family home, under the terms of the will she was not obliged to care for the children, and she was reluctant to do so.

A new family   *Sense & Sensibility*

William's elder brother Francis Austen, lived in Tonbridge, but was unmarried. So Leonora, five, George, six, and Philadelphia, seven, were sent to London to live with their father's youngest brother, Stephen, an *eminent bookseller,* his wife Elizabeth and their five year old son. They all lived above his bookshop, *The Angel & Bible,* in St Paul's Church-Yard, that specialised in religious works.

His younger brother   *Northanger Abbey*

In January 1740, Stephen Austen was elected to the Court of Common Council of the City of London, as a Commoner for Castle Baynard Ward. Later in the year, he purchased the rights to Reverend Thomas Stackhouse's *New History of the Holy Bible, from the beginning of the World to the establishment of Christianity.* Between 1742 and 1744, he published a second edition, lavishly illustrated with pictures of the Tower of Babel, interior and exterior views of the Ark, a plan of the city of Babylon, and the like, which sold very well.

In 1741, George Austen, now nine, returned to Tonbridge, to the care of his uncle Francis, a solicitor at Sevenoaks. He was enrolled in the Tonbridge School, and in 1747, he won a scholarship to St John's College Oxford, where he graduated in Arts and Divinity. In 1754, he was ordained a priest in the Church of England.

Leonora formed a close bond with Stephen's wife Elizabeth, she was always happy to run errands for her, hurrying along the ginnels threaded between St Paul's Church-Yard, Paternoster Row and Newgate Street, carrying messages and sometimes books from *The Angel & Bible.*

In 1745, when Philadelphia turned fifteen, she was apprenticed to a milliner. In 1750, the year she completed her indenture, her uncle

Stephen Austen died, *after twelve days with fever and a violent pain in his head. He had been trepann'd about 28 years since, for a fracture which he received by a fall from his horse.*[242]

His elder brother

After Stephen's death, Francis Austen took charge of Philadelphia's affairs. A few months later, now twenty-one, she wrote to the East India Company asking for permission to visit Fort St David, a hundred miles south of Madras.[243]

Booksellers

Leonora, eighteen, remained with Stephen's widow, Elizabeth. In his will, Stephen had bequeathed to Elizabeth *and her only all my Estate real and personal,* and had appointed her his *sole Executrix.* Elizabeth was now responsible for managing his publishing business, and Leonora's responsibilities increased.

In 1752, two years after his death, Elizabeth Austen married John Hinton, a bookseller on Pater-noster Row, near Warwick Lane. More than a dozen years younger than Stephen Austen, he was an enterprising publisher who had launched a popular monthly periodical in 1747, *The Universal Magazine of Knowledge and Pleasure.* Its contributors included Oliver Goldsmith, it was lavishly illustrated with maps and engravings, and published under a Royal Licence.

Leonora stayed on in the household, *as a companion* to Elizabeth, helping out as she had always done. Jane described the arrangement with gentle derision – they *treat her as if she were their own daughter. She does not go out into Public with them to be sure; but...nothing can be kinder to her than they are; they would have taken her to Cheltenham last year if there had been room enough at the Lodgings, and therefore I don't think that she can have anything to complain of.*

So opposite to all her ideas of Propriety

In January 1752, Philadelphia had left England, on the *Bombay Castle,* an East India Company vessel, *in the adventurous manner often adopted by portionless girls.*[244] Jane knew the brutal truth about her aunt, *that being without means or prospects she was sent out to India with the object of finding a husband.*[245]

In February 1753, at Fort St David, in Cuddalore, Philadelphia, twenty-three, married forty year-old Tyso Saul Hancock, an East India Company surgeon. Her uncle Francis was his agent and attorney.

The eldest daughter had been obliged to accept the offer of one of her cousins to equip her for the East Indies and, tho' infinitely against her inclination, had necessitated to embrace the only possibility that was offered to her of a Maintenance; yet it was one so opposite to all her ideas of Propriety, so contrary to her Wishes, so repugnant to her feelings; that she would almost prefer servitude to it; had Choice been allowed her. Her personal Attractions had gained her a husband as soon as she arrived in Bengal, and she had been married nearly a twelvemonth; Splendidly yet unhappily married – United to a Man of double her own age, whose disposition was not amiable and whose Manners were unpleasing, though his Character respectable.

Phila wrote to her family, her letters *were always unsatisfactory, though she did not openly avow her feelings, yet every line proved her to be Unhappy. She spoke with pleasure of nothing, but of those Amusements which they had shared together and which could return no more, and seemed to have no happiness in view but that of returning to England again.*

Leonora missed her sister, *she was not married, and could yet look forward to a change in her circumstances, but situated for the present without any immediate hope of it, in a family where, tho' all were relations she had no friend, she wrote usually in depressed Spirits, which her separation from her Sister and her Sister's marriage had greatly contributed to make so.*

In 1765, Philadelphia returned to England with her husband, Tyso, and their daughter Eliza. They rented a house in Mayfair and a cottage in Surrey. Philadelphia called on Leonora, it was more than a dozen years since they had seen each other. Motherhood and India had changed Phila, but her sister appeared to have altered very little.

In the name of charity
Sense & Sensibility

Leonora moved quietly within the narrow confines of her service to the Hintons, along little tunnels groaning with books and smelling of yellowed pages. She was *dependent even for her Cloathes on the bounty of others, who of course do not pity her... they consider her very fortunate.*

In January 1768, Susannah Austen, née Kelk, died. She had married William Austen thirty-two years earlier, and since his death she had maintained her life tenancy of his property. On her death, under the terms of his father's will, George Austen inherited his house and land in Tonbridge, which he sold for £1200.

Later that year, Tyso Hancock returned to Calcutta, leaving Philadelphia and Eliza in England. His funds were getting low, he wanted to get rich quickly, to provide for Phila and Eliza, for his family and for Phila's sister Leonora.

In 1769, after Elizabeth Hinton died, John Hinton continued to keep Leonora as part of his household.

A strong sisterly partiality
Pride & Prejudice

In 1770, Phila wrote to Tyso, unhappy about her sister's predicament. He replied that he would be happy to assist Leonora, *with great chearfulness,* but that he did not agree with Phila's view of John Hinton, declaring, *Mr Hinton has behaved very nobly to poor Leonora. He certainly had not the least Obligation to do anything for her.*[246]

Tyso Hancock's hopes of making his fortune came to little. He complained routinely to Phila about her uncle, Francis Austen, and his management of their affairs. In 1773, he worried, *by his Management I may be a fourth time ruined.* Tyso died in Calcutta, two years later, aged sixty-four, insolvent, depressed, ravaged by fever, *gout, gravel & many other Disorders,*[247] most likely addicted to the opium he took to suppress the pain of his ills.

In 1772, John Hinton married Sarah Ivatt, Leonora stayed on, perhaps *considered as one of the fixtures of the house.*[248] During 1773 and 1774, she had a great deal to do, these were very busy years in the Hinton household.

Booksellers   *Sense & Sensibility*

John Hinton was away in Edinburgh much of the time, engaged in *the battle of the booksellers.* He had mounted a case in the Edinburgh Court of Session against three Scottish booksellers, Alexander Donaldson, John Wood and James Meurose, for having infringed his rights, by printing, publishing and selling copies of Stackhouse's *New History of the Holy Bible.*[249]

In July 1773, Hinton lost his case, but the judgement received great public scrutiny, and seven months later, the House of Lords formally intervened.[250]

Not reasonable to expect accommodation   *Persuasion*

In mid 1777, after forty years a member of a London bookseller's household, twenty-five of those in Pater-noster Row with John Hinton, Leonora Austen was moved on. She was sent to live in Islington with the family of Stephen Austen Cumberlege, an employee and former apprentice of John Hinton, and youngest of the five children of John and Elizabeth Cumberlege.

Payments for which I have pledged myself   *Pride & Prejudice*

There appears to have been some negotiation with Leonora Austen's family prior to her move to the Cumberleges. Philadelphia Hancock apparently agreed to pay for her upkeep there, with a £30 annuity to John Cumberlege and a £10 annuity to his son Stephen Austen Cumberlege, paid each June in arrears.

Philadelphia and her daughter Eliza left London for Europe in late 1777. She made the agreed payments through Hoare's Bank in Fleet Street, the first in mid June 1778, with an additional payment of £15 to John's wife Elizabeth. In June 1779, she paid £10 to Stephen-Austen and £40 to his father. She had overpaid John Cumberlege and a few days later, Elizabeth reimbursed her the £10. In total, Philadelphia contributed £215 towards Leonora's upkeep.[251]

The transfer of unchanging attachments   *Mansfield Park*

In May 1781, John Hinton, by now *very rich*,[252] died suddenly. In July 1782, his widow, Sarah Hinton, married Stephen Austen Cumberlege. He arranged for St Thomas' Hospital to transfer John Hinton's lease of their bookshop on Pater-noster Row to his name, and took over publication of *The Universal Magazine of Knowledge and Pleasure.*

In the May 1781 issue, he announced John Hinton's death, assuring readers, *it will continue to be carried on, with the same unremitted attentions to render it equally instructive and amusing that have for a series of years given it such a distinguished share of the public preference.* Stephen Austen Cumberlege published *The Universal Magazine* until 1784, when it was sold to William Bent, bookseller, who continued its publication until 1814.

Philadelphia made her agreed payments to Cumberlege father and son, until June 1782. That year, in January, Jane's father, George Austen began contributing to Leonora's upkeep. Between January 1782 and March 1784, he made eight payments of varied amounts to Stephen Austen Cumberlege, totalling $97.14s, including bank charges of one guinea.[253]

Melancholy and shocking *Sense & Sensibility*

In February 1783, Leonora died, aged fifty-one. She was buried at St Mary's Islington. Jane Austen was seven. Did she remember Leonora in her blue hat? She bristled at the unjust treatment of her aunt, asking, *is that not shameful? That she should be so poor?* She replied to her own question, *It is indeed, with such wealthy connexions as the Family have.*

She had fallen into good hands &
had been given an excellent education *Emma*

Through Kitty, Jane Austen emphasised the importance of education for girls, one broader than, *Drawing, Italian and Music,* generally provided for daughters of the wealthy. She suggests young girls should read novels, not merely *of the lighter kind,* read *Modern history* and develop their critical thinking, grasp the lessons of history, and follow politics, current affairs, and the State of Affairs in the political World. These were among Jane Austen's great strengths and she advocated them for all young girls.

We catch a glimpse of her broader social conscience at the moment Kitty realises her toothache may cause her to miss the Dudley's Ball, *she considered that there were Misfortunes of a greater magnitude than the loss of a Ball, experienced everyday by some part of Mortality.*

Her own share in the story *Emma*

Jane Austen included an incident from her second meeting with D'Arcy Wentworth in *Kitty, or the Bower.* They had first met at the *Bear Inn* in Reading in 1786, when Jane, Cassandra and Jane Cooper dined there with Edward Austen and Edward Cooper. Jane sprained her ankle, D'Arcy bandaged it and carried her, as they all walked back to the Abbey House School.

Next day, he called at the school to check on her progress. The Headmistress, Mme La Tournelle directed him to Jane's little Bower, overlooking the Holy Brook. A little while later, sensing her possible misjudgement, Mme La Tournelle, hobbled down to the Bower on her cork leg, and found them discussing English history. Catching sight of her approach, D'Arcy stood up to leave. He kissed Jane's hand as he departed, not out of any romantic interest, but to provoke the headmistress' authority.

Following this incident, Jane was sent home from Abbey House School in disgrace, never to return. Members of Jane's family felt the school had been at fault for allowing the girls to go out to dinner with the two Edwards. Such a liberty was deemed shocking: *a strange thing to allow*.[254]

Mrs Percival is Jane Austen's portrayal of her headmistress Mme La Tournelle, an overbearing figure, who comes to dominate the story. Her language and authority are those of a school principal, responsible for the moral welfare of her charges, rather than those of an aunt or family guardian. She describes Kitty as *one of the most impudent Girls that ever existed...her behaviour indeed is scandalous*.

Her judgement was harsh, *Oh! Kitty, you are an abandoned creature, and I do not know what will become of you... The welfare of every Nation depends upon the virtue of its individuals, and any one who offends in so gross a manner against decorum and propriety, is certainly hastening its ruin. You have been giving a bad example to the World and the World is but too well disposed to receive such.*

In the middle of the Michaelmas term, George Austen collected Jane from school. In the new year of 1787, he paid the headmistress, Mme La Tournelle only half the fees he paid previously.[255] Cassandra went back to school to join Jane Cooper, while Jane remained at home in the Steventon rectory.

The names of people that fill up my time *Mansfield Park*

Jane included the names of a number of prominent families of consequence in the story. Dudley likely refers to Queen Elizabeth great love, Robert Dudley, fifth Son of the Duke of Northumberland; Stanley, to Thomas Stanley, 1st Earl of Derby, stepfather of Henry VII; Halifax, refers to Charles Montagu, 1ˢᵗ Earl of Halifax, Lord President, one of Cromwell's deputies during the Commonwealth.

Mr Dudley, the rector who followed Reverend Wynne at *Chetwynde*, is *Lord Amyatt's brother*. James Amyatt, of *Freemantle*, Hampshire, was a *nouveau riche*, former nabob and East India Company stockholder. He served as and alderman in Calcutta in 1766, and a member of a the House of Commons between 1774 and 1780 for the seat of Totnes in Devon, and from 1784 to 1806, for the seat of Southampton.

Jane Austen's title *Kitty*, or *the Bower* was later amended by her nephew James Edward Austen-Leigh, he crossed out most references to *Kitty*, and wrote *Catherine* above them. He also changed the surname of Kitty and her aunt from *Peterson*, to Percival, though as with *Kitty*, his editing was not very thorough, and some *Petersons* remain.

James Edward, who was fifteen or sixteen at the time, also wrote in Volume the Third his own continuation of the story, but did not finish it. It appears he made these alterations with Jane's agreement, at this time, 1815-1816, she was encouraging the literary efforts of both James Edward and his half-sister Anna.[256]

Jane may have approved the change the name to Percival to acknowledge her brother Edward and his *family's physician, Dr Percival, the son of a famous Dr Percival of Manchester,* whose father, Thomas Percival had written a volume of moral guidance: *A Father's Instructions; consisting of Moral Tales, Fables, and Reflections, designed to promote the Love of Virtue.*[257]

Edward had given Jane a copy of the book, apparently he imagined it would be a helpful source of moral guidance for her. His gift gives us some insight into Edward's attitude towards Jane. She may well have approved the alteration of the Kitty's surname from Peterson to Percival, as a subtle riposte to Edward. Kitty's surname might change but without doubt, her guardian, who gives her niece tracts to read, such as *Blair's Sermons*, and *Coelebs in Search of a Wife*, to progress her moral improvement, would remain Mrs Percival forever.

Afterword

Major Themes
Of The Juvenilia

Marriage is the central theme of the *Juvenilia* stories, as it is in Jane Austen's later novels. Marriage, in her day, meant commitment for life. It was an important means for a family to increase its standing, property and wealth. Parents were expected to exert their authority in the selection and approval of their children's spouses.

More than two-thirds of the stories in the *Juvenilia* deal with matters of marriage. Only ten of the thirty-one do not: in *Volume the First, Mr Clifford; The beautifull Cassandra; The Mystery; the three Detached Pieces,* and the *Ode to Pity.* In *Volume the Second,* the first and the fourth letters in *A Collection of Letters,* and the first story in *Scraps,*

There are numerous arranged marriages in the Juvenilia

In *The History of England,* Jane Austen reported on thirteen royal marriages, most of them arranged, more than likely for strategic reasons, though that is not always clear. We learn Lady Jane Grey's marital status as she is of walking to the scaffold and sees *the dead body of her husband accidently passing that way.* Three sovereigns never married: Elizabeth I

Edward 5th and Edward 6th. She supposes that Henry the 4th married, as he had four sons, and assumes her readers know the history of Henry the 8th. She mentions only *Anna Bullen*, his 5th, and his *last wife*, not his first, arranged marriage or other brides. She ends her history with the travails of the Stuarts, failing to mention Henrietta Maria, the wife of Charles the 1st, or his unfortunate end.

In *The First Act of a Comedy*, Pistoletta is on her way to London with her father, Popgun, confident he has arranged her marriage to Strephon, but despite his offer to him of his whole estate, once Chloe enters, singing of her love for Strephon, the audience knows he is wasting his time.

Their marriage of *Frederic and Elfrida*, is arranged by their parents. Frederic neither proposes to Elfrida nor seeks her parents' permission, *the parents of Frederic propose to those of Elfrida,* and are accepted with pleasure.

In *Evelyn*, Mr Gower asks Mr and Mrs Webb for *their elder daughter in marriage. Take our girl, take our Maria,* the Webbs reply, and add *a handsome portion* of ten thousand pounds. No-one thinks to ask Maria's wishes. Lord – refuses to allow his son Henry to marry Mr Gower's sister, Rose. He bans Henry son from seeing Rose, and sends him to the Isle of Wight, to overcome his *Constancy*. The ship is wrecked, his son drowns, and Rose is hastened to her grave.

A number of young people in the Juvenilia resist their parent's authority

Elfrida Falknor's resistance in *Frederic and Elfrida* is quite passive, she simply refuses for twenty years to name the day for her wedding to Frederic. In the same story, Mrs Fitzroy refuses her consent for Rebecca to marry Captain Roger, insisting they wait until they are a *good deal older*. After seven days, when the Captain threatens to steep his dagger in her *heart's blood,* she agrees they can be united in three days time.

In *Love and Freindship*, Edward Lindsay refuses to marry Lady Dorothea, his father's choice, rather he enters *an indissoluble engagement* with Laura, *without* his father's Consent, telling him, *Sir, I glory in the*

Act. It is my greatest boast that I have incurred the Displeasure of my Father! Edward's friend Augustus *and his wife* Sophia *have also, nobly disentangled themselves from the Shackles of Parental Authority, by a Clandestine Marriage.*

A number of young women in the Juvenilia seem eminently marriageable

A number of these young women have come out, they attend Balls and Assemblies approved by their parents and guardians. There they will have opportunities to meet young men from suitable families, their annual incomes and assets declared. In time, we might assume, each of them will find a congenial partner and marry in conformity with the *Marriage Act.*

Sophy and Georgiana Stanhope in *The Three Sisters;* Matilda and Margaret Lesley in *Lesley Castle;* Maria Williams, in *Letter the Third,* despite her *distress'd circumstances,* and Henrietta Halton in *Letter the Fifth* of *A Collection of Letters;* Kitty Percival in *Kitty, or the Bower;* and all seem destined for a happy ending!

A large question mark, though, hangs over the future of Augusta and Margaret F- after their coming out in *Letter the First.*

The Marriage Act of 1753 ruled that to be valid, parental approval was required for any party aged under twenty-one, the marriage had to be conducted in a church, by a clergyman, after publication of three banns, or production of a marriage licence.

A number of the marriages in the Juvenilia appear to be within the law

We can probably be confident that the royal marriages in *The History of England* were legal.

Those of the three couples in *Amelia Webster,* who publish notices of their marriages; the marriages of Lady Williams and Charles Adams in *Jack and Alice,* who are *publicly united;* that of Mary Stanhope and Mr

Watts in *The Three Sisters*; and of Susan Fitzgerald and Sir George Lesley in *Lesley Castle*, all appear to be within the law.

Anna Parker in *A letter from a Young Lady*, is determined to make a show of her marriage to the immensely rich, Colonel Martin of the Horseguards. We can probably assume it will be a very public event, and compliant with the *Marriage Act.*

Most marriages in the Juvenilia do not comply with the Marriage Act

In *Frederic and Elfrida,* Miss Fitzroy runs off with the Coachman. Henry and Eliza Cecil have a *private union* conducted by a chaplain (not necessarily a member of the clergy).

Sir William Mountague, seventeen, is under age, he and Emma Stanhope are *privately married.*

The three couples that find each other at the end of *The Visit,* have been circulating the Bottles and *drinking draughts of love* from each others' eyes. Though Lord Fitzgerald mentions marriage, their intentions are not clear.

In *Love and Freindship*, Laura and Edward Lindsay are immediately united by Laura's father who *had never taken orders; their freinds,* Augustus and Sophia had a Clandestine Marriage; the Scottish Lord St Clair had four illegitimate children with Laurina, *an italian opera-girl:* Claudia, Matilda, Bertha and Agatha; Bertha and Agatha each had an illegitimate son, Philander and Gustavos.

In *Lesley Castle,* young Lesley married Louisa before he had known her a month, and she was likely not much older than eighteen. It does not sound legal under English law of the time, though if it was conducted in Scotland, it may well have been. Later, in Naples, after both turn Roman-Catholic, Lesley obtains *one of the Pope's Bulls for annulling his 1st marriage and actually marries a Neapolitan Lady of great Rank and Fortune,* while Louisa is to do *likewise.*

In *Letter the Second* of *A Collection of Letters*, Miss Jane and Captain

Dashwood *married without the consent or knowledge* of her father.

In *The First Act of a Comedy*, Strephon tells the Postilion he is *going to Town* to marry Chloe, but when we learn he has no money, only a *bad guinea*, and he offers to pawn one her letters, it seems most likely he will opt for a *private arrangement*.

In *Evelyn*, Maria Webb is around seventeen, when her parents give her to Frederick Gower. Their nuptials, celebrated the following day, were not legal.

With so many marriages in the Juvenilia, matchmaking may be required

In *Amelia Webster*, brother and sister George and Matilda Hervey, look for partners for each other amongst their friends, this seems to be an accepted role for siblings.

In *Lesley Castle*, Charlotte notices Margaret Lesley has mentioned her brother in several letters, and tells her, in no uncertain terms, she is not interested in marriage.

In *The Visit*, three matches are achieved over a very haphazard dinner party, after servants *bring in the Bottles and Glasses and circulate the Bottle*. Miss Fitzgerald arranges for Sophy Hampton to sit Lord Fitzgerald on her lap. Cloe and Stanly are busy admiring each other, leaving Willoughby to Miss Fitzgerald, who offers him her hand.

In *Letter the Fifth* of *A Collection of Letters*, Lady Scudamore goes to great lengths to interest Henrietta Halton in her cousin Mr Musgrove, though her success is uncertain.

There are young women in the Juvenilia who fall madly in love, sometimes at first sight, but fail to draw any interest from the man they favour.

Things end badly for Charlotte in *Frederic and Elfrida*, who has a *natural turn of mind to make every one happy;* and for Lucy and Alice

Johnson in *Jack and Alice*. We never learn the fate of Emma Marlow in *Edgar and Emma*; Sophia, author of *Letter the Second in A Collection of Letters*, has been crossed in love, her beloved, Willoughby, has married someone else.

Jane Austen finds a husband for rejected Lady Dorothea, and even a wife for *Sensible, well-informed and Agreable* Graham, deprived of Janetta Mcdonald.

Certain powerful older women attempt to dominate and control young women, some by taking an active interest in their affairs of the heart

Lady Scudamore in *Letter the Fifth*, of *A Collection of Letters*, is most intent to promote her cousin Mr Musgrove, she tries to persuade Henrietta Halton to fall in love with him.

In *Jack and Alice*, Lady Williams takes a contrary approach to Alice Johnson and Lucy, actively discouraging their interest in Charles Adams.

Lady Greville in *Letter the Third*, of *A Collection of Letters*, offers favours to Maria Williams that she can't refuse, only to bully and humiliate her. Lady Greville wants her own daughters to shine, she criticises Maria for wearing a pretty new dress to the Ball, and once there, is pleased to presume that no one has asked her to dance.

In *Kitty, or the Bower*, Mrs Percival, Kitty's guardian, *loses every idea of propriety and Goodbreeding* in her efforts to control Kitty's every move. After both Mary Wynne's parents die, leaving their children penniless, Lady Halifax takes her in, but she is never part of the family, she is just a poor relation.

In *Love and Freindship*, that giddy pair, Laura and Sophia, take on the role of older, worldly-wise women with Janetta McDonald, and succeed in persuading her to reject Graham, her fiancé. The pair have a little more difficulty in arranging a *secret Union* between Janetta and the *amiable M'Kenzie*, but eventually experience *the Satisfaction of seeing them depart for Gretna-Green*.

Many young women in the Juvenilia decide to take the initiative, in love and life

Elfrida in *Frederic and Elfrida*, finally emerges from her chrysalis, to take control of her own destiny. In *Jack and Alice*, Lucy is a beacon of independence, Alice less so. In *Edgar and Emma*, Emma takes a first step towards taking charge of her future.

In *The beautifull Cassandra*, her day of adventure could be just the beginning. In *Henry and Eliza*, Eliza is a survivor, and when she has power, she uses it for good. In *Sir William Mountague*, Lady Percival and Emma Stanhope take charge of their lives. In *Amelia Webster*, Matilda Hervey takes charge of her brother's future and succeeds, where Margaret Lesley, in *Lesley Castle*, tries and fails.

In *The Visit*, Miss Fitzgerald, ensures Willoughby is available, and offers him her hand. In *The Three Sisters*, Mary Stanhope, entrapped, tries to negotiate, rather than faking interest in Mr Watts.

In *Love and Freindship*, Laura moves forward as everything collapses around her. In *The History of England*, the narrator maintains her humour and her independent perspective. In *Letter the Third* of *A Collection of Letters*, Maria maintains her detachment and refuses to be cowed by her *distress'd circumstances*. In *Letter the Fifth* of *A Collection of Letters*, Henrietta Halton, maintains her good manners, her enjoyment of life and her independence despite the efforts of Lady Scudamore.

In *Scraps*, Anna Parker is taking charge of a future of which her heart disapproves. Kitty in *Kitty, or the Bower* gives a lot of thought to all she encounters and to cautions and criticism she receives from her aunt; she seems ready to take charge of her life.

Independent young women in the Juvenilia do not all find happiness

There are only a few independent young women who have optimistic outcomes, including Lady Percival in *Sir William Mountague*, *The beautifull Cassandra*, and Charlotte Lutterell in *Lesley Castle*.

Lucy in *Jack and Alice*, considers marrying the Duke of —, because *it will procure* her *a home*, but she is murdered, poisoned, before she can decide.

Emma Stanhope, in *Sir William Mountague*, seeks fourteen shillings compensation for her brother's murder. Sir William offers her himself and his fortune instead. She accepts, and a fortnight later he falls violently in love with someone else.

In *Love and Freindship*, after a period of independence and adventure, Laura retires to the Highlands of Scotland, to live *in melancholy Solitude, with unceasing Lamentations.*

In *Letter the Second* of *A Collection of Letters*, Miss Jane keeps the secrets of her marriage and her children, her father dies without ever learning the truth. She cannot bring herself to use either her maiden name or her married name, and chooses to make a home with a widowed sister-in-law she had never met.

Eliza, in *Henry and Eliza*, has a period of happiness in France, but on her return she is imprisoned by the Dutchess. She escapes from the *Dutchess's Dungeon*, wretched and hungry, and is reduced to begging. But in the end, she gains the *Applause of her own Heart*, after returning to Harcourt Hall, raising an Army and entirely demolishing *the Dutchess's Newgate*.

Jane Austen exposes affected and hypocritical social customs that can be used to confine and degrade young women

The social customs exposed in the *Juvenilia* include: coming out, as in *Letter the First* of *A Collection of Letters*; arranged marriages, that treat young women as objects, or property to be traded up, as in: *Henry and*

Eliza, The Three Sisters, Love and Freindship, The First Act of Comedy, Evelyn and *Kitty, or the Bower*; the requirement on young women to accept impertinent quizzing and to respond politely, as in: *Jack and Alice, Letter the Third, Fourth and Fifth* of *A Collection of Letters*, and *Kitty, or the Bower*; and to allow themselves to be persuaded and criticised, as in *Letter the Fifth* of *A Collection of Letters*, and *Kitty, or the Bower*.

Some young women in the Juvenilia look back over their past lives, with regret

These include Laura in *Love and Freindship*, the young woman behind *Ode to Pity*, and Anna Parker, the *Young lady, whose feelings being too Strong for her Judgement led her into the commission of Errors which her Heart disapproved.*

Parents hold the purse-strings in the Juvenilia, to live independently, young people need money, but have no source of funds other than their parents

For some, theft of money from their family and friends is their only choice, if they are to achieve independence. In *Love and Freindship*, Augustus, Sophia, Philander and Gustavos all take that option. It is unclear though why Eliza, in *Henry and Eliza*, took £50.

Young people in the Juvenilia have no experience in managing money

Eliza and Cecil in *Henry and Eliza*, the beautiful Cassandra, Augustus, Sophia, Laura, Edward, Philander and Gustavos in *Love and Freindship*, have no concept of managing money. Philander and Gustavos have devised a system for budgeting, they divide the money they stole from their mothers into nine parcels, each for a different expense. The ninth is for *Silver Buckles*.

Young women in the Juvenilia need friends, they make friends easily, and rely on them, sometimes unwisely

Jane Austen presents a variety of snapshots of female friendship. In *Volume the First*, Elfrida Falknor and her friends Charlotte Drummond and Jezalinda Fitzroy in *Frederic and Elfrida*; in *Jack and Alice*, Lucy and Lady Williams; in *A beautiful description of the different effects of Sensibility on different Minds*, Melissa, surrounded by her seven friends.

In *Volume the Second*, the friendships between Laura and Isabel, and Laura and Sophia in *Love and Freindship*, in *Lesley Castle*, between Charlotte Lutterell and Margaret Lesley, Charlotte and Lady Susan Lesley, and Eloise Lutterell and Mrs Marlowe.

In *Volume the Third*, Kitty misses her friends the Miss Wynnes, and finds an unsuitable friend in Camilla Stanley, in *Kitty, or the Bower*.

Jane Austen cannot hide her anger at those who gather and spread gossip

In *The Mystery*, the Humbug family gossip amongst themselves, Colonel Elliott passes a secret to Sir Edward Spangle, as *he is asleep and wont hear*.

In *Letter the Fourth* of *A Collection of Letters*, *a young Lady rather impertinent* questions and probes Miss Grenville for information about herself, she wants to know everything, to gossip about it to her friends.

In *The female philosopher*, Louise's gossip about Arabella to her friends the Millars, led them to call on Arabella and her father, with their *Sentiments of Morality*.

The Juvenilia is busy with siblings and their interactions

The siblings in *Volume the First* include: Rebecca and Jezalinda Fitzroy, in *Frederic and Elfrida;* the three Simpson sisters, Caroline, Cecilia and the murderous Sukey, in *Jack and Alice*; the Willmot family, with children *too numerous to be described,* in *Edgar and Emma*; the three

Miss Cliftons of Kilhoobery Park, in *Sir William Mountague*; the Stanhope sisters, Mary, Georgiana and Sophy Stanhope, and their friends Kitty and Jemima Dutton, in *The Three Sisters;* and Mr Williams' *six very fine children* in *The Generous Curate*.

Siblings in *Volume the Second* include, in *Love and Freindship*: Augusta and Edward Lindsay, and the arrival of Lord St Clair helps to identify four cousins. In *Lesley Castle*, there are two pairs of sisters, Margaret and Matilda Lesley, and Charlotte and Eloisa Lutterell and brother and sister, Lady Lesley and William Fitzgerald. In *A Collection of Letters*, sisters, Augusta and Margaret, who are coming out together, and Miss Greville and her sister Ellen, daughters of Lady Greville. In *Scraps*: Julia and Charlotte Millar in *The female philosopher*; Elizabeth and Fanny Johnson in *A Tour through Wales*; and brothers, Robertus and Wilhelminus in *A Tale*.

In *Volume the Third*, siblings include Frederick Gower and his sister Rose in *Evelyn*; and Cecilia and Mary Wynne, and Camilla and Edward Stanley in *Kitty, or the Bower*.

There are few mothers in the Juvenilia, and their behaviour is disturbing

In *Henry and Eliza*, Lady Harcourt exposes her newborn daughter in a field, under a haycock, dreading her husband's *just resentment* that the baby is not a boy; the Dutchess of F.'s *passions* are *strong, her friendships firm and her Enmities, unconquerable*. When Eliza marries *Mr Cecil*, the Dutchess sends *300 armed Men* after them, with orders not to return without their Bodies, dead or alive. Three years later, Eliza steps on Shore at Dover, with a child in each hand, is seized by *officers of the Dutchess,* and conducted to a *snug little Newgate*.

In *Letter the First* of *A Collection of Letters*, a mother tells her friend at great length about her plans for the fake coming out of her two daughters. In *A Tour through Wales*, the mother rides along on her *poney*, while her two daughters run alongside. When all the girls' shoes are all worn out, she lends them a pair of blue *Sattin Slippers*, one each, for them to hop home *delightfully*.

In *Evelyn*, Mrs Webb welcomes Mr Gower to her *House, and to every thing it contains,* and gives him her elder daughter Maria, *Take our girl, take our Maria.* Lady – *felt a deeper sorrow at the loss of her son, en route to the Isle of Wight, than his Lordship's harder heart was capable of.*

In *Kitty or the Bower,* Mrs Stanley, a woman of *large Fortune and High Fashion* encourages her daughter Camilla's focus on the Elegance of her appearance, the fashion of her dress, and the Admiration she wished to excite. She *perfectly agrees* with her daughter's outbursts of snobbery and ill temper.

Fathers in the Juvenilia are a lot kinder

In *Jack and Alice*, Alice, madly in love with Charles Adams, asks her father, Mr Johnson, to propose a union between them. He receives a very negative response from Charles, who insults both him and his daughter. He gives Alice *the sad account of the ill success of his visit.*

The Generous Curate has a very modest income and *six fine children*, whom he treats kindly and with a great deal of patience.

In *Love and Freindship*, grandfather, Lord St Clair, acknowledges his four illegitimate grandchildren, and fulfils his duty to them, presenting each with a £50 note.

In *Evelyn*, Lord –is a *most inflexible man, he and the whole Company* at his castle, find Mr Gower to be *Mad.*

In *Kitty, or the Bower*, Mr Stanley, a man of *Large Fortune and a Member of the House of Commons*, was perhaps too prone to forgive his son's faults

The leading characters of four stories in The Juvenilia are men

Jane Austen is more understanding towards these men than she is to many of her women characters, she draws them with broader strokes and expects far less of them. The four stories with men as their leading characters and no, or very little room for women are: *The Adventures of*

Mr Harley, Memoirs of Mr Clifford, A Tale and Evelyn.

A Tale looks at the interplay between two brothers, the elder with money, property, transport and friends, the younger, *with that happy ease of overcoming difficulties.* The give and take between brothers was something Jane Austen returned to in *Emma, Mansfield Park* and *Sanditon.*

Jane Austen raises a number of social issues in the Juvenilia

Social issues raised in the *Juvenilia* include the infanticide of newborn daughters, in *Henry and Eliza.*

The use of steel traps, set on country properties to catch and deter poachers, as in *Jack and Alice.*

The oppression of the working class: in *Henry and Eliza,* their haymakers punished for idleness with a cudgel; and in *A fragment – written to inculcate the practise of Virtue: the unfortunates who sweat under the fatigue of their daily Labour.*

In *Kitty, or the Bower,* Kitty concludes that: *there were Misfortunes of a greater magnitude than the loss of a Ball, experienced everyday by some part of Mortality.*

Jane Austen argues for the education for young girls

In *The History of England,* Lady Jane Grey is described as an *amiable young woman and famous for reading Greek.*

In *Kitty, or the Bower,* Kitty is very disappointed in her new *Acquaintance,* Camilla Stanley, who *had been attended by the most capital Masters* from the age of six. Her *understanding was unimproved by reading,* her *Mind totally devoid either of Taste or Judgement.* She *appeared to be shamefully ignorant as to the Geography of England.* Kitty *found no variety in her conversation; She received no information from her but in fashions...All her stock of knowledge was exhausted in a very few Days.*

Finale

It was through her writing and the success of her novels that Jane Austen *brisked up.* By December 1815, she had four novels in print, all selling well. In London, her zest for life bursts through her letters: *I am sorry my Mother has been suffering, & am afraid this exquisite weather is too good to agree with her – I enjoy it all over me, from top to toe, from right to left, Longitudinally, Perpendicularly, Diagonally; & I cannot but selfishly hope we are to have it last till Christmas; nice, unwholesome, Unseasonable, relaxing, close, muggy weather!* [258]

Conclusion

Jane Austen's father, George, recognised her efforts and her talent, and encouraged her writing. He gave her the journal she used for *Volume the Second*, and wrote a note on the inside cover of *Volume the Third*, praising her work: *Effusions of Fancy by a very young Lady consisting of Tales in a Style entirely new.*

In December 1794, for her nineteenth birthday, eighteen months after Jane finished her *Juvenilia*, George Austen gave her a portable mahogany writing desk, with an inlaid leather top, *one long drawer and glass inkstand compleat.* She could take her desk wherever she went, to use, and store her manuscripts inside. She wrote in 1798, *no part of my property could have been such a prize before, for in my writing-box was all my worldly wealth.*[259]

In 1795, Jane Austen completed her first full length novel, *Elinor & Marianne*, and in 1797, her second, *First Impressions.*

George Austen was so delighted with *First Impressions*, he decided that it should be published, and he was prepared to meet the cost. On 1 November 1797, he wrote to Cadell & Davies, a leading London bookseller and publisher, at 141 The Strand:

Sir,—I have in my possession a manuscript novel, comprising 3 vols., about the length of Miss Burney's "Evelina." As I am well aware of what consequence it is that a work of this sort shd make its first appearance under a respectable name, I apply to you. I shall be much obliged therefore if you will inform me whether you choose to be concerned in it, what will be the expense of publishing it at the author's risk, and what you will venture to advance for the property of it, if on perusal it is approved of. Should you give any encouragement, I will send you the work.

I am, Sir, your humble Servant

George Austen

Steventon, near Overton, Hants

Cadell declined Reverend Austen's proposal *by return of post.*[260] It was published anonymously, sixteen years later, by Thomas Egerton, revised and renamed *Pride & Prejudice*, "By a Lady."

What a picture of intellectual poverty   *Northanger Abbey*

In *Becoming Jane Austen*, Jon Spence noted: *it is a fact, rarely acknowledged, that there is no conventional source of personal information about her between the ages of eleven and twenty. None of her own letters from this time survive.... There has been a long-observed tacit agreement that Jane Austen's work is off limits to the biographer as a source of information about her life, but it seemed to me that the early stories might reveal the themes and situations that were preoccupying Jane's imagination, even if they could not be directly related to her personal experience.*[261]

Spence received a rap over the knuckles for his impertinence, from an Austenphile – Janeite: *Spence commits the cardinal sin among Austenphiles of pointing to connections between the fictional characters and real-life people – a connection that Jane Austen herself vehemently denied.*[262] His disciplinarian, though, failed to state where or when Jane Austen might have issued this *vehement denial.*

Virginia Woolf warned: *Anybody who has the temerity to write about Jane Austen is aware of two facts: first, that of all the great writers she is the most difficult to catch in the act of greatness; second, that there are twenty-five elderly gentlemen living in the neighbourhood of London who resent any slight upon her genius as if it were an insult to the chastity of their aunts.*[263]

A concerted scheme of Revenge *Lesley Castle*

Anyone with the temerity to suggest Jane Austen had a life, a real life, not one inscribed in the Janeite canon, today risks being sanctioned and blackballed by the international might of an Austenphile – Janeite militia. Their rigid adherence to the Austen family's obfuscation, partial truths, denials and censored histories means that after more than two hundred years, her real history and the significance of a great deal of her writing still remains hidden in plain sight.

I trust that the themes and situations which preoccupied Jane Austen's imagination in the three volumes of her *Juvenilia*, which once seemed so impenetrable, are now more transparent, and that the secrets of her youth and her vibrant life, hidden and denied for so long, have found the light of day.

V.S.Rutherford
August 2020

Endnotes

Preface

1 Henry Austen, *A Biographical Notice of the Author*, published as a preface in the posthumous editions of *Persuasion* and *Northanger Abbey*, London, John Murray, 1816.

2 James Edward Austen-Leigh, *Memoir of Jane Austen*, Richard Bentley & Son, London, 1871, Chapter III.

3 Virginia Woolf, "Jane Austen Practising," in *Essays*, ed. Andrew McNellie, Hogarth, London, 1988, page 331.

4 Margaret Drabble, Foreword to *Jane Austen's Beginnings: The Juvenilia and Lady Susan*, ed. J.David Grey, Ann Arbor, Michigan, 1989, page xiv..

5 Clare Brant, "Obituary: David Nokes." *The Guardian*, 7 December 2009

6 David Nokes, *Jane Austen, A Life*, London, Fourth Estate, 1997, pages 115-116.

7 John Halperin, "Unengaged Laughter" in Grey, *Jane Austen's Beginnings*, op cit, page 46

8 Richard Church, Introduction, *Shorter Works of Jane Austen*, The Folio Society, London,1965

9 Caroline Austen, *Reminiscences*, ed. Deirdre Le Faye, The Jane Austen Society, U.K., 1986.

10 James Edward Austen-Leigh, *op cit*, Preface and Chapter 3.

11 Fanny Caroline Lefroy, "Is it Just?" *Temple Bar:A London Magazine for Town and Country Readers*, Volume 67, January to April 1883, page 270.

12 Mary Russell Mitford to Sir William Elford, April 13, 1815, *The Life of Mary Russell Mitford, related in a Selection from her Letters,* volume I, London, Bentley, pages 305-7.

13 Bruce Stovel, "Further Reading," Chapter 13, *The Cambridge Companion to Jane Austen*, eds E. Copeland & J. McMaster, CUP, 1997.

14 Paul Poplawski, A *Jane Austen Encyclopedia*, Greenwood Press, Connecticut, 1998, page 104.

15   John Halperin, *The Life of Jane Austen*, John Hopkins University Press, Baltimore, 1996, page 5.

16   James Edward Austen-Leigh, *op cit*, Preface and Chapter 3.

17   Virginia Woolf, *The Athenaeum*, December 1923.

18   Virginia Woolf, "Personalities" in *Collected Essays*. Hogarth Press. London. 1966.

19   Zona Gale, 'Jane Austen Outdoes Daisy Ashford,' *New York Times Book Review*, 17 Sept. 1922, pages 1, 24.

20   E. M. Forster, *Aspects of the Novel*, Edward Arnold, London, 1927.

21   Reginald Farrer, "Jane Austen", *Quarterly Review*, 228, July 1917.

22   Robert W. Chapman, *The Times Literary Supplement*, 10 December 1931.

23   Brian Southam, *Jane Austen's Literary Manuscripts*, London, 1964, page 6.

24   John Halperin, *Jane Austen's Lovers*, St Martin's Press, New York, 1988, page 9.

25   Jon Spence, *Becoming Jane Austen*, continuum, London, 2007. The Introduction was omitted from the later editions.

26   Wal Walker, *Jane & D'Arcy, Vol.1 Folly is not always Folly*, and Vol 2 *Such Talent & Such Success*, Arcana Press, Sydney, 2017. https://www.janeanddarcy.com/

27   Jane to Cassandra Austen, 29 January, 1813.

28   Jane to Frank Austen, 25 September, 1813.

Volume The First

29   James Edward Austen-Leigh, op cit, Chap 3

30   Andrew Honey, *Volume the First, conservation report,* Bodleian Library, Oxford, 2019.

31   Jane to Cassandra Austen, 11 June 1799.

Frederic & Elfrida

32   *The European Magazine*. Volume XLVI, July 1804. Quoted from the tablet on the South wall above his tomb in the Church of St Michael at Enborne. In 2016, it no longer appeared to be there.

33   Jane to Cassandra Austen, 13 October 1808.

34   Peggy Hickman, *A Jane Austen Cookbook with Martha Lloyd's Recipes*, David & Charles, Devon, 1977.

35   Three kings of England - Alfred the Great, Canute and William the 2nd and four early kings of Wessex are buried in Winchester Cathedral, along with Jane Austen.

36   Eliza Nugent Bromley, *Laura & Augustus; an Authentic Story, in a Series of letters,* 1784, volume 3.

37   Wal Walker, *Folly is not always Folly*, op cit, pages 110, 131, 117. https://www.janeanddarcy.com/

Jack & Alice

38   Jane Austen used the steel trap as a highly visual and comic device to describe Charles Adams' feelings toward Lucy and her uninvited visit. It was also a powerful social comment about their cruelty and violence. Such traps were set in rural areas to deter and catch poachers, treating them like animals to be caught and killed. They were used to dissuade the lower orders, the starving poor, from trespassing, hoping to catch a rabbit or a ground bird to feed their families. Once caught they would be arrested and charged and transported as convicts to outposts like America and Australia. The traps were made illegal in 1827.

39   "To the Author of the Loiterer", signed Margaret Mitten. *The Loiterer*, issue 43, 21 November 1790.

40   George Lyttleton, from *Advice to a Lady,* 1731.

41   Jane Austen, *Northanger Abbey*, Volume I, Chapter I.

42   Wal Walker, *Folly is not always Folly*, op cit, pages 126, 135-143. https://www.janeanddarcy.com

43 Henry Austen, *op cit.*

44 Claire Tomalin, *Jane Austen A Life, Vintage Books*, New York. 1999, page 109.

45 J. E. Austen-Leigh, op cit, Chapter 5.

46 Jane described by Mrs Middleton, a neighbour in Chawton, quoted by Deirdre Le Faye, "Recollections of Chawton", *Times Literary Supplement*, May 1985, page 495.

47 Fulwar-Craven Fowle, recorded by Mrs Mozley in 1838, quoted by Kathleen Tillotson in the *Times Literary Supplement*, 17 September 1954, page 591.

Edgar & Emma

48 Wal Walker, *Folly is not always Folly,* op cit, pages 124, 130-132. https://www.janeanddarcy.com/

49 Jane to Cassandra Austen, 30 June 1808.

50 Jane Austen, *Pride & Prejudice,* Volume III, Chapter XVII.

Henry & Eliza

51 Eliza de Feuillide to Phylly Walter, 7 May 1784, D. Le Faye, *Jane Austen's Outlandish Cousin*, London, The British Library, 2002, page 59.

52 Jane Austen, *Lady Susan*, Letter VI.

53 Eliza de Feuillide to Phylly Walton, 7 May, 1784. D. Le Faye, *Jane Austen's Outlandish Cousin*, op cit, p.59.

54 Eliza de Feuillide to Phylly Walton, 27 March, 1782, ibid, page 52.

55 Brian Southam, op cit, page 5.

56 *Willson or Wilson*, there are two spellings in the text.

57 Jane Austen, *Pride & Prejudice,* volume I, Chapter X.

58 Wal Walker, *Folly is not always Folly,* op cit, page 27. https://www.janeanddarcy.com/

59 *Whitehall Evening Post*, 12 November 1789.

60 In 1681, a married woman, Mary Naples, was indicted for murdering her *Male Infant*. The child was *not a Bastard*, and his mother did not fit the profile of a *lewd* woman under the terms of the 1624 Statute. Found Not Guilty, she was acquitted. https://www.oldbaileyonline.org/browse.jsp?div=t16810228-5

61 Jane Austen, *Pride & Prejudice*, Volume I, Chapter XVIII.

62 Reproduced in C. Tomalin, op cit, page 40.

63 Jane Austen, *Mansfield Park*, Volume I, Chapter V.

64 Wal Walker, *Folly is not always Folly*, op cit, pages 179-181. https://janeanddarcy.com/

65 Jane Austen, *Sense and Sensibility*, Volume II, Chapter VII.

66 Jane Austen, *Sense and Sensibility*, Volume II, Chapter IX.

The Adventures Of Mr Harley

67 *The Gentleman's Magazine*, Volume 59, Part 1, 1789, page 374.

68 Letter from Abbott of the Inner Temple to the *Whitehall Evening Post*, March 31, 1789 to April 2 1789; and *Public Advertiser*, April 2, 1789.

The Beautifull Cassandra

69 Jane Austen, *Persuasion*, Volume I, Chapter I.

Amelia Webster

70 Fergus Butler-Gallie, *A Field Guide to the English Clergy*, Oneworld, London, 2018, page 35.

71 Wal Walker, *Folly is not always Folly*, op cit, page 86-7. https://www.janeanddarcy.com/

72 Pierre de Beaumarchais to the Comte de Vergennes, 17 December 1777, quoted by S.F.Bemis, "British Secret Service & the French-American Alliance," *The American Historical Review*, Volume 29, No.3, April 1924. Pierre de Beaumarchais was a spy and a playwright. His *Le Mariage de Figaro* was the basis for Mozart's opera of the same name, and for Rossini's *Le Barbier de Séville*.

73 Jane Austen, *Pride & Prejudice*, Volume III, Chapter XVII.

74 Hampshire County Council, *Hantsweb Heritage* 100.

75 Marriage Register of St.Nicholas Church, Steventon, 1755 to 1812, Hampshire Record Office.

76 In 1798, the Duke of Norfolk was dismissed as Lord Lieutenant of the West Riding of Yorkshire, by George III, for proposing a toast to "Our Sovereign – the Majesty of the People," at a banquet for Charles Fox's birthday, on 24 January 1798.

77 Jane Austen, *Mansfield Park*, Volume II, Chapter IV.

78 William Shakespeare, *Henry IV, Part I*.

79 *Whitehall Evening Post*, November 12, 1789.

The Visit

80 "To the Author of the Loiterer," signed Sophia Sentiment, *The Loiterer*, issue 9, 28 March 1789.

81 *High Life Below Stairs, A Farce in Two Acts,* 1759, by James Townley (1714-1778).

82 A hothouse, or greenhouse, would be used to grow berries and other fruits for the household.

83 Wal Walker, *Folly is not always Folly*, op cit, page 138. https://janeanddarcy.com/

84 Jane Austen, *Northanger Abbey*, Volume II, Chapter II.

85 *Whitehall Evening Post*, July 14-16, 1789.

86 Jane Austen, *Northanger Abbey*, Volume II, Chapter V.

87 Jane Austen, *Pride & Prejudice*, Volume II, Chapter XIX.

88 Ibid, Volume III, Chapter I.

89 Ibid, Volume II, Chapter XIX. *Chatsworth* is often claimed to be the estate Jane Austen named *Pemberley* in *Pride and Prejudice*. A closer reading of the last chapter in Volume II and the first in Volume III makes it clear that Elizabeth and the Gardiners may have visited Chatsworth to admire its celebrated beauties, but they travelled on, after Chatsworth, Matlock, Dove Dale and the Peak, to Pemberley. *Wentworth Woodhouse* is 28 miles from *Chatsworth*, travelling north-east through the Peak District National Park.

The Mystery

90 J. E. Austen-Leigh, op cit, Chapter 3.

91 Henry Austen, "The Science of Physiognomy Not to Be Depended On," *The Loiterer*, No.51, 16 January 1790, Oxford.

The Three Sisters

92 Jon Spence, op cit, page 62.

93 Deirdre Le Faye, ed, *Jane Austen: A Family Record,* Cambridge University Press, 2004, page 70.

94 During her Christmas at Steventon in 1787, Eliza de Feuillide suggested the Austens perform *Which is the Man* (1783) by Hannah Cowley, her suggestion was not taken up. Lady Bell Bloomer was attractive young widow, pursued by Lord Sparkle, a fashionable wit and a gambler who rigged local elections.

95 Mary Wollstonecraft, *A Vindication of the Rights of Woman*, London. 1790.

96 Richard Church, op cit, page viii.

A Fragment – Written To Inculcate The Practise Of Virtue

97 Peter Sabor, ed, *Juvenilia, The Cambridge Edition of the Works of Jane Austen*, CUP, 2006, Introduction.

A Beautiful Description Of The Different Effects Of Sensibility, etc

98 The publication in 1740 of *Pamela*, or *Virtue Rewarded* by Samuel Richardson (1689-1761) marked the beginning of the rapid growth of novels with emotional appeal. It ushered in an era of sensibility in art and literature in England that flourished in the second half of the eighteenth century.

99 Jane Austen named her sentimental heroine *Melissa*, following Margaret Mitten's advice: "your heroine must possess a great deal of

feeling and have a pretty name." *The Loiterer*, issue 43, 21 November 1790.

The Generous Curate

100   *The Loiterer*, issue 2, 7 February 1789.

Ode to Pity

101   Pindar's victory odes celebrate winners at Pan Hellenic games held at Olympia, Delphi, Corinth and Nemea, including wrestling and boxing, foot races, horse and chariot races, pentathlons and flute playing.

102   Quoted by William Austen-Leigh and Richard Arthur Austen-Leigh in *Jane Austen, Her Life and Letters: A Family Record*, London. Smith, Elder and Co, 1913, Chapter II.

103   Oxford English Dictionary, second edition, Clarendon Press, Oxford, 1989, Volume XI, page 932. *The common meaning of pity today is the feeling of sorrow and compassion caused by the sufferings and misfortunes of others.*

104   Ovid, 43BC-17AD, *Metamorphoses*, Book 6, translated by John Dryden, Joseph Addison, Laurence Eusden & Sir Samuel Garth. London. Jacob Tonson.1717, Volume II, page 201:
Still my revenge shall take its proper time,
And suit the baseness of your hellish crime.
My self, abandon'd, and devoid of shame,
Thro' the wide world your actions will proclaim;
For tho' I'm prison'd in this lonely den,
Obscur'd, and bury'd from the sight of men,
My mournful voice the pitying rocks shall move,
And my complaining echo thro' the grove.

105   Wal Walker, *Folly is not always Folly*, op cit, page 111-118. https://www.janeanddarcy.com

106   Ibid, page 30.

107   In April 2012, Janeite blogger, Arnie Perlstein, noted *Jane Austen's shocking allusion in Ode to Pity to Shakespeare's most disturbing play,* Titus Andronicus where: *Lavinia eloquently pleads for mercy—or, more accurately, for PITY and receives none—and it is exactly that emotion that I have always felt lurking just beneath the surface of Jane*

Austen's youthful Ode To Pity, and I cannot help wondering what happened to Jane Austen that made her identify so strongly with the tragic Lavinia, the ultimate Shakespearean guiltless victim? http://sharpelvessociety.blogspot.com April 17, 2012.

Love & Freindship

108   From the information Jane Austen provides, that: Edward's Aunt Philippa lived in *Middlesex* (Letter 6th), M—,*the seat of Edward's most particular friend Augustus is but a few miles distant from her (Letter 8th), and the Habitation of Augustus was within twelve miles of Town* (Letter 10th), and knowing that Jane and D'Arcy were driving up the Great North Road, they most likely went to Monken Hadley. The Priory in this village was the family home of William Garrow, D'Arcy Wentworth's friend, the young barrister who defended him successfully in December 1789.

109   Jane Austen, *Northanger Abbey*, Volume I, Chapter XIII.

110   Jane Austen, *Mansfield Park*, Volume II, Chapter II.

111   Letter to the Author of The Loiterer, signed E. (Henry Austen), *The Loiterer*, issue No. 47, 19 December 1789

112   Henry Austen, "Thoughts on Education," *The Loiterer,* No. 27, 1 August 1789, Oxford.

113   Jane Austen, *Persuasion*, Volume I, Chap II.

114   Tobias Smollett wrote that under *the 1707 Act of Union, uniting England and Scotland as one Kingdom, some Scottish Laws and customs were permitted to remain, including old marriage laws, even after English Law had radically altered under Lord Hardwicke's Marriage Act. In Scotland (as formerly in England) a couple had only to get up before witnesses and declare themselves married to be married. Couples not permitted to marry under the new English law (designed to protect the dowries of girls of good family) could speed to Scotland. The Expedition of Humphry Clinker,* London, 2nd ed. London, W. Johnston, 1772, volume 3, page 105.

115   A. P. W. Malcomson, *The Pursuit of the Heiress,* Ulster Historical Foundation, 2006, page 155.

116 Debtor's prisons in London included Marshalsea, King's Bench, Coldbath Fields, Fleet and Clink Prisons, Poultry and Giltspur Street Compters and Wood Street Counter.

117 *Diary or Woodfall's Register*,15 November 1789.

118 In *Pride & Prejudice*, Jane Austen renamed *Wentworth Woodhouse* as *Pemberley*.

119 *Whitehall Evening Post*, July 14-16, 1789.

120 From Jane Austen's description, her coach from Alton to London was most likely a Diligence, a bigger coach with a larger capacity than the coach she travelled in from Stirling to Edinburgh.

121 Jane to Cassandra Austen, 23 August 1814.

122 Footnote to Jane Austen's letter of 23 August 1814, in William Austen-Leigh and Richard Arthur Austen-Leigh, *Jane Austen, Her Life and Letters, A Family Record,* London. 1913.

Lesley Castle

123 Earl Fitzwilliam's London home was at 4 Grosvenor Square, in Mayfair.

124 Jane to Cassandra Austen, Tuesday, 23 August 1796.

125 Paul Poplawski, op cit, page 179.

126 The troublesome little boy D'Arcy unfastened from Jane's neck, four year old Edward Lefroy, became a British Commissary Judge in Surinam, where he laboured to suppress the slave trade. Little William Thomas Lefroy never got well, he died at Ashe two months before his fourth birthday, three months after the birth of his brother Benjamin, Anne Lefroy's seventh and last child. Jane lived to see Benjamin marry her beloved niece, Anna, James Austen's eldest daughter.

127 Jane Austen, *To the Memory of Mrs Lefroy*, in James Edward Austen-Leigh, op cit, Chapter 3. It seems that Jane's friendship with Anne Lefroy had earlier cooled. Mrs Lefroy, who had discouraged Jane's interest in Tom Lefroy, later introduced her to an eligible young clergyman, Reverend Samuel Blackall. Initially, it appears, he was interested in Jane, but his ardour cooled after

he learned more about her past; it seems Anne Lefroy had said too much. Jane to Cassandra Austen, 9 January 1796; 17 November 1798.

128 From a collection of James Austen's poetry, held in the Austen archives at Chawton House in Hampshire.

129 Jane to Cassandra Austen, 29 January 1813.

130 Jane to Cassandra Austen, 21-22 May 1801.

131 In a letter to Cassandra on 25 September 1813, Jane mentioned Henry had sent her an account of his trip to Scotland, adding: *I wish he had had more time & could have gone farther north, & deviated to the Lakes in his way back, but what he was able to do seems to have afforded him great Enjoyment & he met with Scenes of higher beauty in Roxburghshire than I had supposed the South of Scotland possessed.*

132 At the time of Jane Austen's visit to Scotland, the Leslies were merchants in Aberdeen. They occupied several places in the surrounding area including Wart Hill at Meikle Wartle, near Inverurie, and Balgonie Castle near Glenrothes.

133 It is uncertain who was living at Leslie Castle in September 1789, then in the possession of the Leith-Hay family and under the control of their agents. Leslie Castle, gradually fell into disrepair, and was abandoned in a ruinous state. In the 1970's it was restored by Baron David Leslie and today is the headquarters of the world-wide Leslie Clan.

134 The 9th Earl of Kinnoull, Member for Cambridge in the House of Commons, from 1741 to 1758. He was responsible for part funding the Perth Bridge over the River Tay, completed in 1771.

135 In 1789, when Jane and D'Arcy visited Perth, there were people living in Kinnoull Castle, though their names are no longer known. Later, it was occupied by a tenant farmer who built farm-buildings and attached lean-to sheds to the tower walls. Today, these outer buildings have been removed, while the tower still stands, though in a ruined state.

136 Kathryn Sutherland and Freya Johnston, editors of *Jane Austen Teenage Writings,* OUP, 2017, note that "Dunbeath" had been written over 'the N,' an abbreviation of 'the

North." Their brother's estate was 'near Aberdeen," Dunbeath is 184 miles from Aberdeen.

The History Of England

137 Jane to Cassandra Austen, 9 & 14 January 1796.

138 Linda Robinson Walker, "Why Was Jane Austen Sent away to School as Seven", *Persuasions*, Volume 26, No 1, Winter 2005.

139 Deirdre Le Faye, *Jane Austen: A Family Record*, op cit, page 72.

140 Oliver Goldsmith, *The History of England, from the Earliest Times to the Death of George II*, 4 volumes, London, 1771. Jane wrote over a hundred comments in the margins of the third and fourth volumes, reproduced in Juvenilia, ed. Peter Sabor, op cit.

141 Jane Austen, *Northanger Abbey*, Volume I, Chapter XIV.

142 In *Jane Austen's The History of England and Cassandra's Portraits*, by Annette Upfal and Christine Alexander, Sydney, Juvenilia Press, 2009, Upfal argues that Cassandra's paintings are portraits of the Austen family, depicting Jane as Mary Queen of Scots and her mother as Elizabeth I.

143 William Gilpin, *Observations on Several Parts of Great Britain, Particularly the Highlands of Scotland*, London, 1776, page 96.

144 John Whitaker, author of *Mary Queen of Scots Vindicated*, published in 1788.

145 Mrs Anne Lefroy, formerly Anne Bridges, wife of Reverend George Lefroy, Rector of Ashe. Jane Austen's neighbour, and during these years, her friend and counsellor.

146 Mrs Knight, née Catherine Knatchbull, married Thomas Knight, who adopted Jane's third brother Edward.

147 Mary Leigh of Adlestrop, *The Leigh Pedigree*, 31 December 1777, Hampshire Record Office, 23M93/50/1/1.

148 Ibid, both verses quoted by David Nokes, op cit, page 90.

149 Rev. Gilbert White, *The Natural History of Selborne*, Vol.1. London, 1822, pages 331 &

336. Rev. White recorded 8.16 inches of rain that month, at Selborne, near Steventon.

150 Jane to Cassandra Austen, 30 January 1809.

151 The George Washington papers, in the U.S National Archives, includes invoices from Robert Cary & Co for goods despatched to Washington from London on 15 March 1760 and 13 February 1764 from a number of suppliers. On 15 March 1760 on board the *Charming Polly*, Thomas Newnham & Co sent four pounds of Ivory Black, a fine black pigment used to make ink, made from charred ivory; a jar containing twenty-six pounds of raisins, three peck of almonds, and a large quantity of white and brown sugar – for the total sum of £22.8.4. On 13 February 1764, on the *William & Mary*, Thomas Newnham sent quantities of loaf sugar, raisolis, currants, almonds, mace, nuts, cinnamon, cloves, white pepper and white and brown candy– for the total sum of £16.4.11.

152 *London Literary Gazette & Journal of Belles Lettres Etc*, 10 October 1829, page 665.

153 Jane to Cassandra Austen, 8 November 1800.

154 Jane to Cassandra Austen, 8 April 1805.

155 Details of George Austen's students' ordination and clerical appointments from *The Clergy of the Church of England Database 1540–1835*.

156 Rose Willis, *Yate, Victoria County History in Gloucestershire*, 2015. All householders in a parish, including Dissenters, were obliged to pay their tithe to the rector. Robert Neale, a Yate Quaker, was imprisoned in 1678 and 1691 for contempt of the rector. Each year *between 1693 and 1701, the rector's servants entered Neale's property and forcibly took what was owed. In 1694, they "hoved (the gate) off the hooks"* to gain entry.

157 Jane Austen, *Persuasion*, Volume 1, Chapter 3.

158 From *The Letters of Oliver Goldsmith*, ed Michael Griffin & David O'Shaughnessy, Cambridge, 2018.

A Collection Of Letters

159 All Souls College, founded to commemorate the victims of the Hundred Years War,

received its Charter from Henry VI in 1438. In 1639, All Souls purchased the advowson of Harpsden for £300.5s, which entitled it under English law to nominate its candidate for appointment to the living of the parish when it became vacant. During the seventeenth and eighteenth centuries, the rectors of Harpsden were all current or former scholars or fellows of All Souls College, who resided in the parish.

160 *The Wonder – A Woman Keeps a Secret* (1718) by Mrs Susannah Centlivre, and *The Chances* (1647) by John Fletcher, in a version by actor David Garrick staged in 1773.

161 Eliza De Feuillide to her cousin Philly Walter, 26 October 1792, in Deirdre Le Faye, *Jane Austen's 'Outlandish Cousin'*, op cit, page 118.

162 *The Sultan*, or a *Peep into the Seraglio* (1775), by Isaac Bickerstaffe and *High Life below Stairs* (1759) by Reverend James Townley.

163 Eliza de Feuillide to Philly Walter, 26 October 1792, in Deirdre Le Faye, Jane Austen's *'Outlandish Cousin'*, op cit, page 115.

164 Brian Southam, *Jane Austen and the Navy,* National Maritime Museum, Greenwich, 2005, page 37.

165 Jane to Cassandra Austen, 21 January 1799.

166 Jane to Cassandra Austen, 1 November 1800.

167 *The Times*, 18 June 1796.

168 *The Times*, 18 June 1796. Copy of a letter from Captain Williams, of His Majesty's ship, *Unicorn*, to Vice-Admiral Kingsmill, dated Unicorn at Sea, June 10, 1796. Published in the *London Gazette*, 15 June 1796.

169 *The Times*, 14 July 1796

170 *The Times*, 20 June 1796.

171 Jane to Cassandra Austen, 15 September 1796. *The Times*, 13 September 1796, reported in *Ship News*, Portsmouth Sept 11: *the Unicorn frigate, Capt Williams sailed this evening on a cruize.*

172 Jane Austen to Martha Lloyd, 12 November 1800.

173 Jane to Cassandra Austen, 1 December 1800.

174 Jane to Cassandra Austen, 11 February, 1801. Prince Augustus Frederick, Duke of Sussex (1773-1843) continued to live with Lady Augusta. In 1831, a year after her death, he remarried, once more in contravention of the *Royal Marriages Act.*

175 Prince Augustus was Queen Victoria's favourite uncle, he gave her away at her wedding to Prince Albert.

176 Through the 17th and 18th centuries, to the mid 19th, warships were classified under a rating system, that indicated the number of men required to man them at sea and the number of guns. The first and second rates had three continuous decks of guns, fourth and fifth rates had around fifty to sixty guns on two decks.

177 In January 1809, Vice Admiral Sir Alexander Cochrane (1758-1832), commander of the West Indian Station, and Lieutenant- General George Beckwith, marshalled an overwhelming expeditionary force 29 ships and ten thousand men to invade Martinique. The British campaign for Martinique began on 30 January, its successful outcome directed offshore by Beckwith, on board *HMS Neptune,* Cochrane's flagship.

178 Jane to Cassandra Austen, 30 January 1809.

179 The Nore is a sandbank in the Thames estuary extending from Shoeburyness in the North to Sheerness in the South, in the County of Kent. The Nore anchoring-ground, four miles east of London Bridge, was much used by the English fleet in the seventeenth and eighteenth centuries..

Letter The Second – From A Young Lady Crossed In Love

180 James Austen, "To Miss Jane Austen the reputed author of Sense & Sensibility, a Novel lately published," lines 1-2 & 5-6, *The Poetry of Jane Austen & the Austen Family,* ed. David Selwyn, University of Iowa Press, 1997, page 50.

181   Jane to Cassandra Austen, 14-15 January 1796.

182   Was *Persuasion* Jane Austen's *antes de morirme*? Aware she was failing, did she record and hide away her analysis of how she was persuaded to abandon D'Arcy, the heaviest secret of their short time together, and her anger and despair at his failure to return?

183   *Jane Austen's Fiction Manuscripts*, The British Library, London.

Letter The Fifth - From A Young Lady Very Much In Love

184   D'Arcy Wentworth, *Medical Notebook*, page 75, Wal Walker, op cit, *Folly is not always Folly*, p. 111-118. www.janeanddarcy.com

185   Percivall Pott, *Chirurgical relative to the Cataract, the Polypus of the Nose, and Cancer of the Scrotum*, London, T.J.Catnegy, 1775. Pott's work and advocacy led to the *Chimney Sweeper's Act* of 1788, which prohibited the apprenticeship of boys under eight, and required the master to first obtain their parent's permission, to provide his apprentices with proper clothes and accommodation, and ensure they attended church on Sunday. Wal Walker, *Folly is not always Folly*, op cit, page 111-118. www.janeanddarcy.com

Scraps

186   Jane to Cassandra Austen, 5 Sept 1796.

187   Jane to Cassandra Austen, 18 Sept 1796.

188   Jane to Cassandra Austen, 24 August 1805.

189   Jane to Cassandra Austen, 15 June, 1808.

190   Jane Austen, Northanger Abbey, Volume II, Chapter XIII.

191   Jane to Caroline Austen, 20 June, 1808.

192   Jane to Cassandra Austen, 15 June, 1808.

193   Anna Lefroy, *Original Memories of Jane Austen*, quoted by D. Le Faye, *A Family Record*, op cit, p.182.

194   Jane to Caroline Austen, 29 January 1813.

195   Jane to Frank Austen, 25 September, 1813.

196   Jane to Caroline Austen, 2 March, 1815.

The Female Philosopher

197   Adam Smith's *The Theory of Moral Sentiments*, published in 1759, underpins all his later writings, including *The Wealth of Nations* (1776) and *Essays on Philosophical Subjects* (1795)

198   Jane to Cassandra Austen, 1 September 1796 and 15 June 1808.

199   Jane to Cassandra Austen, 29 January and 4 February, 1813.

The First Act Of Comedy

200   Jane to Cassandra Austen, 14 January 1796.

201   Jane to Cassandra Austen, 1 December 1798.

202   Jane to Cassandra Austen, 18 December 1798.

203   Jane to Cassandra Austen, 8 January 1801.

204   Brian Southam, *Jane Austen's Literary Manuscripts*, op cit.

A Letter From A Young Lady

205   Virginia Woolf, *The Common Reader,* Chapter 12.

206   *Whitehall Evening Post*, 10 November 1789.

207   *Gazetteer & New Daily Advertiser,* 13 November 1789.

208   *Whitehall Evening Post*, 12 November 1789. The three false surnames Jane Austen gave were: Wilson, Weaver and Taylor. Weaver was an Austen family name. *Mistella*, a sour white wine issued to sailors, and referred to in the Navy as Miss Taylor, was a family joke, told by her brother Frank.

209   *The Times*, 13 November 1789.

210   *The Times*, 20 November 1789.

211   *The Times*, 17 November, 11 and 12 December 1789. The Duke and Duchess of Cumberland were brother and sister-in-law of King George III.

       Prince Henry, Duke of Cumberland (1745-

1790), son of George II, was a younger brother of George III. His marriage in 1771 to a commoner, Anne Horton, resulted in the Royal Marriages Act of 1772, which gave the reigning sovereign the power to veto a marriage by a member of the royal family. Under the Act, they needed the consent of the reigning monarch to marry.

Anne, Duchess of Cumberland (1743-1808) was great beauty, her portrait was painted several times by Thomas Gainsborough. Widow of Christopher Horton of Catton Hall, Derbyshire, she was the daughter of Simon Luttrell, an Anglo-Irish member of the House of Commons from 1754 to 1780, created Baron Irnham in 1768, and Earl of Carhampton in 1785. His wife, Judith Maria Lawes, was the daughter of Sir Nicholas Lawes, Governor of Jamaica from 1718-22.

Douglas Hamilton (1756-1799), 8th Duke of Hamilton, born in Edinburgh, at Holyrood Palace, succeeded to the title at age thirteen on the death of his brother James, aged fourteen. From 1772 to 1776 Douglas went on a Grand Tour of France, Italy and Germany with his tutor Dr John Moore and Moore's eldest son John, aged eleven, later Lieutenant-General Sir John Moore, commander and hero, killed in the Battle of Coruña, on 16 January 1809. Jane mentioned his death in a letter to Cassandra on 30 January 1809.

212   Jane to James Edward Austen, 16 Dec 1816.

213   Jane to Cassandra Austen, 8 Sept 1816.

214   Jane Austen, *Persuasion*, Volume 1, Chap 4.

A Tour Through Wales

215   James Edward Austen-Leigh, op cit, page 7.

A Tale

216   J.E.Crowley, *The Invention of Comfort: Sensibilities and Design in Early Modern Britain*, John Hopkins University Press, Baltimore, 2003.

217   Jane Austen, *Sense & Sensibility*, Volume II, Chapter XIV.

218   Jane to Cassandra Austen, 27 October 1798; and 21 January 1799.

219   Jane to Cassandra Austen, 24 August 1805; and 9 October 1808.

220   Jane to Cassandra Austen, 24 January 1809.

221   Jane to Frank Austen, 25 September 1813; Jane to Cassandra Austen, 14 October 1813.

222   Jane Austen to Fanny Knight, 18 Nov 1814.

223   Jane Austen to Fanny Knight, 30 Nov 1814.

224   Jane Austen to Fanny Knight, 20 Feb 1817.

225   Jane Austen to Fanny Knight, 13 Mar 1817.

226   Jane Austen's letters to Fanny Knight were published by Fanny's son, Lord Brabourne in 1884.

227   Fanny, Lady Knatchbull to her sister Marianne, 23 August 1869.

Juvenilia, Volume The Third

228   British Library, *Jane Austen's Fiction Manuscripts*, Manuscript Headnote, *Volume the Third*, London.

Evelyn

229   Jane to Cassandra Austen, 9 January 1796.

230   Jane to Cassandra Austen, 5 Sept 1796.

231   Eliza de Feuillide to her cousin Phylly Walter, 30 December 1796, in Deirdre Le Faye, *Jane Austen's Outlandish Cousin, op cit*, page 134.

232   Prepared by Giovanni Leoni d'Este, and known as the *Evelyn Tables*, they are believed to be the oldest anatomical preparations in Europe. Over three hundred and fifty years later, they are still on display in London, in the Royal College of Surgeons' Hunterian Museum, at Lincoln's Inn Fields.

233   Jane Austen set the story about twenty years ago, around 1772, nearly twenty years after the *Marriage Act of 1753, an Act for the Better Preventing of Clandestine Marriage* came into force. Though Maria has her parents permission, there was no time allowed for Marriage Banns to be read over three Sundays from the pulpit, making their marriage is invalid under English law..

234 Jane Austen, *Persuasion*, Volume I, Chap IV.

235 Jane Austen, *Mansfield Park*, Volume II, Chapter XI.

236 Margaret Doody, Introduction, *Catharine and Other Writings* by Jane Austen, Oxford University Press, 1993, page xxxv.

237 Shawn Normandin, "Jane Austen's "Evelyn" and 'the Impossibility of the Gift,'" *Criticism*, vol.60. No.1, pages 21-46.

238 Jane to Cassandra Austen, 20 June 1808.

239 The first of the fake marriage banns Jane wrote in her father's parish register in 1790, was for her marriage to Henry Frederick Howard Fitzwilliam of London.

240 John H. Appleby, "The Founding of St Petersburg in the Context of the Royal Society's Relationship with Russia," *Notes and Records of the Royal Society of London*, Volume 57, No.3, September 2003, pp 273-284.

241 William Bray, ed, *Memoirs illustrative of the Life and Writings of John Evelyn*, in 2 volumes, London, Henry Colburn, 1818.

Kitty, or the Bower

242 *The London Magazine: Or Gentleman's Monthly Intelligencer*, Volume 19, page 603.

243 W. and R.A. Austen-Leigh, *op cit*, Chap III.

244 William Austen-Leigh and Montagu George Knight, *Chawton Manor & Its Owners*, London, Smith Elder & Co, 1911, Chap VII.

245 R.A. Austen-Leigh, *Austen Papers 1704-1856*, Spottiswoode Ballantyne, Colchester, 1942, page 37.

246 Tyso to Philadelphia Hancock, 17 January 1770, ibid, page 43.

247 Tyso to Philadelphia Hancock, 7 November 1773, ibid, page 74.

248 Jane to Cassandra Austen, 8 January 1801.

249 John Hinton asserted his sole common law right to publish the *New History of the Holy Bible*, arguing that on Stephen Austen's death, Elizabeth had inherited the right to publish the book, and that right had transferred to him on their marriage. He sought orders from the Court for the defendants to cease and desist publishing the *New History of the Holy Bible*, damages for each copy of the book they had sold, and possession of all the unsold copies, which he claimed amounted to ten thousand unsold copies.

250 In the judgement in John Hinton's case, nine of the ten Scottish judges opposed granting a perpetual monopoly to London booksellers, ruling that no such common law right existed in Scotland. In February 1774, to hear the arguments for and against copyright, the Lords summoned twelve Common Law judges to attend and to advise them. Eighty-four Lords voted to reject the argument for common law rights, henceforth copyright was to be limited in term and that term would be established by statute. Known as the *Statute of Anne, the Copyright Act 1710, an Act for the Encouragement of Learning, by vesting the Copies of printed Books in the Authors or purchasers of such Copies, during the Times therein mentioned,* was the first statute to provide for copyright regulated by government and the courts.

251 Deirdre Le Faye, *A Chronology of Jane Austen and Her Family*, Cambridge University Press, 2006.

252 Ian Maxted, *Exeter Working Papers in Book History*, online.

253 Deirdre Le Faye, *A Chronology of Jane Austen and Her Family*, op cit.

254 Anna Austen Lefroy, quoted in *A Family Record*, page 49..

255 George Austen paid Mme La Tournelle at Abbey House School: £35.19.00 on 20 August 1785, £36.2.6 on 23 January 1786, and £16.10.0 on 2 January 1787. See Deirdre Le Faye, *A Chronology of Jane Austen*, op cit.

256 Kathryn Sutherland and Freya Johnston, eds, op cit, page xxi.

257 Jane to Cassandra Austen, 7 October 1808.

Major Themes Of The Juvenilia

258 Jane to Cassandra Austen, 2 Dec 1815.

Conclusion

259   Jane to Cassandra Austen, 24 October, 1798.

260   James Edward Austen-Leigh, op cit, Chap 8.

261   Jon Spence, op cit, Introduction.

262   Henry L. Carrigan Jr, "Comment on Jon
      Spence, Becoming Jane." *Library Journal,*
      Rutgers University, NY. Volume 128, issue 9,
      15 May 2003, page 90.

263   Virginia Woolf, "Jane Austen at Sixty,"
      Nation and Athenaeum, 34, 1923, page
      433-4.

Index

Made in the USA
Coppell, TX
19 December 2020